CW00650119

'*Redefining Genocide* is an incisive, bold, and illuminating exploration oı the close links between genocide, colonialism, and ecocide. With flair and insight, it addresses the vulnerability of humanity in the perilous age of the Anthropocene.'

**John Docker, author of *The Origins of Violence***

'Short's discussion of genocide, ecocide and colonialist exploitation is delivered with clarity and intellectual insight. It is both an important reminder of some nearly forgotten histories of inhumanity and a warning about future dangers to the planet.'

**Nigel South, University of Essex**

'An important, path-breaking book. It expands genocide studies into disciplines and concerns that reach far beyond the academy. Policy-makers and activists, as well as scholars troubled by the genocidal potential and local impacts of global developments, must urgently engage with its arguments.'

**Tony Barta, La Trobe University**

'Genocide scholars have a habit of not getting the bigger picture, they concentrate on the politics, the law, or the human psychology but leaving out the crucial environmental underpinning. If you wreck an environment upon which communities depend, their destruction will inexorably follow. Damien Short is one of the few genocide scholars who does get it and this book is to be vastly welcomed for the belated paradigm shift it augurs.'

**Mark Levene, author of *The Crisis of Genocide***

'Hugely original. Damien Short's well-informed analysis gives hope to those of us who believe that the critique of what is taken to be normal or inevitable is the first step towards promoting the respect for cultural pluralism, human dignity and respect for nature.'

**Colin Samson, author of *A World You Do Not Know: Settler Societies, Indigenous Peoples and the Attack on Cultural Pluralism***

## About the author

Damien Short is a reader in human rights at the School of Advanced Study, University of London. He is director of the school's Human Rights Consortium and Extreme Energy Initiative and editor in chief of the *International Journal of Human Rights*.

# REDEFINING GENOCIDE

## SETTLER COLONIALISM, SOCIAL DEATH AND ECOCIDE

*Damien Short*

Zed Books
London

*Redefining Genocide: Settler Colonialism, Social Death and Ecocide* was first published in 2016 by Zed Books Ltd, The Foundry, 17 Oval Way, London SE11 5RR, UK.

www.zedbooks.net

Copyright © Damien Short 2016

The right of Damien Short to be identified as the author of this work has been asserted by him in accordance with the Copyright, Designs and Patents Act, 1988.

Typeset in Plantin and Kievit by Swales & Willis Ltd, Exeter, Devon
Index: Ed Emery
Cover design: Dougal Burgess

All rights reserved. No part of this publication may be reproduced, stored in a retrieval system or transmitted in any form or by any means, electronic, mechanical, photocopying or otherwise, without the prior permission of Zed Books Ltd.

A catalogue record for this book is available from the British Library.

ISBN 978-1-84277-930-9 hb
ISBN 978-1-84277-931-6 pb
ISBN 978-1-84813-546-8 pdf
ISBN 978-1-78360-170-7 epub
ISBN 978-1-78360-171-4 mobi

MIX
Paper from
responsible sources
FSC® C013604

# CONTENTS

# ACKNOWLEDGEMENTS

This book wouldn't have been possible without the input of numerous people along the way. Firstly, I must thank my co-author researchers for the chapters on Palestine (Haifa Rashed), Sri Lanka (Vinay Prakash) and Alberta (Jen Huseman). They were a pleasure to work with. Then there are Dirk Moses, Tony Barta, Mark Levene, Jürgen Zimmerer, Martin Crook and Colin Samson, who have all provided vital intellectual stimulation and invaluable feedback on many parts of this book. I would also like to acknowledge the significant impact that environmental consultant Paul Mobbs has had on my thinking and for sharing huge amounts of material on the threat of extreme energy over the last few years. I must thank my family for their support and encouragement throughout this lengthy project, and my tireless in-laws for their loving, and much-needed, childcare!

# INTRODUCTION

... nations are essential elements of the world community. The
world represents only so much culture and intellectual vigor as
are created by its component national groups. Essentially the
idea of a nation signifies constructive cooperation and original
contributions, based upon genuine traditions, genuine culture,
and a well-developed national psychology. The destruction of a
nation, therefore, results in the loss of its future contributions to
the world. (Lemkin 1944: Section III, 79–95)

Our whole cultural heritage is a product of the contributions of all
peoples. We can best understand this if we realize how impoverished
our culture would be if the so-called inferior peoples doomed by
Germany, such as the Jews, had not been permitted to create the
Bible or to give birth to an Einstein, a Spinosa; if the Poles had not
had the opportunity to give to the world a Copernicus, a Chopin,
a Curie, the Czechs a Huss, and a Dvorak; the Greeks a Plato and
a Socrates; the Russians, a Tolstoy and a Shostakovich. (Lemkin
1945)

Raphael Lemkin, 'the founder of the United Nations Genocide
Convention', was born on 24 June 1900 in the Bialystok region of
Bezwondene, Poland, which was in imperial Russia at the time but
is now Volkovysk, Belarus.[1] Lemkin was fascinated with languages,
history and the law, eventually becoming a lawyer and working for the
Prosecutor's office in Warsaw from 1929 to 1934. As a prosecutor, he
helped to codify the laws of the new Polish Republic, and in 1933 he
presented a paper to the League of Nations International Conference
for Unification of Criminal Law in Madrid based on two concepts
– 'barbarity' (mass slaughter) and 'vandalism' (cultural destruction)
– he had developed and wanted criminalized. Lemkin urged the
international community to ban the destruction, both physical and
cultural, of human groups. In his subsequent seminal text *Axis
Rule in Occupied Europe* Lemkin combined his prior formulations,

barbarity and vandalism, to form a new, more comprehensive concept – *genocide*, combining the Greek word *genos* meaning tribe or race and the Latin *cide* meaning killing.[2] The United Nations' 1948 Convention on the Prevention and Punishment of the Crime of Genocide (the Genocide Convention) was in large part the product of Lemkin's tireless lobbying in the corridors of the United Nations and beyond.[3] The legal definition is the only internationally accepted definition of genocide and is enshrined in Article II (a) to (e) of the Genocide Convention[4] – currently accepted by the Convention's 142 states parties.[5] In effect Lemkin helped create two definitions – the broad sociological concept sketched out in *Axis Rule* and the narrower legal definition articulated in the Genocide Convention.

The legal definition has, somewhat inevitably, been the most influential, while popular understandings reduce its meaning still further by effectively equating genocide with large-scale killing of 'ethnic groups'. The fact that the genocide concept and legal definition emerged from the context of the Second World War ensured that the Holocaust has proved hugely influential, if not paradigmatic, to both scholarly and popular understandings of the term. Arguably the primary conceptual constraint on thinking about the subject is the dominance of a Holocaust-based conception of genocide.[6] Indeed, it is only from around the turn of the millennium that some scholars began to rigorously interrogate Lemkin's thought and its implications for a range of under-discussed cases of genocide, such as settler colonial Australia.

Importantly, Lemkin's work on genocide went well beyond his seminal book *Axis Rule*. Indeed, a plethora of archival papers were donated to the American Jewish Archives in 1965, the American Jewish Historical Society in 1975, the New York Public Library in 1982, while the United Nations archive in Geneva holds a folder of formal letters and communications from Lemkin to key political figures, such as Eleanor Roosevelt, from the period when he was lobbying for the passage of the Genocide Convention.[7] Lemkin's archives contain a wealth of fascinating personal letters, research notes, historical papers, essays on philosophical, anthropological and economic approaches to genocide, and the results of genocide, while his unfinished autobiography and research into historical case studies of genocide have both finally been published.[8] Some of Lemkin's most illuminating and insightful thoughts are contained in these archives and yet little more than a handful of scholars have interrogated them – most notably Dirk Moses, John Docker, Tanya Elder, Donna-Lee Frieze, Dominik Schaller and Jürgen Zimmerer – making their work hugely important to the field of genocide studies.[9]

What emerges from this scholarship is an understanding of genocide that is far more than a condemnatory label or even the international 'crime of all crimes', and an understanding of Lemkin himself as far more than a mere neologist. Genocide is now a robust concept with a rich intellectual history,[10] while Lemkin has been rediscovered and can now be considered a theorist and historian as well as a 'lawgiver'. These more recent studies have clarified the concept of genocide and in particular the role of cultural destruction. While it may be difficult to pin down exactly what is meant by 'cultural genocide', broadly speaking it is used to refer to a method of genocide which destroys a social group through the destruction of their culture. As we shall see in the next chapter, for Lemkin the concept of 'culture' was fundamental to how he conceived of genocide: it destroys a human cultural grouping, a '*genos*'.

Lemkin-inspired studies have also highlighted a vitally important aspect of genocide that had been somewhat ignored by prior scholarship – genocide's inherently colonial character. In Lemkin's 'History of genocide' in particular, he outlines a vital link between genocide and colonization, and yet prior to this new work it may have seemed reasonable to think of Lemkin's concept, as is popularly done, as little more than a synonym for mass murder.[11] As we shall see in the next chapter, such a position is now completely untenable.

This book is the product of my research over the last six years in the fields of genocide studies, indigenous rights, environmental justice and green criminology. My previous monograph, which analysed Australia's official reconciliation process, demonstrated the inherently *interlinked* nature of these fields, both theoretically and empirically. Indeed, it was in the Australian settler colonial context that I first entered the world of genocide studies via the heated debates about the forced removal of indigenous children from their families. Following this period of research I became heavily influenced by the seminal work of two historians: Tony Barta and his structural understanding of genocidal processes along with his idea that settler colonial societies may involve social and political 'relations of genocide'; and the pioneering work of Dirk Moses in developing what we can now call the colonial/cultural turn in genocide studies. It was clear to me that their work could have significant analytical and explanatory potential beyond historical analysis and that a sociological understanding of genocide should embrace their insights. In addition to such socio-historical structural insights, since 2008 my work on ecocide and the environmental dimensions of genocide has drawn me into the burgeoning field of 'green' criminology, which, unlike traditional criminology with its focus on state-defined 'crime', analyses the nature, causes and societal impacts of environmental and social *harms* that are often *legal* and driven by capitalist expansion and our contemporary neoliberal economic order.

## Research strategy and theoretical orientation

The research for the book was based on sociological methods, primarily qualitative in nature, which sought to gain a nuanced understanding of complex socio-political processes. This involved participant observation at activist and protest events and official governmental and non-governmental policy forums at the local, national and international levels; academic workshops and conferences, documentary analysis, and legislative and common law legal analysis. In addition the research involved considerable textual analysis of relevant official policy documents in order to extract key phrases, metaphors and codes that can elucidate the relationship between political agendas, corporate interests and policy outcomes. The research also involved considerable periods in the United Nations and League of Nations archives in Geneva tracing the documented institutional history of the concept and potential international crime of ecocide, alongside research into the politically instrumental side of Lemkin's writings during the construction of the Genocide Convention (e.g. personal letters to key political figures).

While the case studies were not based on extensive deep ethnography they were informed by significant periods of fieldwork and include data from conversations, correspondence and semi-structured interviews with key actors. From my doctoral studies period to the present my primary research site has been Australia and the main focus of my work over the years has been settler colonial/indigenous relations and the issues of land appropriation, environmental destruction and genocide. The other case studies in this book, Palestine, Sri Lanka and Alberta, were undertaken with experienced researchers of those contexts and the chapters co-authored. The analysis contained in the case study chapters should, however, be regarded in many ways as a springboard for further research and analysis as there is so much more information available if one cares to look, particularly when it comes to illuminating the 'lived experience' of the victims and the structures and casual factors at play in the violation of their basic human rights; they deserve entire books in their own right.

The research for this book has been informed by and contributes to a number of related fields of study and theoretical debates: the sociology of genocide, which to date has primarily examined the role played by historical, social, political and economic forces in genocidal destruction alongside individual, collective and structural dynamics; the 'sociology of human rights', in which I have worked for many years and which views human rights as a social construction, the product of the balance of power between political interests (see Short 2009); 'emancipatory cultural politics', whereby understandings of specific cultural processes that are embedded in wider structural social power relationships should be used to bolster specific endeavours for social change and/or to assist specific marginalized peoples, populations or groups in resisting threats to their survival (ibid.). Finally, the book utilizes the insights of a number of 'green criminologists', who take a 'harm'-based approach that acknowledges the fact that many 'legal' activities can be more destructive to the environmental and human and non-human animals than those deemed illegal.[12] Green criminology has much to offer the study of genocide, particularly where genocidal social harm is ecologically induced. In the penultimate chapter, I make the case for the field of genocide studies to embrace the insights of green criminologists and vice versa.

## Chapter outlines

In the first chapter of this book I develop a sociologically robust understanding of genocide and discuss its implications. I outline why the still-dominant understanding of genocide as mass killing is sociologically inadequate and at odds with the ideas of the author of the concept, Raphael Lemkin. Despite the insights of recent scholarship, to date much of the field of genocide studies has failed to appreciate the importance of culture and social death to the concept of genocide. There is still insufficient serious discussion of culturally destructive processes which do not involve direct physical killing or violence through the analytical lens of genocide. This is especially true when it comes to the experiences of indigenous peoples in the world today. When they invoke the term genocide to describe their present-day experiences it is often derided. And yet I show that indigenous peoples' use of the concept is often more accurate and precise than that espoused by many scholars. I end the chapter with a call for more research into seemingly benign processes of indigenous 'cultural diffusion', in a globalized world dominated by neoliberal capitalism where 'land grabs' – carried out by extractive industries, industrial farms and the like – are, through the annexation of indigenous land and associated 'externalities', the principal vectors of what Martin Crook and I have called 'ecologically induced genocide' – although it's important to note that colonized indigenous peoples the world over have been pointing out such a phenomenon for some time. This brings us to a key contribution of this book – ecocide as a method of genocide.

A small number of studies have shown that ecocide, broadly speaking the destruction of ecosystems, can be a method of genocide if, for example, such destruction results in conditions of life that fundamentally threaten a social group's cultural and/or physical existence.[13] These studies date back to the 1970s, but have been largely ignored by the majority of genocide scholars. One of the earliest studies to have demonstrated how capitalism can produce environmental destruction, which in turn leads to genocide, was the 1973 study by Canadian investigative journalists Robert Davis and Mark Zannis – to my knowledge only Dirk Moses out of the key writers in genocide studies seems to have consulted it, yet the study is filled with rich material of undoubted relevance to genocide scholars. Much later, in 1998, Daniel Brook wrote a groundbreaking article, 'Environmental genocide: Native Americans and toxic waste', which made such a case more explicitly. It wasn't until Ward Churchill's (2002) second scholarly work on genocide, however, that the term 'ecocide' found its way into a monograph alongside Lemkin's concept. Even so, Churchill left the connection largely underexplored and didn't explicitly engage with the concept of ecocide and how it relates to genocide, both in theory and practice.

In the second chapter of this book I explore this under-investigated area and show how genocide and ecocide are inherently linked, institutionally, empirically and theoretically. I first became aware of the idea of ecocide – the destruction of ecosystems – as a potential international crime akin to genocide when I met international lawyer and activist Polly Higgins, who has been a prominent advocate for the idea for many years. To test the practicality of Polly Higgins' proposal to make ecocide a crime, a mock trial was held in the UK Supreme Court in September 2011 at which the two chief executives of two fictional oil companies were found guilty by the jury of the crime of ecocide. I met Polly at the follow-up sentencing event on 31 March 2012 at the Institute for Democracy and Conflict Resolution at the University of Essex in Colchester. During her early advocacy on the subject, a journalist had tantalizingly alerted Polly to a prior time when ecocide had in fact been discussed as a potential international crime within the UN system, but the details were vague. She was interested in learning more about this little-known episode, as indeed was I. Consequently, I started an 'Ecocide Project' within our Human Rights Consortium at the School of Advanced Study to look into it. The early legwork was diligently conducted by a wonderfully gifted researcher, Anja Gauger, before being joined by a team of us in the later stages.

In short, we uncovered a fascinating institutional history of a potential crime of ecocide/environmental destruction in the UN system, the repercussions of which are discussed in the chapter.[14] The crucial point identified by our research was that, at certain points in the past, the international community had deemed ecocide/environmental destruction to be so serious that it was included in its draft Code of Crimes Against the Peace and Security of Mankind, and was also seriously considered as a missing method of genocide that could be written into the Genocide Convention. In order to grasp the contemporary conceptual and empirical dimensions of the genocide/ecocide nexus, which have been the focus of my research over the last six years, the chapter moves on to grapple with what Meadows et al. famously described as 'the Limits to Growth'; exploring the implications for the capitalist mode of production and indeed for all humanity of reaching planetary carrying capacity, alongside Ed Lloyd-Davies' '*process* of extreme energy' (2013) – as easier-to-extract resources peak, there is a drive towards more risky and environmentally destructive extraction. Indeed, the latest resource extraction technologies involved are so disturbing that I set up the Extreme Energy Initiative (extremeenergy.org) as an independent interdisciplinary academic forum designed to investigate the human and environmental impacts of technologies such as mountain-top removal, tar sands extraction, underground coal gasification and 'fracking' (sometimes referred to as 'unconventional gas and oil' extraction). I suggest that the rush to scrape the bottom of the fossil fuel barrel is creating a perfect storm for current and future human rights abuses, with ecocidal and genocidal consequences.

In developing my thinking on the connections between genocide and ecocide, I was hugely influenced by a series of interdisciplinary workshops organized by a group of independent academics known collectively as 'Crisis Forum', in which historian and genocide scholar Mark Levene was a central figure. On 8 November 2008 the forum began the series under the title 'Climate change and violence', based on the premise that anthropogenic climate change will be the most serious accelerator to the overall crisis of mankind in the twenty-first century, featuring, among other calamities, more frequent heat waves, droughts, extreme precipitation events, and related impacts, e.g. wildfires, heat stress, vegetation changes and sea level rise (Levene 2004). The first Crisis Forum workshop was aimed at developing an understanding of the implications for human society of anthropogenic climate change via the input of leading climate scientists, such as Kevin Anderson. The central question posed was 'How bad is bad?'. By the end of the workshop it seemed the answer was that if the excesses of global capitalism, in particular the unrestrained production of greenhouse gases, were not dramatically and abruptly curbed, the situation would be somewhere along the spectrum of 'dire' and 'an extinction event'.

The workshop had a profound impact on me at a core level, as a human being partly responsible for the situation – engaged in unsustainable consumption – as a father, concerned citizen and human rights scholar. On a scholarly level the whole series of interdisciplinary workshops highlighted the interconnected nature of human beings and our natural environment but also the interconnected nature of the fields of study and topics discussed. Indeed, one quickly realized that it is impossible to fully comprehend the nature, scale and overall consequences of phenomena such as genocidal episodes without a strong appreciation of a range of environmental factors and ecological issues such as anthropogenic climate change, land use and abuse, soil degradation, water contamination and shortages, biodiversity loss and habitat destruction. Regardless of our attempts to master nature the simple fact remains: humans are ecologically embedded beings and the destruction of our habitat will have dire consequences. Thus, these issues infuse the book both in terms of the theoretical orientation and in the empirical data discussed in the case studies.

In Chapter 3 we move on to the first of the book's case studies, all of which were chosen with a number of important dimensions in mind. First, they are all under-discussed contexts in the field of genocide studies, but contexts that both benefit from analysis through a genocide lens and which tell us something about the variations, commonalities, causal vectors and societal structures involved in such genocidal processes. Secondly, they each add their own unique elements to our understanding, such as the particular histories of group identity formation, levels and modes of inter-group conflict and environmental contexts, while at the same time highlighting key connections, such as the role of colonization, natural resource exploitation and its destruction of ecosystems and neoliberal global capitalism – the form of capitalism that proposes that human well-being can best be advanced by liberating individual entrepreneurial freedoms and skills within an institutional framework characterized by strong private property rights, 'free markets' and 'free trade' (Harvey 2005: 2). Under this system the role of the state is to create and preserve an institutional framework appropriate to such practices, through military, defence, police and legal structures, using force where necessary. Where markets do not exist (in areas such as land, water, education, social security or environmental pollution) then these should be created by state action if necessary (ibid.: 2).

The case studies involve two contexts that have been embroiled in long-term, almost continuously violent, protracted conflict and two cases that involve 'stable' neoliberal multicultural democracies. What we will see is that, despite considerable differences between the two violent conflict case studies and the two stable 'democratic' case studies, they share many similarities when it comes to victim experiences of cultural destruction and habitat destruction. The first case study is Palestine. As Haifa Rashed and I have argued elsewhere (Rashed et al. 2014; Rashed and Short 2012), the Palestinian case has hitherto seen little investigation by genocide scholars. Given Lemkin's focus on colonialism and genocide and subsequent scholarly examination of settler colonial societies as inherently genocidal, we suggest that when considering the Palestinian case through the lens of settler colonialism there is a clear basis for its further exploration within the field of genocide studies. As Docker indicates, the 'conjunction of genocide studies and the history of Palestine-Israel conceived as genocidal, has grave implications for international law' (Docker 2012). This chapter considers the State of Israel's actions against the Palestinian people through a Lemkin-inspired genocide lens, and also the more restrictive legal understanding articulated in the UN Genocide Convention, specifically Article 2 (a–c).

Chapter 4 investigates the case of Sri Lanka, briefly exploring its colonial past and the shaping of social group identities before moving on to discuss the civil war (1983–2009) and post-war social, political and environmental contexts. While the language of genocide gradually appeared over time, especially during the last phase of the war, the chapter looks at the development of a comprehensive identity, a *genos*, among the Tamil population as a result of policy changes and alienation of minorities since independence. The chapter argues that in order to understand the conflict between the Tamils and the Sinhalese there is a need to explore the dominant narratives from one of Sri Lanka's national epics, the Mahavamsa, as it has been instrumental in shaping Sinhalese Buddhist nationalism and legitimizing genocidal practices on the Tamil community. The chapter also looks at the evolution of ethnic identities and their subsequent stratification and the creation of a vulnerable minority population susceptible to the peculiar harm of genocide. The final section of the chapter interrogates key issues in post-war Sri Lanka, including ecocide and environmental destruction, looking principally at the former war zone and rebel-held territories in the north and east.

Following the Sri Lanka case, in Chapter 5 we move on to investigate a classic settler colonial context – Australia. While debates about genocide in Australia have, for the most part, focused on past frontier killings and child removal practices, I discuss *contemporary* culturally destructive policies, and the colonial structures that produce them, through the analytical lens of the concept of genocide. Even though direct physical killing and genocidal child removal practices may have ceased in Australia, some indigenous people persuasively contend that genocide *is a continuing process* in an Australia that has failed to decolonize. After many years of fieldwork and research on Australian settler/indigenous politics I concur with these views. I argue that the contemporary expression of continuing genocidal relations in Australia can be seen principally, and perversely, in the colonial state's official reconciliation process, the native title land rights regime and the more recent interventionist 'solutions' to indigenous 'problems' in the Northern Territory, alongside the invasion of extreme energy technologies and their ecocidal consequences.

In the final case study, Chapter 6 examines another 'democratic' settler colonial context – Alberta, Canada, and the impacts of the poster child of extreme energy and ecocide, the 'tar sands' mega-oil production project, sometimes described in Tolkien terminology as Canada's Mordor, and its effect on the downstream indigenous communities of the Treaty 8 region.[15] While the project has brought income to some, and wealth to the few, its impact on the environment and ecosystems is truly staggering. It is difficult to comprehend the scale of destruction even when viewing the plethora of images on the Internet. I encourage readers to view the tar sands images of the Extreme Energy Initiative's gifted and aptly named photographer, Garth Lenz (garthlenz.com), to get a sense of the enormity of the tar sands ecological devastation. But of course, ecocidal tar sands extraction and processing do not just destroy local ecosystems. The effects on downstream indigenous groups are truly staggering. Their ability to hunt, trap and fish has been severely curtailed and, where it is possible, people are often too fearful of toxins to drink water and eat fish from waterways polluted by the 'externalities' of tar sands production. The situation has led some indigenous spokespersons to talk in terms of a slow industrial genocide being perpetrated against them. The chapter begins with a discussion of the treaty negotiations which paved the way for tar sands development before moving on to discuss the impacts of modern-day tar sands extraction and the applicability of the genocide concept.

In many ways finishing the case studies with Alberta is particularly insightful as the case starkly illustrates core interrelated, interconnected themes of this book: a colonial history of land grabs that continue into the present, neoliberal capitalist pressures to secure more land and resources, environmental destruction, ecocidal extreme energy and vulnerable disadvantaged social groups highly susceptible to the harm of genocide; and finally the case has profound implications for humanity with the potential catastrophic contribution the tars sands are making to global $CO_2$ emissions and anthropogenic climate change.

The final chapter briefly summarizes the key concepts and empirical material of the book before moving on to ask a crucial question for both genocide studies as a field of academic inquiry, and for humanity and the planet as a whole: *where to from here*? With the looming threat of runaway climate change in the twenty-first century, the advent of the geological phase classified by geologists and earth scientists as the Anthropocene (Zalasiewicz et al. 2008: 4–8) and the attendant rapid extinction of species, destruction of habitats, ecological collapse and the self-evident dependency of the human race on our biosphere, ecocide (both 'natural' and 'man-made') will become a primary driver of genocide. It is therefore incumbent upon genocide scholars to attempt a paradigm shift in the greatest traditions of science (Kuhn 2012) and produce a sustained engagement with the rich scholarly tradition of 'political ecology' and 'environmental sociology' (Crook and Short 2014: 298) alongside the emerging field of 'green criminology'[16] in order to produce a theoretical apparatus that can illuminate the links between, and drivers of, ecocide and genocidal social death (Card 2003: 63–79) in the world today. Fittingly, I finish the book with the biggest issue of all: what does all this mean for humanity and the ecosystems we are part of and depend on but are systematically destroying?

# 1 | DEFINITIONAL CONUNDRUMS: A SOCIOLOGICAL APPROACH TO GENOCIDE

## Introduction: sociology and genocide studies

The discipline of sociology was as slow to engage with Holocaust and genocide studies as it was with the theory and practice of human rights.[1] The legacy of classical sociology's emphasis on 'value-free' 'scientific' methodology, which precluded normative considerations (Short 2009: 97), was perhaps the main reason why both areas of potential study remained under-explored by sociologists for so long. Back in 1982 Irving Horowitz suggested that when it comes to such things as human rights violations and genocide 'many sociologists exhibit a studied embarrassment … feeling that intellectual issues posed in such a manner are melodramatic and unfit for scientific discourse' (Horowitz 1982: 3). Zygmunt Bauman was equally blunt when he commented that 'phrases like "the sanctity of human life" or "moral duty" sound as alien in a sociology seminar as they do in the smoke-free sanitized rooms of a bureaucratic office' (Bauman 1990: 9–10). For a time, the dominant view of sociologists working in the field was that the discipline had not been significant in shaping our understanding of genocide as a concept and as a practice.[2]

In the years prior to serious sociological engagement with genocide studies, the Holocaust came to be seen as a paradigmatic, or even the only true, example of genocide.[3] This bias towards the Holocaust, combined with a legal scholarly focus on the United Nations Convention on the Prevention and Punishment of the Crime of Genocide 1948 (The UN Convention), produced a dominant view of genocide that focused on intentional mass killing of certain groups under the direction of the state.[4] Nevertheless, as with the study of human rights, over time sociologists began to make some important contributions to genocide studies. Given that a primary task of the sociologist 'is the construction of a special kind of general concept', as Thomas Burger put it, it was not surprising that sociologists sought to engage in the debates over the *meaning of* genocide.[5] Indeed, some of the most frequently cited definitions are from sociological studies dating back to the early 1990s, while sociologist Leo Kuper's seminal text was published in 1981.[6]

In the definitional debates the major contentious issues have been: identifying the social groups capable of being victims of genocide, the centrality afforded mass killing, the type of genocidal 'intent' required and the exclusion of cultural genocide. Concerning potential victim groups, Alison Palmer, for example, points out the UN Convention 'definition excludes not only groups such as mentally handicapped or homosexuals, both of whom were targeted for destruction by the Nazis, but also political groups' (Palmer 2000). Adam Jones in his textbook captured the general consensus that has developed since the 1980s:[7] 'I consider mass killing to be definitional to genocide … in charting my own course, I am wary of labelling as "genocide" cases where mass killing has not occurred' (Jones 2006: 22).

In the early 1990s two influential sociological studies engaged with the definitional debates and made contributions of lasting significance. In a book on the *History and Sociology of Genocide*, which emerged from their teaching throughout the 1980s, Frank Chalk and Kurt Jonassohn advanced a now frequently cited definition of genocide that sought to overcome some of the problems associated with defining groups by arguing that it is in fact the perpetrator that defines the victim group in genocides. For Chalk and Jonassohn (1990: Note 7) genocide is: 'a form of one-sided mass killing in which a state or other authority intends to destroy a group, as that group and membership in it are defined by the perpetrator'.

Many social scientists now formulate their definition of genocide to include any group, be it a political, economic or cultural collectivity, with such groups being defined, as above, by perpetrator selection. In support of this position some authors cite examples from the two most prominent genocides. For example, Alison Palmer argues that during the Nazi genocides it was they who identified who qualified as a Jew or a mentally or physically handicapped person, regardless of the victim's self-perception (Palmer 2000). While in Rwanda identity cards specified the categories Hutu and Tutsi, such cards presented at checkpoints did not necessarily spare individuals 'whose skin was a bit too light, who were a bit too tall or whose necks were a bit too long' (Levene 2005: 80). As Levene suggests, 'if they looked like Tutsi they might as well be Tutsi. Ultimately, no social or any other science can determine how perpetrators define a group, whether this has some relationship to social reality, or is entirely something which has developed in their own heads' (ibid.: 80). This definition of victim group is thus infinitely open-ended, allowing for the construction of groups from the paranoid imagination of perpetrators.

Defining genocide in this way allows for the possibility that certain groups may be selected for destruction *when prior to this act of selection no such groups existed*. Although Chalk and Jonassohn did not draw specifically on labelling theory, their understanding of genocide is certainly informed by its insights. Labelling theory emerged out of the sociology of deviance and was fundamentally based on symbolic interactionist epistemology. Howard Becker's seminal 1963 work *Outsiders* (1997 [1963]) is a classic example, which posits that the construction and destruction of enemies (or so-called 'deviants') depends on their labelling as such by the powerful (on this point see Fein 1993: 14). As justification for their position Chalk and Jonassohn cite W. I. Thomas's famous dictum that 'if people define a situation as real it is real in its consequences' (Chalk and Jonassohn 1990).

Even so, sociologist Helen Fein, in her seminal special edition of *Current Sociology*, suggests that the victims of genocide are generally members of previously existing *real groups*, whether conceived of as collectivities, races or classes, and *who acknowledge their existence*. In formulating her own definition of genocide, Fein sought to circumvent the problem of excluding certain types of groups by using the term 'collectivity'. Fein argued that the 'UNGC definition of genocide can be reconciled with an expanded – but bounded – sociological definition if we focus on how core concepts are related'. Taking the root *genus*, Fein argued that Raphael Lemkin and the UN framers had in mind 'basic kinds, classes or sub-families of humanity, persisting units of society', whose definition should be 'consistent with our sociological knowledge of both the persistence and construction of group identities in society' (Fein 1993: 23–4). For Fein the distinctive sociological point is that such groups are usually ascriptive – based on birth rather than choice – often inspire enduring particularistic loyalties, and 'are the seed-bed of social movements, voluntary associations, congregations and families; in brief they are *collectivities*' (ibid.: 23). She thus settled on the following definition: 'Genocide is sustained purposeful action by a perpetrator to physically destroy a collectivity directly or indirectly, through interdiction of the biological and social reproduction of group members, sustained regardless of the surrender or lack of threat offered by the victim' (ibid.: 24).

For Fein, then, any social collectivity could be a victim of genocide so long as the offending actions were 'purposeful' and 'physically' destructive. Such requirements were her attempt at answering two key issues in defining genocide: what should count as sufficient 'intent to destroy' and what sorts of action can count as genocidal destruction. As she points out, one of the main problems with the notion of 'intent to destroy' is that most authors conflate 'motive' with 'intent'. The words 'as such' in the UN Convention are no doubt partly to blame for this confusion as they require that groups be intentionally targeted *because of who they are* and not for any other reason such as economic gain or self-defence. Given that perpetrators may well have multiple reasons for genocidal action it is not surprising that Fein advocated a more sociologically realistic approach – *sustained purposeful action*. Under such a formula intent can also be *inferred from action*, which is entirely consistent with a long-established principle in British common law.[8] However, when considering *the type of action* that counts as genocidal her requirement that a group be 'physically' destroyed is sociologically inadequate and at odds with Lemkin's understanding.

Recent sociological engagement has continued to engage in definitional debates, exploring the contentious areas of group definition, the centrality of mass killing and the role of intent, but within a wider attempt to explain *exactly what genocide is* – I have in mind here the work of Powell (2007) and Shaw (2007). These contributions will be discussed in the next section, where I argue that much sociological work on genocide, barring a few notable exceptions, has downplayed or ignored both the importance of 'cultural genocide' to the concept of genocide itself and the relationship between genocide and colonialism; a relationship which has come under increasing scrutiny from historians writing in the field of genocide studies.[9] A hugely significant dimension of these studies has been the recovery of Lemkin's own historical writing (some of which remains unpublished), and recovering the meaning of genocide for Lemkin is, as Martin Shaw points out, a necessary beginning for the sociology of genocide (Shaw 2010a: 146).

Dirk Moses, Ann Curthoys and John Docker in particular have demonstrated that Lemkin was working on a far more ambitious history of genocide than any undertaken since his death, and that he was more open to the diverse manifestations of genocidal relations than many guardians of his heritage believed.[10] Utilizing some of the key insights from such studies in the balance of this chapter I discuss why we should view *cultural genocide* as *central* to our understanding of genocide itself. By extension I argue that the concept is an appropriate term to describe *the current experiences* of many indigenous peoples living under settler colonial rule which has proceeded, as Patrick Wolfe observes, with a 'logic of elimination' (Wolfe 2006: 388). He writes:

> So far as Indigenous people are concerned, where they are *is* who they are, and ... to get in the way of settler colonization, all the native has to do is stay at home. Whatever settlers may say – and they generally have a lot to say – the primary motive for elimination is not race (or religion, ethnicity, grade of civilization, etc.) but access to territory. Territoriality is settler colonialism's specific, irreducible element. (Ibid.: 388)

For indigenous peoples, then, 'land is life – or, at least, land is necessary for life. Thus contests for land can be – indeed, often are – contests for life' (ibid.: 387).

## Cultural genocide as genocide

Writing about sociological approaches to human rights, Michael Freeman makes an important observation:

> the institutionalisation of human rights may ... lead, not to their more secure protection but to their protection in a form that is less threatening to the existing system of power. The *sociological* point is not that human rights should never be institutionalised, but, rather, that institutionalisation is a social process, involving power, and that it should be analysed and not assumed to be beneficial. (Freeman 2002: 85)

Freeman's warning is just as applicable to the UN Convention as it is to many of the other United Nations Agreements on Human Rights[11] and national rights institutionalization projects.[12] Indeed, the narrowed-down final text of the UN Convention was the product of the balance of power between political interests and the exhaustive work of one highly significant individual – the term's inventor, Raphael Lemkin – in attempting to retain as much of his original conception as possible.[13] During the UN debates over the contents of the draft UN Convention cultural genocide proved to be one of the more contentious elements.[14] It elicited strong defensive responses from the colonial powers sensitive to criticism of their policies in non-self-governing territories (see Kuper 1981: 31; Churchill 1997: 411), such that the protection of cultural groups was ultimately left to conventions on human rights and minority rights (Morsink 1999). This outcome, as we shall see, dismayed Raphael Lemkin as it removed a key *method* of genocidal practice. It was also a seriously unfortunate position for indigenous peoples worldwide since their unique status is not adequately covered by the conventions on minority rights, which is why they pushed for their own international rights declaration for so long.[15]

As mentioned earlier, it was 1933 when Lemkin spoke at the International Conference for Unification of Criminal Law in Madrid, and urged the international community to converge on the necessity to ban the destruction, both physical and cultural, of human groups, invoking the linked concepts of 'barbarity' and 'vandalism'. In his subsequent work *Axis Rule in Occupied Europe*, Lemkin combined the concepts of barbarity and vandalism to form a new, more comprehensive one – *genocide*.[16]

Lemkin envisaged the crime of genocide consisting of the deliberate destruction of a nation or ethnic group:

1. by killing its individual members, i.e. physical genocide (derived from Lemkin's notion of 'barbarity');
2. by undermining its way of life, i.e. cultural genocide (derived from 'vandalism').

In a passage from *Axis Rule in Occupied Europe*, Lemkin wrote:

> Genocide has two phases: one, destruction of the national pattern of the oppressed group: the other, the imposition of the national pattern of the oppressor. This imposition, in turn, may be made upon the oppressed population which is allowed to remain, or upon the territory alone, after removal of the

population and the colonization of the area by the oppressor's own nationals. (Lemkin 1944: 79)

The second element of Lemkin's prior formulation, vandalism – the destruction of culture – was now a technique of group destruction (see Moses 2010). Lemkin's central ontological assertion here was that culture integrates human societies and consequently is a necessary precondition for the realization of individual material needs. For Lemkin, culture is as vital to group life as individual physical well-being.

> So-called derived needs, are just as necessary to their existence as the basic physiological needs ... These needs find expression in social institutions or, to use an anthropological term, the culture ethos. If the culture of a group is violently undermined, the group itself disintegrates and its members must either become absorbed in other cultures which is a wasteful and painful process or succumb to personal disorganization and, perhaps, physical destruction ... [Thus] the destruction of cultural symbols is genocide ... [It] menaces the existence of the social group which exists by virtue of its common culture. (Cited in Moses 2008)

'This quotation', according to Moses, 'gives us clues to Lemkin's conception of genocide. He was more concerned with the loss of culture than the loss of life' (ibid.: 12), as culture is the social fabric of a *genus*. Indeed, in Lemkin's formulation, culture is the unit of collective memory, whereby the legacies of the dead can be kept alive and each cultural group has its own unique distinctive *genius* deserving of protection (see Jones 2006: 13). National culture for Lemkin is an essential element of world culture and nations have a life of their own comparable to the life of individual. On this point Lemkin wrote:

> The world represents only so much culture and intellectual vigour as are created by its component national groups. The destruction of a nation, therefore, results in the loss of its future contributions to the world. Moreover, such a destruction offends our feelings of morality and justice in much the same way as

does the criminal killing of a human being: the crime in the one
case as in the other is murder, though on a vastly greater scale.
(Lemkin 1944: 91)

After finishing *Axis Rule* Lemkin set about researching for his
intended magnum opus, a comprehensive multi-volume 'History
of Genocide', covering ancient, medieval and modern periods. His
notes for this project have recently been explored by a few genocide
scholars and their reports make for revealing reading. Lemkin's
notes are particularly instructive on the 'methods and techniques of
genocide', which include:

> physical – massacre and mutilation, deprivation of livelihood
> (starvation, exposure, etc. often by deportation), slavery
> – exposure to death; biological – separation of families,
> sterilization, destruction of foetus; cultural – desecration
> and destruction of cultural symbols (books, objects of art,
> loot, religious relics, etc.), destruction of cultural leadership,
> destruction of cultural centres (cities, churches, monasteries,
> schools, libraries), prohibition of cultural activities or codes of
> behaviour, forceful conversion, demoralization. (McDonnell
> and Moses 2005)

These methods of genocide are so pervasive throughout Lemkin's
unpublished notes that it seems he viewed physical genocide and
cultural genocide not as two distinct phenomena, but rather *one
process that could be accomplished through a variety of means*, such as
those listed above. This understanding is based on a functional view
of national structure where the physical and cultural aspects are
seen as interdependent and indivisible. From this perspective the
destruction of a nation could occur when *any* structural element was
destroyed. Even if the national group did not possess recognized
sovereignty Lemkin thought it had an inherent right to exist just
like the sovereign individual – and such groups provided the
essential basis of human culture as a whole – such that the concept
of 'genocide' was designed specifically to protect that life (Powell
2007: 534).

Lemkin defined genocide in terms of the violation of a nation's
right to its collective existence – genocide in this sense is quite

simply the destruction of a nation. Such destruction can be achieved through the 'mass killings of all members of a nation'; *or* through 'a coordinated plan of different actions aiming at the destruction of essential foundations of the life of national groups'. It is this latter point that is missed or ignored by those authors like Helen Fein who insist on the centrality of *physical* destruction to the concept of genocide. As Dirk Moses suggests, the extraordinary implication here is 'that Lemkin did not properly understand genocide, despite the fact that he invented the term and went to great trouble to explain its meaning. Instead, most scholars presume to instruct Lemkin, retrospectively, about his concept, although they are in fact proposing a different concept, usually mass murder' (Moses 2010: 3).

Lemkin's conception also poses a serious problem for those theorists that suggest perpetrators define the victim group, since it is quite conceivable that a perpetrator can invent a categorization that does not exist in any meaningful sense; e.g. recall Mark Levene's example of Rwanda: 'if you looked like a Tutsi you might as well be a Tutsi'. Is this the sort of offence Lemkin had in mind when he invented the term genocide? It may well be that Levene's example is better described as an individual murder or a crime against humanity within a broader genocidal context, *but not a genocidal act in and of itself*, if we presume that the victim did not belong to the type of group (with a cultural identity capable of making future contributions to the world) whose life the concept of genocide was designed to protect.

In 'What is Genocide?', a thought-provoking contribution to genocide studies, sociologist Martin Shaw attempts to move us away from problematic group definitions towards a focus on what he describes as the 'missing link' of genocide studies: 'civilians' (Shaw 2007: 113). He writes:

we should focus on what all genocidal campaigns have in common: not the destruction of a particular group type (the groups attacked vary greatly between cases) but the civilian character of the attacked population ... Although victims are targeted for their supposed particular identities, the civilian character – not a particular identity type – is the *common* feature of both group targets and individual victims across *all* genocides. The focus on civilian enemies demarcates genocide from war

and defines its comprehensive immortality and illegality. Thus
the concept of 'civilian' is central to the understanding of
genocide. (Ibid.: 117)

While the identification of *civilians* as victims is an important
element of genocide, distinguishes the concept from war and is
in keeping with Lemkin's use of the words 'subjects', 'civilians'
and 'populations' (Lemkin 1944: 79) to describe some victim
characteristics, this understanding does not seem to offer much of a
distinction between genocide and crimes against humanity – which
are 'directed against any civilian population'; it also downplays
the importance of culture to the master concept.[17] Indeed, the
foundational conceptual ingredient of genocide for Lemkin was *culture*
not 'civilian'. For Lemkin culture animates the *genos* in genocide
– the social group exists by virtue of its common culture. For this
reason it is not surprising that during the process of construction of
the draft UN Convention, Lemkin argued that 'Cultural Genocide
is the most important part of the Convention' (Moses 2008: 12–13),
and yet, owing to political influences and adaptations during the
drafting process, the final legal definition was narrower than Lemkin
had originally intended, largely omitting the cultural method.[18] In his
1958 autobiography, *Totally Unofficial Man*, Lemkin wrote:

> I defended it successfully through two drafts. It meant the
> destruction of the cultural pattern of a group, such as the
> language, the traditions, the monuments, archives, libraries,
> churches. In brief: the shrines of the soul of a nation. But there
> was not enough support for this idea in the Committee ... So
> with a heavy heart I decided not to press for it. (Cited in Docker
> 2004: 3)

Lemkin had to drop an idea that, in his words, 'was very dear to me'
(ibid.).

The codified definition is the only internationally accepted legal
definition of genocide and is enshrined in Article II (a) to (e) of the
Genocide Convention.[19] While this definition was based on Lemkin's
initial concept of genocide, as Curthoys and Docker point out there
has been considerable confusion between two basic definitions of
genocide: 'the discursive definition in chapter nine of *Axis Rule* and

the codified definition of the 1948 Genocide Convention' (Curthoys and Docker 2008: 13).

*Lemkin and settler colonialism* Out of the two definitions that Lemkin helped to create, the legal definition has, inevitably, been the predominant definition of genocide. Furthermore, the fact that the genocide concept was formed during the context of the Second World War ensured that the Holocaust deeply influenced its conception and the subsequent understanding of the term by scholars. Indeed, views such as that the Holocaust is the 'ultimate expression' (Horowitz 1982, cited in Curthoys and Docker 2008: 27) of genocide has led to it commonly being the example case that other potential genocides are compared against. Despite the important sociological interventions mentioned above, by the mid-1980s the perception that genocide 'equals mass murder' was 'an orthodoxy of sorts'.[20] Shaw concurs with this view: 'because Genocide has been narrowed down to Nazi-like extermination policies, few recent cases have been recognised'. Only that of Rwanda (1994) has been overwhelmingly accepted, since it involved physical destruction (Shaw 2007: 48) and the designated perpetrator regime was no friend of the international community's power brokers.

For Moses, this reductionist interpretation of genocide dismisses the validity of the experience of other genocide victims: 'the establishment of the Holocaust as *the* threshold of trauma in western modernity conveniently renders invisible the experience of trauma that has driven the vengeful yet redemptive politics of minorities and displaced peoples for centuries, including, significantly, the Palestinian one' (Moses 2011: 13). This trend has meant that 'from a legal perspective, genocide unaccompanied by mass killing is rare, and has stood little chance of being prosecuted' (Jones 2006: 13). However, it is significant that it isn't actually necessary for anyone to be killed in order for genocide to take place under the Genocide Convention's definition. So, rather than prioritizing mass killings; Lemkin's focus lay with the destruction of the rudiments of social and cultural existence:

> Generally speaking, genocide does not necessarily mean the immediate destruction of a nation, except when accomplished by mass killing of all members of a nation. It is intended rather to

signify *a coordinated plan of different actions aiming at the destruction of the essential foundations of the life of national groups*, with the aim of annihilating the groups themselves. The objectives of such a plan would be *disintegration of the political and social institutions of culture, language, national feelings, religion, and the economic existence of national groups, and the destruction of the personal security, liberty, health, dignity, and even the lives of the individuals belonging to such groups.* Genocide is directed against the national group as an entity, and the actions involved are directed against individuals, not in their individual capacity, but as members of the national group. (Lemkin 1944: 79, emphasis added)

A key strand of recent genocide scholarship focuses on the link Lemkin made between colonization processes[21] and genocidal practices,[22] at the heart of which is an understanding of the importance of territory as a primary cause of violence (Zimmerer 2014: 273). As Jürgen Zimmerer points out,

> Space is a finite quantity for which people (by definition indefinite in their numbers) compete. The need for land can be real or imagined (it can include imaginative landscapes, for example, plans for settlements, economic or agricultural use, or fear of land shortage). Early globalisation in the form of European colonialism affected this in three ways: The movement of people (settlement), the inclusion of distant regions in the emerging world economy (agriculture, mining, hunting, trading with certain impacts on people living there) and an increase in communication over vast distances (exchange of personnel, representations, learning experiences) … Colonialism, in particular settler colonialism, can be seen as the control of space (land) on the basis of race. It is – if nothing else – land grabbing by the colonisers on a truly global scale. Genocidal violence accompanied the colonial settlement process, particularly in settler colonies. (Ibid.: 273)

Racist colonial ideologies of 'superiority' and 'progress' served land grabs by placing the indigenous inhabitants outside the sphere of moral concern. It's important to note, however, that the primary driver of colonial genocide is an expansionist economic system, which rationally requires more and more territory to control and exploit. In this sense rational (economic) choice is facilitated by ideology and not driven by it (ibid.: 275).

When Lemkin defined the genocide concept, he defined it as 'intrinsically colonial' (Moses 2008: 9). Indeed, he stated that once the 'national pattern' of a victim group had been destroyed, the act of genocide involved the imposition of the 'national pattern' of the colonial oppressor, while the oppressed population can be allowed to remain following the colonization of the area by the oppressor's own nationals (Lemkin 1944: 79). Taking up this connection, some contemporary writers such as Churchill (in Jones 2004: 80) concur that where the practice of imposing the 'national pattern' of the colonial oppressor is the result of 'policy', it should indeed be considered genocidal. Jean-Paul Sartre stated that 'Colonialization is … necessarily a cultural genocide' (Sartre 1967). This view has since been expanded by others such as Card, who describes genocide as a 'social death' (Card 2003). For Abed, it is this 'social death' that makes acts genocidal (Abed 2006). This focus on the genocidal nature of destroying a group culture is, as we have seen, similar to Lemkin's own position. He wrote: 'the destruction of cultural symbols is genocide' (Lemkin, cited in Moses 2008: 12). To destroy their function 'menaces the existence of the social group which exists by virtue of its common culture' (ibid.). Lemkin also recognized that national groups do not last for ever, and differentiated between cultural change and cultural genocide, when nations either 'fade away after having exhausted their spiritual and physical energies' (Lemkin, cited in Moses 2010) or 'when they are murdered on the highway of world history. Dying of age or disease is a disaster but genocide is a crime' (ibid.).

As already mentioned, owing to political opposition, the cultural element of genocide is largely absent from the final text of the Genocide Convention. It was, however, present in the draft stages and the term 'cultural genocide' was also included in Article 7 of the draft UN Declaration on the Rights of Indigenous Peoples.[23] While the term is not present in the final text, its initial inclusion suggests that the concept is still a valid one, despite the lack of support at state level. As Moses points out, 'although indigenous people often regard assimilation and development policies as genocidal or at least culturally genocidal, we know that they have no legal protection from the UN Genocide Convention. "Cultural genocide" is of rhetorical effect only' (Moses 2010: 39). Despite its lack of currency from a legal perspective, 'cultural genocide' was integral to Lemkin's understanding of genocide (ibid.), and as such I consider this method in each of the case studies in this book.

When considering genocide within a colonial context it is also important to acknowledge that Lemkin never stipulated that the crime of genocide was limited to state actors (ibid.). This is also made explicit in Article 4 of the Convention, which states that 'persons committing genocide ... shall be punished, whether they are constitutionally responsible rulers, public officials or private individuals.'[24] This is extremely relevant when examining the genocidal nature of settler colonialist societies, as in some cases the settlers may commit acts of genocide despite it not being the official state practice. This consequently raises the question as to what extent any genocides committed by such settlers can be defined as a function of the colonialist agenda itself. If some rogue settlers commit such acts, it is unfair to blame the colonial authorities, or assume there was a deliberate intent endorsed and enforced by them. It is, therefore, a complex issue. The Australian academic Tony Barta perceives one possibility as being a 'genocidal society' 'as distinct from a genocidal state – one in which the bureaucratic apparatus might officially be directed to protect innocent people but in which a whole race is nevertheless subject to remorseless pressures of destruction inherent in the very nature of the society' (Barta 2000: 239).

Thus the motives of the colonizers may be 'muddled and obscure' (Curthoys and Docker 2008: 29). It could be argued that the physical destruction of indigenous people cannot be described as 'genocide' since they are not intentionally being targeted for who they are, but rather are simply in the way of the colonizers and the land they seek to possess, or, as Rose deftly stated, 'to get in the way of settler colonization, all the native has to do is stay at home' (Bird Rose 1991: 46). Many scholars have sought to counter that argument, including Césaire, who declared that 'no one colonizes innocently' (Césaire 1955) and Curthoys, who concluded that: 'to seek to take the land whatever the consequences ... is surely a genocidal process' (Curthoys 2008: 246). Abed asserts that many indigenous groups are 'territorially bounded' (Abed 2006: 326). For him, therefore, removing these groups from their land or to control their interaction with it is inevitably a genocidal practice. As Wolfe explains: 'Land is life – or, at least, land is necessary for life. Thus contests for land can be – indeed, often are – contests for life' (Wolfe 2006: 387).

The production of new, permanent societies – forged on the back of an entrenched logic of racism which sought to protect the culturally white character of the population, and utterly destroy the indigenous world – establishes settler colonialism not as 'an essentially fleeting stage', but rather a 'persistent defining characteristic of this new world settler society' (Elkins and Pederson 2005: 1). As Wolfe illustrates with reference to Australia, 'the determination "settler-colonial state" is Australian society's primary structural characteristic rather than merely a statement about its origins' (Wolfe 1999: 163). Settler colonialism, therefore, is a 'structure not an event' (ibid.: 390); it is a phenomenon, which consists of complex social formations, and significantly it exists and develops continually with time, and thus Wolfe proposes that 'structural genocide' be the term used in such settler colonial contexts (ibid.: 403).

The structurally defining settler colonial logic typically produces societies marked by 'pervasive inequalities, usually codified in law, between the settler and indigenous populations' (Elkins and Pederson 2005: 4). This settler–indigene division is usually pervasive throughout the economy and the legal and political systems, manifested by institutionalized settler privilege. It is on this basis that later we will be considering its relationship to genocide: if, since the initial point of colonization, contests for land, and therefore life, are ongoing, it seems logical to assume that the destruction of the native population – within the colonized territory – becomes a likely possibility. This settler privilege inherent in this form of colonialism arguably 'denies human rights to human beings whom it has subdued by violence … since the native is subhuman, the Declaration of Human Rights does not apply to him' (Sartre 1990: 22). We can see that, for Lemkin, genocide was the attempted annihilation of a group by a variety of actions aimed at undermining the foundations necessary for the survival of the group as a group. So what of indigenous peoples in the world today, and specifically those living under settler colonial rule? How should we think about the continued assimilationist pressures they face from the spread of global capitalism?

## Indigenous peoples: genocide or cultural change?

Even where national groups do not possess recognized sovereignty, like many indigenous peoples living within colonial settler states, Lemkin thought national collectivities had an inherent right to exist just like the sovereign individual. He also thought that a nation possesses a biological life and an interrelated and interdependent cultural life such that an attack on its physical existence is also an attack on its cultural existence, *and vice versa*. Lemkin clearly understood the importance of cultural destruction to group life and that such destruction will have dire *physical* consequences – which is especially true of indigenous peoples.

Regardless of whether indigenous peoples live in wealthy states like Canada, the USA, Australia or countries in South America and Africa, their stories of dispossession, environmental degradation, and appalling social statistics including endemic suicide, very high levels of infant mortality and exotic diseases, are remarkably similar. Indeed, a study by the Commonwealth Policy Studies Unit highlights 'the extraordinary similarity of experiences of Indigenous Peoples across the Commonwealth – between those in First World Countries and those in Third World countries'.[25] Such 'conditions of life' are leading increasing numbers of indigenous representatives to describe their *present* situation in terms of genocide. As Australian aboriginal academic and activist Larissa Behrendt states: 'use of the term "genocide" to describe the [indigenous] colonial experience has been met with scepticism from some quarters ... Yet the political posturing and semantic debates do nothing to dispel the feeling Indigenous people have that this is the word that adequately describes our experience as colonised peoples' (Behrendt 2001: 132).

The genocidal 'logic of elimination' (Wolfe 2006) that informed frontier massacres in places like Australia and North America, and the assimilationist agendas that emerged once it was clear that the natives would not 'die out', can in more recent times be found underpinning settler colonial expansionist land grabs driven by global capitalism. Indeed, after 1945 traditional colonial terror was transformed into a 'genocide machine' as the nature of capitalist domination became less overtly racist and more attuned to American corporate imperatives (Davis and Zannis 1973). Driven by corporate agendas governments frequently dispossess indigenous groups through industrial mining and farming, but also through military operations and even national park schemes – all of which routinely take no account of core indigenous rights.[26] But of all such activities it is industrial extractive industries which pose perhaps the biggest threat to indigenous peoples' survival, for it is not just the accompanying dispossession which they bring but also the ecocidal 'externalities' of pollution and environmental degradation. A particularly acute example of such is the 'tar sands' mining project in northern Alberta, Canada, which we will examine in Chapter 5, an undoubted 'ecocide' that is producing horrendous environmental destruction with quite predictable consequences for human health (Stainsby 2007). Environmental pollution from the tar sands[27] has been linked to high levels of deadly diseases such as leukaemia, lymphoma and colon cancer (Petersen 2007) in indigenous communities.[28] For George Poitras, a Mikisew Cree First Nation member affected by tar sands mining in Fort Chipewyan, Alberta, the battle with industrial mining over land and resources comes down to the fundamental right to exist: 'if we don't have land and we don't have anywhere to carry out our traditional lifestyle, we lose who we are as a people. So if there's no land, then it's equivalent in our estimation to genocide of a people' (cited in ibid.).

We can see here that the victims of these policies seem to appreciate Lemkin's assertion that genocide attacks the 'essential foundations of the life of national groups',[29] much more than those writers who insist on the centrality of violent destruction for a finding of genocide. On this question, however, there is a more subtle point to discuss in Lemkin's writings. Dirk Moses recently pointed out that Lemkin appears to consider cultural destruction genocidal *only in conjunction* with attacks on the physical and biological elements of a group (Moses 2008: 13). While more recently Thomas Butcher made a similar argument, reading Lemkin's conception of genocide as *requiring* a 'synchronised' attack owing to the 'ontological character', i.e. the holistic nature, of group identity (Butcher 2013). This is even though in the same article we read Lemkin's categorical assertion that 'the destruction of cultural symbols is genocide' and that Lemkin's functional holism meant that he characterized the core elements of social groups as 'interdependent, meaning that a change to one element affects multiple other elements'. Indeed, rather than the 'necessity' of a 'synchronised attack', Lemkin's functional holism is much more convincingly interpreted as akin to the workings of the body – whereby disease of one organ may well produce breakdowns in others and ultimate death.

Even so, in articulating his position on this point, Moses, like Butcher, drew attention to the cases of genocide Lemkin studied, where 'attacks on culture were inextricably interwoven with a broader assault encompassing the totality of group existence' (Moses 2008: 13). In other words, Lemkin's case studies involved attacks on culture as *part of* a broader offensive on the totality of group existence, and consequently he came to view cultural and physical destruction as interrelated, interdependent elements of a singular genocidal process. This position would seem injurious to the genocide claims of some indigenous peoples today since violent physical destruction is not presently occurring in places like Australia and Canada (although this is less certain in many other countries where indigenous people are resisting natural resource extraction, e.g. Botswana, Brazil, Peru and Mexico). But to take such a view involves invoking a snapshot view of history divorced from past context and experience. Indeed, most indigenous peoples will have suffered forms of violent physical destruction at some point in the history of their colonization such that their current cultural destruction should be seen as the tail end of a singular genocidal process that invariably began with direct physical destruction. Moreover, physical destruction need not be direct but can of course be achieved indirectly through inflicting on the group 'conditions of life' (such as dispossession and environmental destruction) which lead to that end. Those indigenous peoples who are currently invoking the term genocide to describe their current experiences, such as the Mikisew Cree above, are invariably referring to both physical (albeit indirect and latent) *and* cultural destruction.

When thinking through Moses' and Butcher's reading of Lemkin on this point it is worth noting that when concerned with creating the international offence of genocide, Lemkin's functional holism did not lead him to consider cultural destruction genocide *only in conjunction with physical attacks* or only as part of a *synchronized attack*. Given Lemkin's support for the original UN Convention draft (the Secretariat's)[30] it seems that he considered the cultural method of genocide to be such a serious crime, in and of itself, as to be *stand-alone punishable as genocide*, provided it was 'with the purpose of destroying [the group] in whole or in part or of preventing its preservation or development' (also note the absence of the final

Convention's 'as such' motive requirement). In the Secretariat's draft cultural genocide ('destroying the specific characteristics of the group') had its own section – Article II (3) – as a means of committing genocide *in and of itself*. To be found guilty of genocide under Article II (3), the accused party would not also have to be charged under Article II (1) or (2). It is just the same with the remnants of the idea in the final UN Convention (Articles II d and e), which are also stand-alone crimes of genocide that need not be accompanied by direct physical killing.

Even so, there is some debate on how cultural genocide differs from other forms of cultural change. On this issue Lemkin's unpublished works are again illuminating. Docker cites Lemkin's plea that cultural genocide 'must not be confused with the gradual changes a culture may undergo' (Docker 2004: 3). Lemkin was concerned to distinguish cultural genocide from 'the continuous and slow adaptation of the culture to new situations', outside influences and the 'assimilation of certain foreign culture traits' and the like, which he preferred to call a 'process of cultural diffusion' (ibid.). Cultural change, for Lemkin, was induced by outside influences resulting in weaker societies adopting the social and political institutions of more efficient ones or becoming absorbed by them because they better fulfil basic needs (Moses 2008: 11). The key point for Lemkin in making the distinction between cultural diffusion and cultural genocide was that the former was a slow and relatively spontaneous process (ibid.).

Considering the issue in a colonial context involving indigenous peoples, Lemkin suggested that with the loss of hunting grounds they were forced to accept 'the economic and social system of the white man', 'cultural change' of a 'radical and perhaps inhumane type (considering the misery of the generations undergoing the change)' but not necessarily genocidal (ibid.: 14). But such diffusion would become cultural genocide (and physical genocide) if insufficient measures were taken to assist the change from nomadic life, with the Indians through cession and warfare being left 'landless and foodless' (ibid.). On this understanding *sufficient measures* could involve indigenous peoples being permitted, by a settler state, to retain control of a land base of sufficient size as to allow for meaningful political and cultural autonomy and physical and cultural preservation; then any gradual cultural changes they would undergo would not constitute genocide since they would be of a more organic and *autonomous* nature.[31]

It has been argued, however, that Lemkin had a somewhat static view of culture and unwittingly participated in the discourse on indigenous extinction, common in the cultural evolutionism of anthropology since the nineteenth century, and which significantly downplayed indigenous agency, adaptation and survival (Moses 2008: 16). Furthermore, when writing about the Maya in twentieth-century Mexico, Lemkin suggested that although the 'condition of the Indians has been improving ... their *cultural heritage has been irrevocably lost*' (ibid.). He went on to concede that 'one million Indians still speak Maya dialect today', but stated that while they still tilled the land as their forefathers had done, 'they have lost their civilized habits, their remarkable skills and knowledge long ago' (ibid.). In contrast to perhaps the dominant twentieth-century conceptions of 'culture' and 'social structure' as somewhat static phenomena reproducing over time in the same fixed form,[32] writers like Norbert Elias maintained that change is integral to social structure – what seems fixed and stable is actually undergoing a continuous process of change. If we fail to recognize this we may misperceive change as a sign of pathological breakdown or decay (Powell 2007: 538). Despite the cultural adaptation that has seen the 'survival' of many indigenous peoples today there is still value in Lemkin's point regarding twentieth-century Maya culture that is pertinent to the issue of cultural genocide. To pinpoint this it is useful to reflect on the nature of the *genos* in genocide and its relationship to the notion of social structure.

Drawing on Norbert Elias's relational sociology, sociologist Christopher Powell suggests we replace the concept of social structure with that of social 'figuration', meaning the action or process of forming into a figure and the resulting shape, as the former concept has negative associations with stasis. Applying this idea to the concept of genocide, Powell suggests that a '*genos*' must connote a type of social figuration. The collective object designated by Lemkin's use of '*genos*' must, like other social structures, have the general property of being a dynamic relational network formed through practical social interactions in historical time (ibid.). However, as Mohammed Abed argues, the collective object must also display certain features if it is to be logically and ethically susceptible to the harm of genocide (see Abed 2006). Thinking carefully about the *genos* in genocide and the social phenomena that Lemkin was trying to protect, not just any social figuration is capable of being the victim of genocide. As Abed suggests, its members must consent to a life in common, its culture must be comprehensive and its membership should not be easily renounced. Under these conditions, the flourishing of the group's culture and social ethos will have profound and far-reaching effects on the well-being of its individual members such that the destruction of its cultural and social institutions will eventuate in the individuals suffering the harms and deprivations peculiar to the crime of genocide (ibid.).

Thus, if we consider the *genos* in genocide to be a social figuration – made up of a fluid network of consensual practical social relations which form a comprehensive culture, from which an exit would be arduous – *then genocide is the forcible breaking down of such relationships* – the destruction of the social figuration. This destruction, as Lemkin suggested, can be achieved in a variety of ways *not restricted to physical killing*. It could be through some form of 'ethnic cleansing' to ensure that people are no longer connected to each other or through suppression of language, religion, law, kinship systems and other cultural practices through which the people maintain the relations among themselves, or through the imposition of severe conditions of life that break down social solidarities, etc.

Writing in 1845, Friedrich Engels described how the imposition of extreme conditions of life on a group could result in a form of 'social murder':

> ... society in England daily and hourly commits what the working-men's organs, with perfect correctness, characterise as social murder, ... it has placed the workers under conditions in which they can neither retain health nor live long; it undermines the vital force of these workers gradually, little by little, and so hurries them to the grave before their time ... society knows how injurious such conditions are to the health and the life of the workers, and yet does nothing to improve these conditions. That it knows the consequences of its deeds; that its act is, therefore, not mere manslaughter, but murder. (Engels 1958: 109)

Relating a very similar idea specifically to the harm of genocide, the philosopher Claudia Card suggests that '*social death is utterly central to the evil of genocide* not just when a genocide is primarily cultural but even when it is homicidal on a massive scale' (Card 2003, emphasis added). Card emphasizes how social vitality is constituted via contemporary and intergenerational relationships that form an identity which gives meaning to a life. It follows, then, that a major loss of social vitality is a loss of identity and consequently a serious loss of meaning for one's existence. It is just such a focus on *social death* and not mass killing that allows us to distinguish the peculiar evil of genocide from crimes against humanity and mass murder. Genocidal murders are but an extreme means to achieve social death. Such death could be produced without specific 'intent to destroy' but could occur through sporadic and uncoordinated action or be a by-product of an incompatible expansionist economic system.[33] It might even result from attempts to do good: to enlighten, to modernize, to evangelize (Powell 2007: 538).

Yet if a *genos*, like all social institutions, is itself a process of change and transformation and adaptation, how can we adequately distinguish 'cultural change' from 'cultural genocide'? Following Powell's reasoning, if we take a *genos* to be a continuous changing and transforming social figuration, *'the effect of genocide is to disrupt that process'* (ibid., emphasis added). He elaborates:

A living, breathing social figuration (as it were) decays and grows at the same time, producing new ideas, new institutions, new practices, from which emerge the 'future contributions to the world' that Lemkin wrote of. Genocide violently interrupts this process. We may count among the means by which genocide may be committed the measures that interrupt the reproduction of the figuration over time, the passing on of culture to children, the renewal of social institutions, and also the measures that prevent change, through the silencing of innovation in thought, art, technology, everyday practice, or through forcible confinement to a fossilized 'tradition' that is not allowed to be transformed. (Ibid.: 539)

Many indigenous peoples openly accept and often encourage the importing of ideas and practices from other cultures that ultimately have little impact on their uniqueness (Samson 2009). For example, in Australia and the Americas, instead of taking Christianity or science as objectively true, indigenous peoples often selectively use them as enriching or useful to their own non-European way of life (see ibid.). Even though there is no absolute zero point of cultural authenticity, for many groups (but of course not all) that define themselves as indigenous peoples today indigeneity is synonymous with attachments to land.[34] The externally orchestrated *forcible* disruption of this relationship will gravely interrupt the reproduction of their social figuration over time and critically endanger their distinct existence.[35] Colin Samson writes:

> The loss of interconnection between territory, subsidence, livelihood and cultural practises are in almost all cases the results of impositions that do not enrich a people's experience. Among many of the world's indigenous peoples, descents into community-wide trauma and dysfunction have been precipitated by removal from lands. (Samson 2009)

Since cultures are complex and have the capacity to change rapidly, emerging as well as dying out, Pretty et al. (2008) use four intrinsic components to assess these changes; (i) beliefs, meanings and worldviews, (ii) livelihoods, practices and resource management systems, (iii) knowledge bases and languages, and (iv) institutions, norms and regulations. Crucially all four *must be sustained if cultural continuity is to be successfully attained.* So while culture is in a sense always 'changing', it is the *context and manner in which it changes* that is important to the question of genocide. Thus, when Lemkin talked of Mayan cultural heritage – 'their remarkable skills and knowledge' – being 'irrevocably lost ... long ago', he was making a valid comment that did not deny the Mayan peoples today their right to identify as Mayan but which drew attention to the fact that their present social figuration has been *forcefully* influenced by a colonization process that dispossessed them and violently interrupted the reproduction of their figuration[36] over time to the extent that important cultural continuities with the past (that cut across all of Pretty et al.'s four components) were radically violated, and quite possibly 'irrevocably lost'. It is just such an interruption of a social figuration that is genocidal.

Genocide is far more than a label or an international crime. It is a sociological concept with a rich intellectual history that connects the idea to colonization processes and their socially destructive effects.

Despite this, it is arguable that 'genocide as mass killing' is still the dominant understanding, but as this chapter has shown, such a view is contrary to Lemkin's formulation and conceptually flawed. Even so, we have seen that key sociological definitions of genocide have, somewhat strangely, downplayed the 'social' dimension implicit in a *genos*, preferring to argue out or ignore a key method of group destruction – destruction of culture. Consequently this contribution has relied on interdisciplinary observations to make *sociological* points. If we take the *genos* in genocide to be a social figuration which forms a comprehensive culture (along Abed's lines) then *genocide is the forcible breaking down of such relationships* – the destruction of the social figuration, which as we have seen can be accomplished by non-violent means. Mass killing is but one way a social figuration can be broken down, crippled or destroyed completely; '*social death is what makes* some act or series of acts genocidal' (Abed 2006: 312), not the *method* by which such destruction is achieved.

Furthermore, this chapter has argued that the dominant understanding of genocide as mass killing is at odds with the ideas of the term's originator, Raphael Lemkin, who 'rejected the idea that "the destruction of the national pattern of the oppressed group" necessarily involves the mass physical death of group members' (ibid.: 309). He argued that destroying the social relations on which a group's identity and communal life are based can be genocidal (ibid.). Indeed, we have seen that cultural destruction is '*central* to Lemkin's conception of genocide' (Moses 2008: 12), and consequently this chapter further contends that cultural genocide *is genocide* and strictly speaking does not need the 'cultural' descriptor since it simply serves to describe *a method* of genocide. In so doing we avoid the problem that Wolfe warns of whereby *only* physical genocide is seen as 'the real thing' (Wolfe 2006: 118).

Those indigenous peoples fighting to retain or regain their lands are fighting for their *life as distinct peoples* since, for them, their spirituality and cultural vitality are based in and on and with their lands. If we take this point seriously, when this relationship is *forcibly* interrupted and breaks down we can only conclude that genocide is occurring. Indeed, when indigenous peoples, who have a physical, cultural and spiritual connection to their land, are *forcibly* dispossessed and estranged from their lands they invariably experience 'social death' and thus genocide. Furthermore, when indigenous lands are used by extractive industries the inherent corporate preference for externalizing environmental costs can lead to physical as well as cultural destruction. The tar sands project is a prime example of this, as we shall see in Chapter 5.

In my view what is needed from academics in the field is more research into the *context and manner* in which indigenous cultures are 'changing' in the face of continuing settler colonial expansionist projects driven by global capitalism and a 'logic of elimination' (Wolfe 2006). Moreover, such research should unashamedly utilize the analytical lens of *genocide* as assaults on the 'essential foundations of life of national groups' is what the concept was designed to highlight and prohibit.

## 2 | THE GENOCIDE–ECOCIDE NEXUS

The neologism 'ecocide', 'eco' meaning ecosystem and 'cide' meaning destruction, has been around for some time. In 1970, during the time of the Vietnam War, a group of scientists coined and propagated the term 'ecocide' to denounce the environmental destruction and potential human health catastrophe arising from the herbicidal warfare programme known as Operation Ranch Hand (Zierler 2011: 14). The scientists' accusation was notable for being levelled against their own government and for effectively forcing national policy to renounce first use of herbicides in future wars (ibid.: 14). Much as happened with genocide, the term 'ecocide' has since entered the popular lexicon and come to mean something somewhat different to its original conception. Unlike genocide, however, the term ecocide has since *expanded beyond its original meaning and context*. As early as 1971 environmental activists soon adopted 'ecocide' as their own, with one writer arguing that 'the message of our day is ecocide, the environment being murdered by mankind ... Our dense, amber air is a noxious emphysema agent; farming – antihusbandry – turns fertile soil into a poisoned wasteland; rivers are sewers, lakes cesspools, and our oceans are dying' (ibid.: 14).

More recent works have used the word 'ecocide' to condemn the Euro-American colonial destruction of indigenous peoples' land-based cultures; the destruction of rainforests around the equatorial world; the corporate takeover and consequent destruction of a Pacific island; the neoliberal debt crisis in developing countries; the alarming trend of accelerated species extinction in recent decades; and the environmental ravages wrought across Eurasia in the pursuit of a totalitarian command economy (ibid.: 14). Nowadays, ecocide is often used in the context of the most pressing environmental issue facing the world, anthropogenic climate change, while some activists have preferred to use the term 'climate genocide' when denouncing carbon-dioxide-emitting corporate operations and the governments that back them and fail to place strong curbs on emissions rates. Nevertheless, despite such usages it's important, as it is with the concept of genocide, to properly understand the historical origins of the concept, its original intended meaning and practical utility.

Since the 1970s the movement to eradicate ecocide has attracted interest from legal theorists, political scientists and environmental activists, but unlike in the field of genocide studies, there has been no serious definitional debate or conceptual consideration of 'ecocide', nor is there a rich intellectual history of case studies and comparative research on which to draw. This is perhaps because ecocide is still a concept and not an international crime; for while Lemkin had developed a robust concept of genocide prior to its institutionalization in international law in 1948, the field of genocide studies developed well after the crime's codification. Crucially, the Genocide Convention, as we saw earlier, was a key reference point for much scholarly work, and without a similar international crime it is unsurprising that, despite a regrettable amount of potential data sets, there is no coherent field of ecocide studies as yet. This chapter, then, rather than surveying a field of ecocide studies and advocating an understanding of the concept, will first delve into the institutional history of ecocide within the UN system and its connection to the crime of genocide before moving on to discuss a high-profile contemporary articulation of ecocide and the empirical underpinnings of the nexus between genocide and ecocide in the world today.

Our Ecocide Project research into the history of ecocide in the UN system revealed that members and delegates of several UN institutions, including the Sub-Commission on Prevention of Discrimination and Protection of Minorities,[1] the Legal Committee of the General Assembly and the International Law Commission discussed, at different times over a forty-year period, how to define and criminalize severe environmental destruction. These institutions met frequently to discuss the elements and issues involved in formulating such an international crime, including the level of intent required for an offence to constitute 'ecocide' or 'severe damage to the environment'.[2]

In the years following the implementation of the 1948 United Nations Genocide Convention many governments began to voice their concerns about its effectiveness. Genocide was still a reality in many parts of the world and the Convention seemed to offer little to those groups it was designed to protect. This was, in part, due to the narrow interpretation of what constituted genocide described above and the omission of much of the cultural method in the Genocide Convention. Concern at the lack of utility eventually led to an extensive United Nations (hereafter UN) inquiry into the effectiveness of the Genocide Convention, and it is in just such a review that we find the first attempt to criminalize environmental destruction in international law.[3]

Early discussions of ecocide were triggered by extreme environmental damage that was being inflicted on Vietnam, Cambodia and Laos through the use of chemical warfare as part of the US campaign there. Because this was the context in which discussions of ecocide began, and because of the urgency and extremity of the harm being done, early definitions of ecocide tended to be restricted to wartime situations in which intent to cause environmental destruction was present and central. The term 'ecocide' was first recorded at the Congressional Conference on War and National Responsibility in Washington, a two-day conference on the question of American war crimes in Vietnam, where Professor Arthur W. Galston 'proposed a new international agreement to ban ecocide',[4] arguing that:

> After the end of World War II, and as a result of the Nuremburg trials, we justly condemned the wilful destruction of an entire people and its culture, calling this crime against humanity genocide. It seems to me that the wilful and permanent destruction of environment in which a people can live in a manner of their own choosing ought similarly to be considered as a crime against humanity, to be designated by the term ecocide. I believe that the most highly developed nations have already committed auto-ecocide over large parts of their own countries. At the present time, the United States stands alone as possibly having committed ecocide against another country, Vietnam, through its massive use of chemical defoliants and herbicides. The United Nations would appear to be an appropriate body for the formulation of a proposal against ecocide. (Zierler 2011: 14)

In making a link with genocide, Galston was suggesting that environmental destruction can have a genocidal impact but also that the environment can be seen as a victim of ecocide in the same way a social group of people can with genocide. Even so, Galston, it appears, was no environmentalist. Following interviews with Galston, David Zierler (2011) argues that he 'was not motivated to preserve some indigenous ecological Eden from Western technological predations. If Ranch Hand was an operation of resource extraction, it would not be ecocide.' Such a position places Galston's understanding firmly at odds with contemporary articulations (which we shall explore later), but unlike with Lemkin's conception of genocide, I would suggest that Galston's articulation of ecocide doesn't command the same level of intellectual respect. Lemkin went to great lengths to justify the integrity of his concept, its etymology and its application – the same cannot be said of Galston and ecocide.

In its early incarnation, then, ecocide was envisaged as a crime that would be committed in a war context. In 1972, at the UN Stockholm Conference on the Human Environment, Mr Olaf Palme, then prime minister of Sweden, spoke explicitly in his opening speech of the Vietnam War as an 'ecocide' (Björk 1996). Other heads of state, including Ms Indira Gandhi from India and the leader of the Chinese delegation, Mr Tang Ke, also denounced the Vietnam War on human and environmental terms (ibid.). Even so, the Stockholm Conference itself had a broader focus beyond environmental destruction in times of war. Indeed, it drew international attention to environmental issues, especially in relation to environmental degradation and trans-boundary pollution.

While there was no reference to ecocide in the official outcome document of the Stockholm Conference, the potential for a law criminalizing ecocide was widely discussed in the parallel unofficial events, including at the 'Folkets Forum' – the People's Summit – where a working group on the Law of Genocide and Ecocide was established (ibid.). 'Almost every popular movement and group of NGOs addressed the issue. A demonstration with 7,000 participants was held' (ibid.). Dai Dong, a branch of the International Fellowship of Reconciliation,[5] sponsored a 'Convention on Ecocidal War' (CEW), which took place in Stockholm, Sweden.[6] The CEW brought together many people, including Professor Richard A. Falk, expert on the international law of war crimes, and Dr Arthur H. Westing and Dr Egbert L. Pfeiffer, who were both biologists, and was coordinated by John Lewallen (Björk 1996). The CEW called for a UN working group on Ecocidal Warfare, which would, among other matters, seek to define and condemn ecocide as an international crime of war (ibid.). A draft International Convention on the Crime of Ecocide was prepared for UN consideration by Falk and reproduced in a journal article he published in 1973 (Falk 1973). It recognized that the Genocide Convention was deficient and that there was a need for another international law that could address ecological crimes. Falk's draft convention, though, primarily envisaged ecocide as a military offence, which could be committed in times of war or peace, provided the requisite intent was present.

As with the crime of genocide there was much academic debate over what would constitute the crime and, in particular, whether intent to commit destruction of ecosystems was a necessary element of the crime. John H. E. Fried, a specialist in international law and member of the Lawyers' Committee on Nuclear Policy, believed ecocide to denote 'various measures of devastation and destruction which ... aim at damaging or destroying the ecology of geographic areas to the detriment of human life, animal life, and plant life' (Fried 1972). Even so, it was recognized by others, such as Falk, that ecocide often occurs simply as a consequence of human economic activity rather than being a result of a predetermined, intended direct attack on the environment. Indeed, even though Falk's draft (1973) Ecocide Convention constructed a primarily military offence, he explicitly acknowledged at the outset that 'man has consciously and unconsciously inflicted irreparable damage to the environment in times of war and peace'. Meanwhile Westing stated that 'intent may not only be impossible to establish without admission but, I believe, it is essentially irrelevant' (Westing 1974).

### Ecocide and environmental destruction in the UN system: revising the Genocide Convention?

Even though Falk's draft Ecocide Convention was never adopted it was considered by the Sub-Commission on Prevention of Discrimination and Protection of Minorities (Sub-Commission) when it prepared a study for the UN's Human Rights Commission into the effectiveness of the Genocide Convention. The Sub-Commission was asked to consider the addition of ecocide as *a method of genocide* as well as the possible reintroduction of the cultural method into the Genocide Convention. The study was prepared by the Special Rapporteur, Mr Nicodème Ruhashyankiko, with the final draft published in 1978. At this time many Sub-Commission members were supportive of the idea that additional instruments be adopted.[7] Within the Sub-Commission Mr Abdelwahab Bouhdiba voiced support for criminalizing ecocide; 'any interference with the natural surroundings or environment in which ethnic groups lived was, in effect, a kind of ethnic genocide because such interference could prevent the people involved from following their own traditional way of life'.[8] However, Ruhashyankiko concluded:

> from the review of the problem of ecocide regarded as a war crime, in chapter IV of the present study, it follows that the question of ecocide has been placed by States in a context other than that of genocide. The Special Rapporteur believes that an exaggerated extension of the idea of genocide to cases of ecocide which have only a very distant connexion with that idea is liable to prejudice the effectiveness of the Genocide Convention.[9]

Nevertheless, in a follow-up to the Ruhashyankiko report, the concept of ecocide surfaced again when the Sub-Commission considered the same basic issue in 1985 – whether or not to expand the Genocide Convention. This time the Special Rapporteur was Mr Benjamin Whitaker.[10] The report stressed the opinion of the members of the Sub-Commission who were vocal in their support for the inclusion of a crime of ecocide.[11] Even so, in a non-committal conclusion, Whitaker recommended that 'further consideration should be given to this question'.[12] In subsequent discussions in the Sub-Commission, once again members spoke out in favour of the creation of a law criminalizing ecocide within the Genocide Convention. A draft resolution, prepared for the Commission on Human Rights, submitted as part of the review, recommended that Whitaker expand and deepen the study of the notions of 'cultural genocide', 'ethnocide' and 'ecocide'. In addition, a draft article on cultural genocide had also been prepared[13] although not adopted. Ultimately, in the Sub-Commission's final report on its 38th session,[14] it was recommended that Special Rapporteur Whitaker further investigate the expansion of the Genocide Convention to include the cultural and ecocidal methods of genocide and report back in its 40th session, which did not happen – it was only a recommendation and not a concrete stipulation.

*The UN's International Law Commission* While ecocide failed to make it into a revised Genocide Convention – which also failed to appear – the issue of criminalizing environmental destruction in international law did not go away. In the 1980s the UN's International Law Commission (ILC) considered the inclusion of an environmental crime within the Draft Code of Crimes Against the Peace and Security of Mankind[15] ('the Code'). This document eventually became the Rome Statute of the International Criminal Court, adopted in 1998 and entering into force on 1 July 2002. As of July 2012 there are 121 state parties to this internationally legally binding statute.[16] It now codifies four named international crimes – genocide, war crimes, crimes against humanity, and acts of aggression.

The ILC is mandated to promote the progressive development of international law and its codification.[17] Members of the ILC are 'persons of recognized competence in international law [... that] sit in their individual capacity and not as representatives of their Governments'.[18] The ILC sits in session annually from May to July and prepares a report to the Legal Committee, which sits from October to November.[19] From the very outset of the United Nations, the ILC had been assigned by the General Assembly in 1947 to formulate 'the principles of international law recognized in the charter of the Nuremberg Tribunal and in the judgment of the Tribunal' and to 'prepare a draft code of offences against the peace and security of mankind, indicating clearly the place to be accorded to the [aforementioned] principles'.[20] The Code was on the agenda of the ILC from 1949 to 1957 and 1982 to 1996. The gap in time arose out of difficulties in defining the Crime of Aggression and, as a result, the General Assembly postponed the drafting of the Code. The Code was revisited between 1982 and 1996; in 1982 Mr Doudou Thiam was appointed as the Special Rapporteur on the topic. His work picked up at the last adoption of the Code by the ILC in 1954.[21] The first reading began in 1985. The second and final reading began in 1992 and was adopted in 1996. In total, Thiam issued thirteen reports before the Code's final adoption in 1996 and his death three years later.

The years 1984–96 proved to be pivotal; during this time there had been extensive engagement in the ILC about the inclusion of a law regarding extensive environmental damage in the Code. Article

26 of the Code stated, 'an individual who wilfully causes or orders the causing of widespread, long-term and severe damage to the natural environment shall, on conviction thereof, be sentenced ...'. This was in light of legal precedent[22] and corresponded with Article 19 of Part I of the draft Articles on State Responsibility: 'wilful and severe damage to the environment' – legislation that the ILC was working on concurrently with the Code.[23]

Between 1984 and 1986 consideration of whether to include in the Code 'acts causing serious damage to the environment'[24] led some members[25] in 1986 to reopen the debate on whether ecocide was a crime of intent.[26] Criticisms centred on the inclusion of the element of intent and on the fact that the final draft of Article 26 did not address environmental crime by name – it contains no reference to ecocide. For the purposes of the Code previous drafts were removed and Article 26 was reduced to 'wilful and severe damage to the environment'. After the element of intent had been added, the governments of Australia, Belgium, Austria and Uruguay went on record criticizing the redrafting, in recognition of the fact that ecocide during peacetime is often a crime without intent as it occurs as a by-product of industrial and other activity.

Belgium stated: '[t]his difference between articles 22 [war crimes][27] and 26 ['wilful and severe damage to the environment'] does not seem to be justified. Article 26 should be amended to conform with the concept of damage to the environment used in article 22, since the concept of wilful damage is too restrictive.'[28] Australia objected on the grounds that 'the requisite *mens rea* in Article 26 should be lowered so as to be consistent with Article 22',[29] and Austria went on record stating that 'since perpetrators of this crime are usually acting out of a profit motive, intent should not be a condition for liability to punishment'.[30]

However, the ILC – instead of removing reference to the element of intent from the Article – determined to remove Article 26 altogether. Reactions within the ILC to the announcement of the withdrawal of Article 26 were recorded only in part. Based on the observations recorded at the time, we know that the decision taken was not based on agreement between the parties. Subsequent off-the-record discussions between ILC members failed to further the progress of the debate about the law of ecocide: in 1995 it was decided at least twice to hold informal meetings 'to facilitate the consultations and ensure a truly frank exchange of views'.[31] Consequently, in 1995, at the ILC's 47th session, it was decided to establish a further Working Group that would meet at the beginning of the 48th session to examine the possibility of covering the issue of wilful and severe damage to the environment in the draft Code of Crimes Against the Peace and Security of Mankind.[32] The group came together at the beginning of the ILC's 48th session in 1996, to consider this far more limited inclusion of crimes of environmental damage in the Code.[33] The members of the Working Group included Thiam, Mr Christian Tomuschat, Mr Mochtar Kusumaatmadja, Mr Alberto Szekely and Mr Chusei Yamada.[34] As the group was not listed with the other working groups at the beginning of the 1996 *Yearbook of the ILC*, it has not been possible to detect exactly which members took part in its discussions.

We do know that this Working Group issued a report on the topic entitled 'Document on crimes against the environment'[35] by Tomuschat. In his recommendations he suggests:

a)  retaining environmental crimes as a distinct and separate provision; or
b)  including environmental crimes as an act of crimes against humanity; or
c)  including environmental crimes as a war crime.

Despite this document, none of his recommendations was followed up. Worse still, in 1996, at a meeting of the ILC, the then chairman, Mr Ahmed Mahiou, unilaterally decided to remove the crime of ecocide completely as a separate provision. Without putting it to a vote, a decision was made by him despite the remit of the Working Group – 'to work on crimes against the environment'. Szekely immediately objected.[36] What was finally put to the vote was far more narrow in scope; all that was left to decide on was whether to include environmental damage solely in the context of a war crime or to include it as a crime against humanity, which would be applicable in peacetime. The result was that the Drafting Committee was notified only to draft the far narrower remit of environmental damage in the context of war crimes, and not in the context of crimes against humanity.[37]

The exclusion of a crime addressing damage to the environment during peacetime was sudden. Documentation as to why this occurred is hard to find. Our research found just one explanatory comment by the Special Rapporteur of the Code, Mr Thiam of Senegal, who stated in his 13th report[38] that the removal was due to comments of a few governments from 1993[39] that Thiam describes as being largely opposed to any form of inclusion of Article 26. And so it was that Article 26 was removed completely from the Code. Following further amendments by the Drafting Committee the final legal definition of a crime against the environment adopted by the ILC, and which made it into the final Rome Statute, can be found in Article 8 on 'War Crimes': the intentional creation of 'widespread, long-term and severe damage to the natural environment' – importantly only within a war context.[40]

Mr Christian Tomuschat, a long-term member of the ILC from 1985 to 1996 and a member of the Working Group on the issue of wilful damage to the environment, published a short article in 1996 on the development of the provision on crimes against the environment during the drafting and codification process of the Code, in which he argued that:

> One cannot escape the impression that nuclear arms played a decisive role in the minds of many of those who opted for the final text which now has been emasculated to such an extent that its conditions of applicability will almost never be met even after humankind would have gone through disasters of the most atrocious kind as a consequence of conscious action by persons who were completely aware of the fatal consequences their decisions would entail. (Tomuschat 1996)

Thus the Rome Statute's Article 8 (b IV) on War Crimes is the only provision in international crime to hold a perpetrator responsible for environmental damage. Of course, the Article does, however, limit the crime to wartime situations and to intentional damage. In addition to drafting the Code, the ILC also drafted international articles on state responsibility, and a provision linking state responsibility and damage to the environment was adopted in 1976.[41] The ILC prepared draft articles for an act that concerned itself with international liability for trans-boundary harm 'carried out in the territory or otherwise under the jurisdiction or control of a State'.[42] One of its draft provisions of 1976 defines environmental damage as an international crime.[43] Making states liable for trans-boundary harm was extensively scrutinized by the ILC and the term 'trans-boundary harm' came to refer largely to damage done to the environment by events such as the pollution of the air, sea or rivers, consequences of nuclear pollution, or oil spills.

### Ecocide: the missing 5th Crime Against Peace

Although the Code of Crimes Against the Peace and Security of Mankind morphed into the lesser Rome Statute, some states transferred the draft Crimes Against Peace, including ecocide, into their own national penal codes. Vietnam,[44] no doubt as a consequence of its experiences during the long Vietnam War, was the first county to include a crime of ecocide in its domestic law, followed by Russia[45] in 1996 after the collapse of the USSR in 1991. Although ecocide had been taken off the table at the United Nations, the crime itself was adopted by states that preferred to include all the draft Crimes Against Peace in their national penal codes. In the aftermath of the collapse of the USSR, over a period of seven years, new states that were formed drew up their own national penal codes. Some have included ecocide as a named Crime Against Peace, specifically Armenia,[46] Belarus,[47] Republic of Moldova,[48] Ukraine[49] and Georgia.[50] Georgia identifies the crime of ecocide to 'be punishable by imprisonment extending from eight to twenty years in length'. In addition, three other countries have done the same: Kazahkstan,[51] Kyrgyztsan[52] and Tajikistan.[53]

It is reasonable to draw certain conclusions from this institutional history: elements of the international community clearly approve of the legal concept of ecocide and have chosen to deliberately set out the crime in their own national penal codes. Ecocide/environmental destruction was a draft crime that made significant progress through the UN system and in some of the national penal codes there is explicit reference to the fact that ecocide constitutes a crime against the peace and security of mankind, which can be taken as an explicit reference to its earlier institutional standing in the draft Code of Crimes Against the Peace and Security of Mankind. The important point to take from all of this is that at certain points in the past, the international community had deemed ecocide/environmental destruction to be so serious that it was included in its draft Code of Crimes Against the Peace and Security of Mankind, and was also seriously considered as a missing method of genocide that could be written into the Genocide Convention.

So that was a major aspect of the genocide–ecocide nexus – its important institutional history, initially driven by outrage over the Vietnam War and its environmental destruction. In order to grasp the contemporary conceptual and empirical dimensions of genocide and ecocide, the focus of my research over the last six years, it is necessary to grapple with the implications of what Meadows et al. (1972) called 'the Limits to Growth' and Ed Lloyd Davies' '*process* of extreme energy' (see Lloyd-Davies 2013; Short et al. 2015).

*Limits to growth and extreme energy* The 1972 Club of Rome report *The Limits to Growth* (Meadows et al. 1972) utilized a system dynamics computer model to simulate the interactions of five global economic subsystems, namely: population, food production, industrial production, pollution, and consumption of non-renewable natural resources, the results of which posed serious challenges for global sustainability. A more recent study collated historical data for 1970–2000 (Turner 2007) and compared them with scenarios presented in *The Limits to Growth*. The analysis shows that thirty years of historical data compares favourably with key features of the 'standard run' scenario, which results in collapse of the global system midway through the twenty-first century. The key driver behind the *Limits to Growth* prediction – and arguably the one most poised to quickly cause global economic collapse – is the depletion of non-renewable energy sources, especially of oil and natural gas.[54] Despite the best efforts of the fossil fuel industry to propagate a paradigm of energy abundance, especially in the United States (Heinberg 2014), global production of conventional oil has already peaked and – barring incredibly unlikely huge new discoveries of easily extracted oil – must soon decline as predicted in *Limits to Growth* (Murray and Hansen 2013). New discoveries of oil and natural gas liquids[55] have dropped dramatically since their peak in the 1960s, and the world now consumes four to five barrels of oil for every one discovered (Mobbs 2013a; Heinberg 2014: 25). Because oil production from conventional fields drops globally by 5 per cent each year, it is thus assured that such fields will eventually 'run out'.[56]

This downward global trend in oil discovery and supply has not gone unnoticed by the major international actors, namely states and multi- and transnational corporations, which have taken various actions since the end of the Cold War to secure access to remaining conventional oil supplies. An examination of major international conflicts in the Persian Gulf region alone since 1990 demonstrates the determination of countries such as the United States to maintain control of conventional energy resources.[57] Indeed, conventional energy supplies have become so precious to many states that 'energy security' (Barnett 2001) is now an overriding objective within which foreign and domestic policies situate the procurement of oil (and other energy sources) as a matter of national security. Such a discourse often elevates concern for the global fossil fuel market over other considerations such as the environment and human rights.[58]

This change in rhetoric to boost the perceived necessity of fossil fuels is furthered by the influence of major energy corporations upon state governments (Short et al. 2015). As numerous internationally reaching corporations, such as Exxon Mobil and ConocoPhillips, have developed larger economies than many sizeable states,[59] their power has correspondingly grown. Since such companies' business models centre on fossil fuels, examples of corporate–state collaboration to further non-renewable energy use may be found in varying arenas, from the more than fifty million dollars Koch Industries spent on lobbying the US government between 1998 and 2010 (Mayer 2010) and the formation of the American Legislative Exchange Council (which brings private corporations together with elected US state officials to draft new legislation) (Bedell 2014), to direct connections between advisers to the UK Cabinet Office and energy sector companies such as Centrica and Riverstone (Mobbs 2013b). Because of the overly close, arguably corrupt and undemocratic, relationships[60] between politicians and corporate interests, it could be argued that the exclusion of 'the underground injection of natural gas for purposes of storage' and '… of fluids or propping agents … pursuant to hydraulic fracturing operations related to oil, gas, or geothermal production activities' from the US Safe Drinking Water Act;[61] the British government's determination to make unconventional energy extraction through hydraulic fracturing an 'urgent national priority';[62] the failure of the European Union to create legally binding environmental legislation for hydraulic fracturing;[63] and George W. Bush's administration's policy of attempting to 'refute the science of global warming and install in its place economic and environmental policies that not only ignore but deny the views of the scientific community on climate change' (Lynch et al. 2010) are – at the very least in part – results of the wishes of the energy sector. As the 200 largest listed fossil fuel companies spent $674 billion on developing new energy reserves (five times as much as they spent returning money to shareholders) in 2012,[64] the energy industry remains invested in pushing the 'limits' as far as they can go.[65]

Though corporations may lobby otherwise,[66] resource limitations to growth are not the only significant, impending ecological threats to humanity and ecosystems worldwide. Carbon dioxide atmospheric concentrations 'have increased by 40% since pre-industrial times', with concentrations of carbon dioxide, methane and nitrous oxide at their highest level in at least 800,000 years,[67] and the rate of carbon dioxide release is unprecedented, at least in the last 300 million years. The result of this level of pollution – inherently tied to an insistence on using and depleting non-renewable energy sources (Hönisch et al. 2012) – is the phenomenon of climate change, in this context represented by the anthropogenic increase in the Earth's surface temperature. Since 1880, the average global temperature has increased by roughly 0.85 degrees Celsius, with most of the increase – 0.72 degrees Celsius – occurring in the past fifty years (IPCC 2013). The effects of this global warming are diverse and range from shrinking glaciers and ice sheets to the highest rate of sea level rise in the past 2,000 years and increasingly frequent extreme weather events; all of which clearly result from 'human influence on the climate system'.[68]

Knowing that these results of humanity's addiction to fossil fuels are imminently approaching, global use of oil, natural gas and coal should be immediately curbed. At present, however, fossil fuels still remain the world's main source of energy, accounting for around 81 per cent of global primary energy use (Office of the Chief Economist 2011). This is undoubtedly due, at least in part, to the current, Western-propagated largely fossil-fuel-dependent neoliberal economic model, wherein corporations, being legally bound to pursue profit above all other considerations, continuously, and most often successfully, lobby for favourable legislation, deregulation and tax incentives. As Bakan noted in his seminal text *The Corporation: The Pathological Pursuit of Profit and Power* (2005), under corporate law, the primary legal duty of the corporation is 'simply to make money for shareholders' and failing to pursue this end 'can leave directors and officers open to being sued'.[69] Thus, the multitude of multibillion-dollar companies that depend upon the continued global use of fossil fuels have not only a vested interest in advocating for further non-renewable energy extraction, but arguably, in the current energy market, a legal duty to do so – and at the very least an obligation to continue pursuing oil, coal and natural gas extraction as long as it is profitable (and legal) to do so. Thus, while the use of renewable energy sources is growing,[70] they are forced to compete with an established and highly subsidized[71] non-renewable market, rather than be allowed to replace it.[72]

*Extreme energy* As conventional reserves are depleted[73] and demand for energy rises, there is increasing pressure to exploit unconventional energy sources.[74] Michael Klare (2011) first coined the term 'extreme energy' to describe a range of relatively new, higher-risk, non-renewable resource extraction processes that have become more attractive to the conventional energy industry as the more easily accessible supplies dwindle. Edward Lloyd-Davies points out, however, that this definition of extreme energy as a category is highly problematic as it is dependent upon specific examples; it lacks 'explanatory or predictive power' (Lloyd-Davies 2013), and leaves open the question of who decides which extractive techniques qualify. A conceptual understanding would suggest that extreme energy is a 'process whereby extraction methods grow more intense over time, as easier to extract resources are depleted' (Short et al. 2015). The foundation of this conception is the simple fact that those energy sources which require the least amount of effort to extract will be used first, and only once those are dwindling will more effort be exerted to gain similar resources. Extreme energy, in this sense, is evident in the history of energy extraction – in the change from gathering 'sea coal' from British beaches and exploiting 'natural oil seeps', to opencast mining and deep-water oil drilling. Viewed in this light, the concept of extreme energy becomes a lens through which current energy extraction efforts can be explained and the future of the energy industry predicted. Using this extreme energy lens necessitates an understanding of 'the amount of energy which is needed to obtain energy', as in this process it is that value which is continually rising. This value may be calculated as either 'net energy' or 'energy return on investment (EROI)', whereby net energy is the available energy for use after subtracting the energy required for extraction, and EROI is the percentage of energy produced divided by the amount required for extraction. When charted together, the net energy available to society is seen to decrease along with EROI in a curved mathematical relationship, which forms the 'energy cliff' – i.e. the point at which EROI becomes increasingly low and net energy drops to zero.[75]

In the extreme energy process the economic system can be conceptualized as consisting of two distinct segments, the part which is extracting, refining and producing energy (the energy industry) and everything else, which just consumes energy. What needs to be clearly understood is that the energy industry is in the rare position where the commodity which it produces is also the main resource it consumes. Therefore, as energy extraction becomes more extreme, while the rest of the economy will be squeezed by decreasing energy availability and rising prices,[76] the energy industry's rising costs will be offset by the rising revenues it receives. The net result will be a reallocation (through the market or otherwise) of resources from the rest of society to the energy industry, to allow the energy industry to target ever more difficult-to-extract resources. This process is ongoing as easier-to-extract resources are depleted, and data from recent extraction methods, such as hydraulic fracturing and tar sands extraction, shows that industry is increasingly lurching towards the net energy cliff. Such action on the part of some of the largest and most commercially successful transnational corporations may only be understood as the logical result of the extreme energy process[77] – there simply are not enough easier-to-extract resources available.[78]

Despite the obvious negative implications of these developments, the process shows no sign of stopping, but continues towards the precipice at an ever-increasing rate, fuelled by ever-increasing levels of energy consumption. Perpetuated by the global economic 'growth' fixation (Purdey 2010), increasing amounts of energy are consumed each year (International Energy Agency 2013), driving the process over the edge. Of course, industry is not willing to halt the process (Lloyd-Davies 2013) as intense demand further pushes up the price of energy,[79] allowing extraction to remain economical – as long as enough resource is extracted at each site and the price stays high. The result is that higher energy consumption leads to faster resource depletion, which in turn results in the acceleration of the extreme energy process. Within this neoliberal economic context of increasing demand and profit potential the results of extreme extraction techniques (Heinberg 2014), and the consequences of continuing the process, are easily trumped in the interests of short-term profiteering and 'energy security'. Indeed, as Stephanie Malin notes, neoliberal 'normalization' of unconventional energy extraction emerges most saliently regarding environmental outcomes and economic development (Malin 2013). Despite the prospective consequences of reaching our limits to growth, and with considerable evidence demonstrating a strong correlation between extraction effort and damage to both society and the environment, the extreme energy process continues to accelerate with potentially disastrous consequences (Lloyd-Davies 2013; see also Huseman and Short 2012; Humphreys 2008).

The depth of connections already established between the extreme energy process and our human right to a 'minimally good life' illustrates the otherwise overlooked insidious nature of this insistence upon striving towards the energy precipice. Human rights violations due to climate change and the release of pollutants are yet another side effect of humanity's dependence on fossil fuels, which grows in magnitude with each decade. The tropics and subtropics have seen droughts increase in intensity and duration since the 1970s,[80] and diseases such as malaria are affecting larger portions of the population (Patz et al. 2005). Two hundred thousand deaths in the United States each year result from air pollution,[81] while a heat wave across Europe in 2003 (most likely resulting from global climate change; Stott et al. 2004) left roughly 30,000 people dead.[82] There is strong evidence to suggest that the worst consequences of anthropogenic climate change on human rights have not yet been felt. As predicted in *The Limits to Growth* (Meadows et al. 1972), the effects of climate degradation will rapidly increase with temperature throughout the twenty-first century,[83] resulting in large-scale deaths across Europe due to heat stroke,[84] worsening droughts across continents,[85] further loss of food and water, and a potential, eventual, extinction-level event for humanity if global emissions are not reduced in accordance with the latest climate science modelling. Such events, along with resulting unrest, wars and mass migrations (IPCC 2014), threaten people's rights to life and health worldwide.

The rush to scrape the bottom of the fossil fuel barrel is thus creating a perfect storm for current and future human rights abuses, with ecocidal and genocidal consequences. As resources become scarcer our scramble to use them grows, increasing the political prioritization of fossil fuel extraction over ecosystems, human health and security; while increasing demand also ensures that such resources will run out sooner, which in turn will result in further human rights violations as requirements for food, healthcare and other basic needs are no longer met, to say nothing of the abuses to human security, which would also necessarily increase. These violations will most likely increase exponentially as resources are depleted – at least, that is, until the sharp population decline predicted in *The Limits to Growth* occurs.[86]

In a recent paper Martin Crook and I show how Karl Marx's classic critique of political economy, and his value analysis more specifically, helps explain the ecologically destructive forces unleashed by capitalist extractive and farming industries. Capitalism is structurally geared towards the social production of commodities in accordance with the imperatives of capital accumulation and exchange value and not in harmony with nature's laws of conservation, sustainability and natural metabolic cycles. As we shall see later in the book, the Athabasca 'tar sands'[87] are a prime example of the artificial fragmentation of the local ecosystem in an attempt to extract oil, with no regard for the anti-ecological effects this transfer of energy and materials has on the local environment and critically downstream indigenous peoples. One of the central ecological contradictions of capitalism is the exponential increase in the throughput of materials and energy needed by the relentless need for 'growth' and the natural limits of production. Disequilibrium exists between capital's ferocious pace in the throughput of energy and materials and nature's laws, temporal rhythms and metabolic cycles, which eventually provokes an inevitable shortage of materials and an accumulation crisis.[88] The result is that the price of the relevant raw material will go up as the amount of socially necessary labour time objectified in each individual product or use value rises in relative terms. This process is exemplified by extreme energy as the supply of fossil fuels begins to run up against natural limits, thus raising the relative amount of objectified labour in a given quantity of fossil fuel, leading, in the medium to long term, to a rise in the average price of fossil fuels. Indeed, within the process of extreme energy, where more complex and costly techniques are required for the extraction of ever-scarcer sources, the very same process unfolds (see Crook and Short 2014). So extreme energy 'as a process' can be seen as both an expression of material shortages and a competitive market response in an attempt to correct the imbalance through the extraction of ever more extreme substitutes. The net effect is to put further pressure both on local ecosystems and the biosphere more generally.

Thus capitalism sets in motion a rampant process of accumulation, which carves up nature and increases the material throughput of production to ever more ecologically unsustainable levels, disturbing the social metabolism of human civilization and leading to a 'metabolic rift' of man from nature (see ibid.). The process of extreme energy, and the role of extractive industries within it, are manifestations of the anti-ecological imperatives of capital accumulation, and the drive towards 'unconventional' extraction techniques is a particularly virulent expression of the metabolic rift and the anti-ecological nature of the capitalist value/nature contradiction. The resort to more costly and more environmentally destructive forms of energy extraction within the extreme energy process signifies a particular form of environmental crisis under capitalism caused by material shortages and the natural limits of production.

*'Fracking': the latest step in the extreme energy process* In addition to the infamous 'tar sands' (see Huseman and Short 2012) in Alberta, Canada, the march towards the net energy cliff is arguably spearheaded in the West by the most recently developed family of extreme energy extraction methods known as 'fracking', a colloquial expression which usually refers to the extraction of shale gas, coal-bed methane (CBM) – termed Coal Seam Gas (CSG) in Australia – and 'tight oil'. The term, however, has become somewhat loaded, such that it is necessary to outline the contrasting uses, and define the senses in which it is invoked in this book.[89] In public discourse about 'fracking' different sides often talk past each other, owing to very different understandings of what the issues are, and differing definitions of the term itself. These differences fall along a spectrum

that can be understood in terms of the interests of the parties involved.

Exploitation of unconventional oil and gas is a new, more extreme form of fossil fuel extraction, targeting much less permeable rock formations than previous conventional oil and gas extraction. It is characterized by the drilling of dense patterns of, usually horizontal, wells (up to eight per square mile or more) in conjunction with other more intense processes such as hydraulic fracturing and de-watering. Different rock formations can be targeted, such as shale (Shale Gas & Oil) and coal (Coal Bed Methane), but the negative impacts are very similar and potentially both ecocidal (Hulme and Short 2014) and genocidal. For many local people affected, 'fracking' has come to mean petroleum extraction companies turning up where they live and coating the area in hundreds or thousands of well pads, compressor stations and pipelines alongside large volumes of truck traffic; some liken it to an 'invasion' and 'occupation' (Perry 2012: 81), bringing with it a large variety of negative consequences for them and their environment.

The word 'fracking', however, is derived from 'fraccing', a much more narrowly defined industry slang for 'hydraulic fracturing', one particular stage of unconventional petroleum (oil or gas) extraction. A scaled-up form of hydraulic fracturing (high volume), involving injecting fluids under high pressure to crack the rock, is often used to release hydrocarbons during unconventional oil and gas extraction. The communities living with the consequences of unconventional oil and gas extraction are mainly concerned with the impact it has on them and their environment. Unconventional oil and gas extraction is a complex process, involving pad construction, well drilling, casing, stimulation (often including but not limited to hydraulic fracturing), extraction, and transport, along with well plugging and abandonment (or failure to do so). All these stages have a consequent impact on their local environment and, owing to the fact that fracking requires so many more wells covering much larger areas, these impacts mount up to a far greater extent than for conventional extraction and production.

In an era of peaked conventional supplies (see Heinberg 2014) extractive industries are principally concerned with finding new fossil fuels to extract in order to ensure continued profits, the cumulative impacts of which are likely to be seen as little more than simple 'externalities' for the companies involved. Focused as they are on getting gas and oil out of the ground regardless, the industry and their government supporters are concerned to utilize the technologies which can be used to do just that. Moreover, they work on a drilling-site-by-drilling-site basis, and the cumulative impact of the whole process seems to be of little concern. It is also useful in their public relations to focus on micro details rather than the macro picture, and a narrow definition of 'fracking', as simply hydraulic fracturing, helps promote the impression that fracking is simply conventional extraction plus hydraulic fracturing, rather than an entirely different process with very different impacts.

Quite possibly one of the reasons the term 'fracking' has become synonymous with unconventional oil and gas extraction more generally lies in the choices made by the industry in its early promotional pitches to investors. Indeed, in the early part of the last decade, it seems that to raise funds for exploration a simple technological explanation was preferred when pitching to non-experts. The industry chose to focus attention on hydraulic fracturing as the key ingredient out of a complex array of technological processes. It's not difficult to understand why the idea of a new, high-tech well completion method, 'massive slick-water hydraulic fracturing', which was going to single-handedly revolutionize the industry by allowing access to a wealth of previously untapped resources, was an attractive sales pitch to investors. A more accurate view of unconventional oil and gas, as requiring much more effort, drilling greater numbers of much more expensive wells in order to produce much less oil/gas, does not sound like such an attractive proposition in comparison. It is therefore unsurprising that the terminology used to describe the industry (and understanding of the issues involved) has become somewhat skewed by this initial spin.

Given our concern here with the harms of unconventional extraction on people and the environment, the issues raised are the wider ones surrounding the overall effects of the entire more intense extraction process, rather than ones specific to particular technologies the industry may or may not use. For this reason it is far more appropriate to use this wider definition of 'fracking', rather than the more narrowly defined industry slang that has the effect of limiting discourse to just the narrow technical process of hydraulic fracturing itself, as if it could occur in an isolated vacuum without its necessary production infrastructure. Even so, it should still be acknowledged that since there are often significant levels of confusion surrounding the use of the term, the particular understanding being used should always be defined. Thus, to be clear, in this book 'fracking' is being used in its wider sense to include all of the required industrial elements of hydraulic fracturing, from huge quantities of water, to compressor stations, truck traffic and waste disposal.

In the countries where 'fracking' development has taken place it has been controversial and divisive. Supporters of unconventional gas development often claim that it reduces gas prices, creates employment opportunities and provides 'energy security', all the while producing lower carbon emissions than coal. Its detractors often contest all such claims, usually pointing to contrary data emerging from the USA and Australia. Indeed, in numerous studies from both countries, local communities most affected by developments often cite considerable negative impacts on the environment and human health, including groundwater contamination, air pollution, radioactive and toxic waste, water usage, earthquakes, methane migration, and the industrialization of rural landscapes,[90] the cumulative effect of which has led to calls for the United Nations Human Rights Council (HRC)[91] to condemn fracking as a threat to basic human rights, particularly the rights to water and health. Fracking development is fast becoming a human rights issue.[92] The United Nations Environment Programme (UNEP) has issued a 'Global Alert'[93] on the issue of fracking development, warning of significant environmental risks to the air, soil and water (contamination and usage competition); ecosystem damage; habitat and biodiversity impacts; and fugitive gas emissions – which will endanger carbon reduction targets. In terms of public health, UNEP[94] warned of risks of pipeline explosions; release of toxins into air, soil and water; and competition for land and water resources needed for food production; and that unconventional gas would likely be used 'in addition to coal rather than being a substitute'[95] and would thus pose a threat to the development of sustainable economies.

Most of the academic papers on the impacts of fracking have focused on such issues as the macroeconomic benefits of a 'shale gas revolution', the 'green' credentials of shale gas,[96] and the levels of environmental impact and responsibility for it.[97] The few human impact investigations have come from investigative journalists

(Brasch 2012), small NGOs[98] and documentary film-makers.[99] While valuable, such studies have been limited in scope and were not comparative. Recently anthropologists and sociologists have started to document the social and political discourses of fracking, and the surrounding social conflicts in discrete Australian communities (De Rijke 2013a, b, c) and perceptions of risk and opportunity in American communities,[100] but they predominantly engage in discourse and perception analysis rather than invoking an impact-based analysis. Taking a broader, more structurally aware approach, a recent study has shown that 'neoliberal logic' has led stakeholders to self-regulate their behaviour in order to facilitate fracking, by seeing its current role in rural industrialization, its potential environmental and health outcomes, and its economic outcomes as part of a 'new normal' (Malin 2013). The consequences of this normalization of loss of agency therefore raise fundamental questions about the ability of communities to resist extractive operations and make informed choices about the sources of their energy.

'Green criminologists' have also called for a more theoretically robust approach to the study of ecological harms and crimes (Stretesky et al. 2013). A recent study by Shelley and Opsal (2014) into the social and ecological impacts of energy extractive practices on local communities implies that green criminologists are starting to investigate this issue, documenting not only illegal actions but also legal processes and outcomes that are 'harmful' to humans, animals and the environment. Green criminologists point to the relevance here of German sociologist Ulrich Beck's 1992 'risk society' thesis (Carrabine et al. 2008: 386), whereby modern industrial societies create many new risks not found in nature but which are largely manufactured through new modern technologies – which were unknown in earlier days. Such risks are associated with the many new technologies that generate new dangers to lives and to the planet itself. These dangers are humanly produced, may have massively unforeseen consequences, and may take many, many thousands of years to reverse. For Beck, these 'manufactured risks' are taking us to the edge of catastrophe, posing 'threats to all forms of life on this planet' and presenting us with an 'exponential growth of risks and the impossibility of escaping them' (see ibid.: 386). The emergence of 'green crimes and harms', such as those produced by extreme energy technologies, are part of these new risks which bring new patterns of environmental harm and potential human rights abuses (Short et al. 2015).

In a recent paper, De Rijke noted 'the extraordinary expansion of the unconventional gas industry has ... led to questions about social power and the rights of individuals and local communities, the role of multinational corporations in politics and rural service provision, as well as related questions regarding fundamental processes of democracy, capitalist economies and social justice ...', while the 'close relationship between governments and powerful multinational corporations brings to the fore questions about political influence and human rights' (De Rijke 2013a: 17). Thus, to address these 'important conundrums', De Rijke advocated further academic research into fracking from multiple perspectives, including social impact assessments. Given the weight of evidence of human impacts that is emerging from countries with a mature fracking industry, such as the United States and Australia, I have suggested that it is time to meet De Rijke's call through the human rights lens, i.e. the creation of comprehensive interdisciplinary human rights impact assessments (HRIAs) of fracking. Such assessments would highlight exactly what is at stake for local communities facing the potential ecological devastation that extreme energy technologies usually bring, and would also allow policy-makers to see disaggregated impact data on groups such as indigenous peoples for whom such development may well have genocidal impacts – a discussion we will have later in the chapters on Canada and Australia.

In the next section we will look at the resurrection of the idea that ecocide could, and should, be an international crime in its own right and not subsumed within genocide, war crimes or crimes against humanity. In particular, we will see that some of the most frequently cited examples that proponents of such a law have in mind when invoking the term ecocide often involve 'unconventional' extreme energy technologies and their production sites, such as Alberta's 'tar sands' and 'fracking' in general.[101]

## The crime of ecocide today

In recent years a campaign to criminalize ecocide in its own right, and as a strict liability offence (see Higgins et al. 2013), was instigated by international lawyer and environmental activist Polly Higgins.[102] The Eradicating Ecocide[103] campaign draws attention to the numerous examples of ecocide and its human consequences worldwide, at a time when preventing further ecological destruction couldn't be more pressing. Eradicating Ecocide is one of a number of campaigns[104] that highlights the particularly devastating impact environmental destruction has on indigenous peoples who depend on the health of their local environment not only for their own physical well-being but also for their spiritual and cultural health. Even so, the focus goes beyond the plight of indigenous peoples to eradicating ecocide for the good of the planet, its ecosystems and all those beings that depend on them.

As we have seen, we do not currently have an international crime of ecocide and hence there is no law to prosecute those who are destroying our environment and ecosystems (see ibid.). Far from it, under our current neoliberal capitalist order, governments the world over positively encourage such destruction in the name of economic growth (see Crook and Short 2014). We do have an international crime of environmental destruction as a war crime, but this has no applicability in times of peace and 'environmental destruction' doesn't capture our environmental embeddedness, nor the full scale of our predicament, or the role of capitalism and resource extraction in its development. In his seminal text *The Enemy of Nature*, Joel Kovel outlines why we should talk in terms of an 'ecological crisis' rather than an 'environmental' one. His contribution to this area is worth quoting at length:

> Society and nature are not independent bodies bouncing off each other, like billiard balls. Therefore, the crisis is not about an 'environment' outside us, but the evolution, accelerating with sickening velocity, of an ancient lesion in humanity's *relation* to nature. To think in terms of such a relation is *ecological* thinking, which requires that we see the world as an interconnected whole. From this standpoint we are part of that whole, to which we connect as a natural creature whose relation to nature requires that nature be transformed. In other words, our 'human nature' is to be both part of the whole of nature and also distinguished from it by what we do to it. This boundary is called *production*; it is the species-specific activity

that defines us, and its outcome is the economy, the polity, our culture, religion, and the way we inhabit our bodies. Thus human life is complicated, restless, and full of conflict, as every intelligent person knows. We do not have an environmental crisis, then, but an *ecological crisis*, in the course of which our bodies, ourselves, and the whole of external nature are undergoing severe perturbations. Since production is the key to human nature, the ecological crisis is also about what can be called the *conditions of production*. These include energy resources, technologies, and also the bodies who have to get to work each day. (Kovel 2007a)

The Eradicating Ecocide campaign may not endorse an overtly anti-capitalist agenda but in its preference for the concept of 'ecocide' rather than 'environmental destruction' it invokes a holistic understanding of the problem as an *ecological* crisis, and the concomitant need for the protection of ecosystems, rather than an abstract and external 'environmental' crisis. Indeed, Higgins defines 'ecocide' as: 'the extensive damage to, destruction of or loss of ecosystem(s) of a given territory, whether by human agency or by other causes, to such an extent that peaceful enjoyment by the inhabitants of that territory has been severely diminished'.

This definition is the basis of the Eradicating Ecocide campaign's proposed amendment to the Rome Statute, the treaty that established the International Criminal Court (ICC), which entered into force on 1 July 2002.[105] In short, it is envisaged that any extensive damage, destruction to or loss of an ecosystem can constitute ecocide. 'Extensive' can be either widespread, long lasting or severe. To define these terms the campaign invokes the 1977 United Nations Convention on the Prohibition of Military or any other Hostile Use of Environmental Modification Techniques (ENMOD):

- Widespread: encompassing an area on the scale of several hundred square kilometres.
- Long lasting: lasting for a period of months, or approximately a season.
- Severe: involving serious or significant disruption or harm to human life, natural and economic resources or other assets.

Under the Rome Statute, the ICC can only investigate and prosecute the core international crimes when states are unable or unwilling to do so themselves. These are the existing four Crimes against Peace (genocide, crimes against humanity, war crimes and the crime of aggression), hence the argument that 'ecocide is the missing fifth Crime against Peace' (Gauger et al. 2012).

Higgins outlines two types of ecocide. The first is human-induced or 'ascertainable ecocide' – ecocide caused by human agency, where an individual responsible for the activity can be identified. Usually, Higgins points out, this is corporate-induced ecocide, and she invokes the poster child of extreme energy – the ecological disaster that is the Athabasca tar sands in Alberta, Canada, which we will discuss later on in the book. The second is ecocide by 'other causes', such as catastrophic events like floods or earthquakes, referred to in law as an 'act of God'. These can be termed 'non-ascertainable ecocide' as no one perpetrator can be identified. Of course, this type of ecocide cannot be stopped, but when human-induced ecocides, which destroy carbon sinks and create escalating carbon emissions, are stopped, it is possible that this could reduce the frequency of climatic extremes and mitigate the negative impacts of naturally occurring ecocides.

Following on from Higgins' initiative, a global grassroots supporting campaign has emerged called 'End Ecocide on Earth'.[106] The ultimate goal of the initiative is for ecocide to be recognized as a crime around the world. In their own words: 'this means not only national ecocide crimes in all states but also the recognition that ecocide is an international crime which can be enforced with an international court. To that end, ecocide should be incorporated into the Rome Statute as an international Crime against Peace under the jurisdiction of the International Criminal Court. It is in our collective power to make this change happen, in the years to come till 2017. This is the radical change we need, and we are building a global movement to make it a reality.' Pursuant to their goal the initiative has a three-pronged approach:

1) a 'Global Call for International Justice for the Environment & Health' – the initiative, along with nine other organizations, wrote the 'Charter of Brussels', a global call requesting the establishment of a European and an International Criminal Court of

the Environment and Health. The Charter calls for the recognition of environmental crimes as crimes against Humanity and Peace by the United Nations. At the time of writing, the Charter was open for signatures by individuals and organizations and the ultimate plan was to hand it over to Ban Ki-moon, UN secretary-general, during the COP21 Climate Conference in December 2015 in Paris.

2) 'Social Mobilization Campaign for COP21' – a plan to mobilize tens of thousands of volunteers and supporters in the streets to demonstrate their dedication to protecting the planet and future generations by demanding a halt to dangerous industrial activities.

3) 'Concrete proposal of Criminal Law recognizing Ecocide' – a proposed amendment to the Rome Statute to be drafted by an expert working group in order to include, within the ICC prerogatives, environmental and health crimes. The initiative hopes that organizations joining the Charter's global call and the expert working group will commit to lobby on behalf of the initiative decision-makers in their country, asking them to support the proposed amendment to the Statute of the International Criminal Court.

Leaving aside the thorny issue of likely political opposition, the process of revision of the Rome Statute is remarkably simple in that one member state can propose the amendment to the UN secretary-general, who then distributes the proposal to the other member states during a general assembly or convenes a revision conference. It remains to be seen whether or not a potential crime of ecocide can progress farther within the international system this time around, when the need is much more urgent and pressing than it was in the preceding decades, since, despite this, as we saw earlier, the likely opposition forces are now much stronger – corporate power and influence have grown and the relationships between industry and governments have become even closer. The current anti-ecological, ecocidal rush to deploy the latest extreme energy technologies highlights this depressingly well, raising serious concerns over not just ecosystem protection, but human rights protections and in some cases potential genocidal consequences – as we shall see in later chapters.

If we consider the ostensibly democratic context of the UK, for example, on the surface it may seem that extreme energy technologies like fracking are considered necessary for 'the economic well-being of the UK' and hence 'in the national interest', and are simply being prioritized over individuals' fundamental civil and political rights; but if we look a little deeper, a more politically disturbing picture emerges, especially considering recent evidence likening the precarious nature of the US 'fracking boom'[107] to that of a government-supported 'Ponzi scheme' (Mobbs 2014). Indeed, as Noam Chomsky warns, 'the terms, United States, Australia, Britain, and so on, are now conventionally used to refer to the structures of power within such countries: the "national interest" is the interest of these groups, which correlates only weakly with the interests of the general population' (Chomsky 1999). When investigating the trajectory and impacts of extreme energy developments, a critical awareness of the 'close relationship between governments and powerful multinational corporations', which De Rijke (2013a: 15) warned of with unconventional gas production in Australia, is vital. For example, in the UK much of the public fracking debate has been conducted in a context which involves a government wanting to 'go all out for shale' while at the same time having a 'lead non-executive director' at the Cabinet Office, Lord Browne, who is also the chairman of shale gas company Cuadrilla Resources. There have been illuminating 'freedom of information' requests in the UK that have demonstrated collusion between key politicians and industry figures on such matters as how best to 'manage' public perceptions and manufacture consent in order to 'fast-track' fracking development.[108] Environmental consultant and extreme energy expert Paul Mobbs has highlighted numerous political–industry connections that are deserving of public attention and which raise fears of 'malfeasance' in public office (Mobbs 2013b). Mobbs argues, 'politicians might call for a "balanced debate on shale", but arguably it is they who are peddling a manufactured rhetoric.[109] This is because the political process has been hijacked by lobbyists paid by the industry, whose manipulative tendrils reach right inside the Government.'[110] This chapter has illuminated the conceptual and empirical nexus between genocide and ecocide, the pivotal anti-ecological role of capitalist accumulation and the process of extreme energy and the limits to growth.

In the following case studies we will see that *all* of these issues are at play to varying degrees. Indeed, in all the case studies, first and foremost the primary resource at stake is land. In the first two cases, Palestine and Sri Lanka, where violent conflict continues into the present, social identity features prominently in political rhetoric, which can serve to obscure more structural concerns such as access, ownership and use of natural resources. When there are population pressures due to 'settlements', competition over valuable resources increases and then, as Zimmerer notes,

> ideology, traditions of inclusion and exclusion, and histories of violence come into play ... Nonetheless, if we accept that resource scarcity can create genocidal violence then we should alter our understanding of the role of ideology, of intention, and ultimately of prevention. Ideology will still be important; however, it might not be the initial cause of violence in each and every case. Rather, resource scarcity – real or perceived – could serve as a cause as well as part of an ideology, whereby ideology becomes the means by which allegedly superfluous human beings are identified. (Zimmerer 2014: 275)

When it comes to the case studies of Australia and Canada, while social and cultural identity issues are fundamental to understanding what is at stake, political disagreements are fought on supposed rational grounds of best 'development' practice and often overtly centre on land acquisition and use, with the environmental, physical and cultural repercussions of state and corporate behaviour often seen as mere 'externalities'.

# 3 | PALESTINE

*with Haifa Rashed*[1]

## Introduction

This first case study will analyse the Israel/Palestinian situation[2] by considering the most context relevant of Lemkin's eight 'techniques' of genocide; specifically – political, physical, economic and cultural; and additionally the ecocidal method (Crook and Short 2014). Prior to investigating the Palestinian case in detail, the chapter will seek to define the '*genos*' that we are discussing and will invoke the insights of philosopher Mohamed Abed, who was discussed in Chapter 1. To recap, Abed was interested in the characteristics groups need to display to be logically and ethically susceptible to the peculiar harm that is genocide; when 'the members of a group consent to a life in common, the culture of the group is comprehensive, and the social structure of the group makes leaving it arduous, then its social vitality (or lack thereof) will have profound and far-reaching effects on the well-being of its individual members' (Rashed and Short 2012: 1147). While this formulation will evidently cover many more groups than imagined 'national' communities, their cultural life and vitality would be capable of producing the 'future contributions to the world' that the concept of genocide was designed to protect (Short 2010a).

Since the creation of Israel in 1948 and after subsequent political developments (particularly the occupation of the West Bank and Gaza Strip after the Six Day War in 1967), the Palestinian population has been fragmented into different geographical locations, which include Gaza, the West Bank, the diaspora – 'the largest refugee diaspora in the world' (Cook 2010: 1) – and also Israel itself.[3] For the purposes of this chapter, therefore, when referring to the 'Palestinians', we include all Palestinian Arabs and their descendants, irrespective of where they currently reside.

## Political genocide

*Zionist settler colonialism in Palestine*

> In line with [the] policy of imposing the German national
> pattern, particularly in the incorporated territories, the occupant
> has organized a system of colonization of these areas ... The
> Polish population have been removed from their homes in order
> to make place for German settlers ... The properties and homes
> of the Poles are being allocated to German settlers. (Lemkin
> 1944)

As we saw in Chapter 1, a recent trend in genocide studies has
been to examine the connections between genocide and colonialism
with some genocide scholars concluding that settler colonialism is
an inherently genocidal process.[4] As Wolfe explains, 'Land is life
– or, at least, land is necessary for life. Thus contests for land can
be, indeed often are – contests for life.' Furthermore, the notion
that Israel constitutes a settler colonial state has long been a feature
of Palestinian and Arab critical thought, and in Western radical
circles.[5] It has been increasingly explored more widely in recent
years.[6] Arguably, early Zionist settlers were aware of their colonial
intentions. Masalha describes how 'for over half a century, in the
period between 1882 and 1948, terms such as Zionist "colonies"
and Zionist "colonisation" were universally and unashamedly used
by senior Zionist leaders' (Masalha 2012: 60).

A common feature of European settler colonialism was European
settlers seeking 'to construct communities bounded by ties of
ethnicity and faith in what they persistently defined as virgin or
empty land'.[7] As we have stated previously (Rashed et al. 2014:
15), Israeli politicians are propagating this narrative of denial to
this day, threatening the prospect of a just and peaceful resolution
to the conflict. It isn't possible to uphold the rights of millions of
Palestinians if their presence is not acknowledged. For Pappé this
discourse of elimination 'is the point where ethnic cleansing becomes
genocidal. When you are eliminated from the history book and the
discourse of the top politicians, there is always a danger that the
next attempt would be your physical elimination.'[8] As we shall
see, public incitement to genocide was present in the discourse of
Israeli politicians during Israel's 2014 invasion of the Gaza Strip,

'Operation Protective Edge'. Many commentators have referred to Israel's actions during this operation as being 'genocide' and the use of this term is perhaps not surprising when we consider that both sides of the Israel/Palestine 'conflict' have long accused the other of conspiring to genocide.[9] Indeed, the international advocacy organization Genocide Watch includes Israel-Palestine in its list of countries at risk of genocide,[10] considering both Israeli Jews and Palestinian Arabs to be potential victims as well as perpetrators.[11] As Shaw remarks: 'It has long been contended, after all, that the Arabs in 1948 aimed at genocide of the Jewish people – "to throw the Jews into the sea" as the popular phrase put it – an argument put by the Israeli scholar Yehoshafat Harkabi who also claims that they aimed at "politicide", the destruction of the Jewish political entity' (Shaw 2010b: 1).

Thus examining the Israeli/Palestinian case from a genocide perspective should not be an unprecedented endeavour; yet determining which is the victim group when both groups claim to be may not be straightforward. For French philosopher Alain Badiou, the actions of the Israeli state are a case of history repeating itself:

> For what lurks here is the realization of this inversion of meaning, which would be the project of a genocide of the Palestinians. Already, the will to disperse them at all costs, to drive them further and further away, to wipe them out on every occasion, to shoot at their children, is declared and undertaken with systematicity. A Palestinian Diaspora – terrible recommencement! – is being formed in the world today. Ought the name of the Jews, in straying furthest from its historical meaning, become the place from where the creation, in the abandoned former place, of a new 'wandering' begins? Ought 'Palestinian' become the new name of the true Jews? (Badiou 2006: 169–70)

In fact 'no people is destined always to be victims. All peoples have been victims and executioners by turns, and all peoples count among their number both victims and executioners' (Rodinson 1983, cited in Docker 2004: 11). Lieberman notes that a common feature of ethnic cleansing is that 'perpetrators repeatedly claim to be victimized by groups targeted for removal' (2010: 50), and while

Israelis often argue that they are reacting militarily in self-defence, the possibility exists for what Moses terms the *subaltern genocide*, namely the destruction of the colonizer by the colonized (Moses 2008: 31). Similarly, Curthoys, referring to non-indigenous Australians, describes a common perception among the non-indigenous members of settler colonial societies, that 'they, like so many others, from the United States to Israel and elsewhere, see themselves as *victims*, not oppressors' (Curthoys 2003, cited in Brantliger 2004). Bearing in mind the above assertions regarding the fluidity of genocide, if we view the Zionist Israeli state and settlements as part of an ongoing settler colonial project, then the Palestinian case is clearly of relevance to genocide studies.[12]

## Physical genocide

> Conditions leading to genocide [include] ... Colonial expansion or milit. conquest. (Lemkin n.d., cited in Docker 2004: 7)

*The 'Nakba'* Palestinians refer to the events surrounding the creation of the State of Israel in 1948 as the 'Nakba' or 'catastrophe'. 'Nakba studies' and the Palestinian historical narrative were not widely recognized in Western academic circles until the 1990s, whereby the revisionist Israeli 'New Historians'[13] challenged the dominant narrative of their country's establishment.[14] The magnitude of 'a tragedy that engulfed the population of an entire country' (Pappé 2006: 9) is evident: in 1948, 'half of the indigenous people living in Palestine were driven out, half of their villages and towns were destroyed, and only very few of them ever managed to return' (ibid.: 9). 'Plan Dalet' was the name of the military plan for these evictions and it was the last of a number of military operational plans prepared by the Haganah – a Jewish military organization formed in the 1920s (Sakhnini 2005). The plan was launched to conquer and 'ethnically cleanse the country and was not a defence against an Arab invasion' as such. The Arab armies that did enter Palestine did so after the British left on 15 May, by which time 'the Zionists had already conquered a major part of the country and driven out most of its inhabitants'. Plan D, and expressly its inclusion of phrases such as 'destruction of villages' and 'expulsion of the [village] population to [territory] outside the borders of the state' (Benvenisti 2000: 109), can be taken as the model example of the Zionist concept of 'transfer' – a euphemism denoting the organized removal of the indigenous population of Palestine to neighbouring countries (Masalha 1992: 2) and also, therefore, as potential proof that there existed 'a program of premeditated ethnic cleansing' (Benvenisti 2000: 109). Chomsky and Pappé describe how: 'Jews expelled, massacred, destroyed and raped[15] in that year, and generally behaved like all the other colonialist movements operating in the Middle East and Africa since the beginning of the nineteenth century ...' (Chomsky and Pappé 2010).

One of the most well-known massacres took place in Deir Yassin, where Jewish forces indiscriminately shot at inhabitants, then rounded up the remaining inhabitants before shooting them (Pappé 2006: 90). While the battle between the different narratives surrounding the events of 1948 continues, even the University of Oxford's Professor of Israel Studies Derek Penslar has stated that he has accepted the 'vast bulk of findings' by the New Historians regarding the Nakba, saying, 'what happened to the Palestinians, the Nakba, was not a genocide. It was horrible, but it was not a genocide. Genocide means that you wipe out a people. It wasn't a genocide. It was ethnic cleansing' (Kalmus 2013). He is not the only scholar to conclude that the 'Nakba' was caused by an 'ethnic cleansing' operation.[16] In our view, 'ethnic cleansing' can be recognized as a form of genocide. If we take the example of Serbian acts of 'ethnic cleansing', which were, according to Cambridge professor Elihu Lauterpacht, nominated by the Bosnian government as its ad hoc judge, directed against 'an ethical or religious group as such', and were 'intended to destroy that group, if not in whole certainly in part' (cited in Shaw 2007: 51), it would appear that the above position holds up in a legal capacity.

Certainly with a broader sociological understanding of genocide, forced removal of groups with 'territorially bounded culture' can leave the group 'socially dead even if nonlethal coercive means are used to expel its members' (Abed 2006: 326), and 'if individuals are unable to connect to the culture and social ethos of their community, they will suffer the harms and deprivations peculiar to the crime of genocide' (ibid.: 329). Furthermore, if genocide related to settler colonialism can be understood as a process, then it is ongoing and not limited to the events in 1948. As Shaw concludes: 'Israel is – not uniquely, because many societies, settler and other, have genocidal histories – based on genocide, and much of its history to the present day represents the slow-motion extension and consolidation of that violent beginning.'[17]

This concept of continuing injustice of an ongoing Nakba is not a new one for Palestinians.[18] In Patrick Wolfe's (2012: 136) view we should think of the events of 1948 not as 'a point of origin' but as the 'intensification' of a pre-existing Zionist settler colonial project. Thus in this sense the activities in the decades that followed demonstrate a *further intensification* of the settler colonial process and the genocidal tendencies which inevitably exist in parallel. Indeed, one example of genocidal tendencies is the ongoing Zionist policy of 'transfer', which arguably manifests in the phenomenon of house demolitions, which is described by activists, journalists and politicians as 'ethnic cleansing'.[19] Such demolitions are a frequent occurrence in the West Bank and East Jerusalem.[20] In his final report as UN Special Rapporteur on the situation of human rights in the Palestinian territories occupied since 1967, Richard Falk described the current situation in East Jerusalem as being a 'microcosm of the fragmentation of territory taking place across the West Bank. Israel actively seeks to undermine the Palestinian presence to serve its goal of preserving a Jewish majority.'[21] He further stated that the Palestinians in East Jerusalem are 'subject to a gradual and bureaucratic process of ethnic cleansing' which has consisted of: revocation of residency permits (from 1996 to 2013 an estimated 11,023 Jerusalem Palestinians lost their resident status and right to live in occupied East Jerusalem)[22] as well as 'demolitions of residential structures built without Israeli permits (often virtually impossible to obtain), and forced evictions of Palestinian families, in violation of the basic right to adequate housing, enshrined in the International Covenant on Economic, Social and Cultural Rights'.[23]

Such demolitions are not restricted to the occupied Palestinian Territories – they also take place within Israel itself, to Israeli citizens.[24] The intention of these policies was clearly stated by Ariel Sharon in an interview in 1988: 'You don't simply bundle people on to trucks and drive them away ... I prefer to advocate a positive policy ... to create, in effect, a condition that in a positive way will induce people to leave.'[25] Thus, while the daily living reality for a Palestinian citizen of Israel inevitably differs from that of a Palestinian living in East Jerusalem, the West Bank or Gaza, the underlying techniques employed by the Israeli government *are the same*. If we view the Nakba – including the 'transfer', denial, elimination and discrimination against Palestinians – as an ongoing event and as part of a process of settler colonialism, then the concept of genocide is clearly relevant to how we should understand the Israeli/Palestinian situation.

In terms of physical destruction, thousands more Palestinians have been killed by Israeli forces since the Nakba. As Pappé observes, 'there has never been an end to Israel's killing of Palestinians' (Pappé 2006: 258). Extrajudicial killings of Palestinians by Israeli forces in the Occupied Territories are a frequent occurrence.[26] Furthermore, since 1948 there have been further massacres of Palestinians by or with the cooperation of Israeli forces, including of Palestinian refugees in the Lebanese refugee camps Sabra and Shatila in 1982[27] – declared an 'act of genocide' by the United Nations General Assembly[28] – in Jenin and Nablus in 2002[29] and in Gaza in 2008/09, 2012 and 2014. These were conducted in different locations (including outside of historic Palestine) and at different times but *against the same group*. This is where questions of genocide are raised. Clearly any of these incidents could be examined to see whether they constituted an 'act of genocide' or a genocidal massacre in themselves. Even so, from a broader Lemkin-inspired perspective it is also imperative to consider each individual event in the overall ongoing settler colonial context in which it is carried out. It is important to remember that while Lemkin perceived 'mass killings' to be an unsatisfactory definition for the concept of genocide,[30] he did state that it is one of the principal ways that 'the physical debilitation and even annihilation of national groups in occupied countries is carried out' (Lemkin 1944: 88). We will now consider the most recent example of a massacre committed by Israeli forces, which has widely been described as 'genocidal': Operation 'Protective Edge' in the Gaza Strip.

## Operation 'Protective Edge'

> Perhaps the truest thing that has been said about Gaza these past two months is that if the bombing continues, we suffer a quick death. And if the bombing stops, we die a slow death.[31]

'Operation Protective Edge', the latest military operation in the Gaza Strip, took place in July/August 2014. After the hostilities had ended, the UN estimated that 2,150 Palestinians had been killed,[32] 10,500 injured[33] and 110,000 people displaced. The operation was described as 'genocide' by various diplomats,[34] journalists,[35] public figures,[36] activists[37] and academics,[38] including Ilan Pappé, who reiterated his analysis of Israel's 'incremental genocide in the Gaza ghetto'.[39] Furthermore, various international political leaders, including Nawaz Sharif, the prime minister of Pakistan,[40] the presidents of Venezuela and Bolivia[41] and Palestinian Authority president Mahmoud Abbas described Israeli violence against the Palestinians in Gaza as 'genocide'.[42] Turkish prime minister (now president) Recep Tayyip Erdoğan went a step farther, stating, 'since [the creation of the state of Israel] in 1948 we have been witnessing this attempt at systematic genocide every day and every month'.[43] This assertion that the perceived genocide is systematic and ongoing is in line with our argument of applying a settler colonial Lemkinian genocide analysis to the situation.

During the bombing, there was a rise in aggravated hate speech towards Palestinians,[44] including from Israeli politician Ayelet Shaked, whose widely reported Facebook posting (originally authored by Uri Elitzur, a former Netanyahu associate and journalist)[45] referred to 'the entire Palestinian people [as] the enemy', claiming that 'they are all enemy combatants, and their blood shall be on all their heads. Now this also includes the mothers of the martyrs ... they should go, as should the physical homes in which they raised the snakes. Otherwise, more little snakes will be raised there.'[46] Following the invasion, the Knesset deputy speaker Moshe Feiglin stated: 'I'm not talking about going back to Gaza as a colonialist as we did in 1967, no. I'm talking about going back to Gaza as the owner of the land, as we did in Yafo [Jaffa] in 1948. Those who fought you in the past or don't accept your sovereignty today should be destroyed or sent away.'[47]

His view that the only option for those who don't accept Israeli sovereignty over Gaza is destruction or being 'sent away' is arguably incitement to genocide. It is certainly in line with the Zionist policy of 'transfer' of Palestinians. The fact that these views were expressed by leading Israeli politicians is disturbing, and the UN Special Advisers on the Prevention of Genocide and on the Responsibility to Protect issued a joint statement describing how they were 'disturbed by the flagrant use of hate speech in the social media, particularly against the Palestinian population', referring to 'messages that could be dehumanising to the Palestinians and have called for the killing of members of this group ... incitement to commit atrocity crimes is prohibited under international law'.[48] Specifically, such incitement is prohibited under Article 3 (c) of the UN Genocide Convention. The Russell Tribunal's emergency session in September 2014 considered the impact of Operation Protective Edge and concluded that there was evidence of an increase in anti-Palestinian speech within Israel 'which constitutes the international crime of direct and public incitement to genocide, and [given] the failure of the Israeli state to fulfil its obligations to prevent and punish incitement to genocide, the RToP is at this time compelled to place the international community on notice as to the risk of the crime of genocide being perpetrated'.[49]

During the military operation the Israeli government claimed its actions were in self-defence,[50] and thus it could be argued that the civilian casualties are a product of disproportionate reciprocal violence rather than an intentional coordinated plan of violent destruction. Yet as Chomsky and Pappé stated after Operation Cast Lead in 2008, we should remember that 'it is the decision to employ such fierce military force in a civilian space that should be discussed' (Chomsky and Pappé 2010: 193–4). A spokesman for the UN Office for the Coordination of Humanitarian Affairs stated of Operation Protective Edge that there was 'literally no safe space for civilians'[51] and a first sergeant involved in the military operation later described how there were 'no rules of engagement. If you see anyone in that area, that person is a terrorist.'[52] It is vital that when considering whether these events can be fruitfully analysed through a genocide lens they be assessed within the wider context of continual Zionist colonization and dispossession of Palestinians. Given that these massacres were set amid the context of the blockade of the Gaza Strip and the consequent inevitable destructive impact that it has on civilian life, the civilian death toll is just one aspect of the destructive nature of such a bombardment. After all, 'killing members of the group' is only one technique of genocide.

### Economic genocide

Genocide Convention Article II:
(c) Deliberately inflicting on the group conditions of life calculated to bring about its physical destruction in whole or in part; ...[53]

The crime of genocide involves a wide range of actions, including not only the deprivation of life but also the prevention of life ... and also devices considerably endangering life and health ... all these actions are subordinated to the criminal intent to destroy or to cripple permanently a human group.[54]

The detrimental impact of Israeli policies on the Palestinian economy has been documented in East Jerusalem[55] and the West Bank, but the most acute example can be found in the Gaza Strip. Sara Roy coined the term 'de-development' in relation to the Gazan economy,[56] stating that 'the lack of economic development inside the Gaza Strip has been a result of specific Israeli policies which have aimed to restrict and have, in effect, undermined the ability of the Gazan economy to create the necessary infrastructure required for sustained economic growth'.[57] A recent UN report also used the term 'de-development' to refer to the Gaza Strip, stating that:

> If the current blockade and insufficient levels of donor support persist, even with a reversion to the status quo that prevailed before the latest military operation, Gaza will become economically unviable and the already grim socioeconomic conditions can only deteriorate. The likely outcome will be more conflict, mass poverty, high unemployment, shortages of electricity and drinking water, inadequate health care and a collapsing infrastructure. In short, Gaza will be unliveable, as emphasized by the United Nations (2012).[58]

The same report determines that socio-economic conditions in Gaza are 'at their lowest point since 1967'.[59] Here a doctor in Gaza describes the effects of the Israeli blockade (in place since 2007) on all aspects of Gazan life thus:

> It is a tragedy, honestly. No salaries, no water, no electricity, no open borders, no leisure, no travel, nothing to do in Gaza. The suffering extends to all aspects of life: domestic, personal, scientific development, education. These conditions are bearable for short periods: a few weeks, a few months, at most maybe a year. But when you have to live like this for many long years, it becomes abundantly clear how this affects your psychology.[60]

The year 2014 was reported to be the worst for the Gazan economy in decades, with unemployment affecting over 50 per cent of the population and the poverty rate rising to 80 per cent.[61] Back in 2009, the International Committee of the Red Cross (ICRC) stated that 'Gaza's alarming poverty is directly linked to the tight closure imposed on the territory … The crisis has become so severe and entrenched that even if all crossings were to open tomorrow it would take years for the economy to recover.'[62] A report from the United Nations Relief and Works Agency describes the longer-term prospects for the Gazan economy 'fundamentally unviable under present circumstances'.[63] The blockade and the economic sanctions placed on the Gaza Strip after Hamas' election victory coupled with the blockade that commenced in 2007 restricting the movement of people and goods has produced a 'catastrophic humanitarian situation'[64] throughout the Gaza Strip, leaving the people of Gaza 'worse off than they were in the 1990s'.[65] These reports were all made prior to the most recent military operations that took place in Gaza in 2012 and 2014, respectively. A statement by thirty aid agencies which operate in Gaza stated in February 2015 that 'the Israeli-imposed blockade continues, the political process, along with the economy, are paralyzed, and living conditions have worsened'.[66] At the same time, Oxfam estimated that at current rates it could take more than a hundred years to rebuild homes, schools and health facilities in Gaza, unless the blockade is lifted.[67]

Leaked diplomatic cables from Israeli officials to the USA stated that Israel intended 'to keep the Gazan economy on the brink of collapse without quite pushing it over the edge'.[68] Wanting the Gazan economy 'functioning at the lowest level possible consistent with avoiding a humanitarian crisis' indicates that the economic restrictions and subsequent humanitarian situation experienced in the Gaza Strip have been intentionally strategized. The Gazan economy has been severely affected by the reduction of the fishing zone open to Palestinian fishermen[69] and the establishment of a 'buffer zone' along the border between Gaza and Israel, which incorporates 35 per cent of Gaza's arable land.[70] A document created by the Israeli government detailing the estimated minimum number of calories that Gaza residents would need to consume to avoid malnutrition was revealed in 2012. According to an UNWRA spokesman, 'The facts on the ground in Gaza demonstrate that food imports consistently fell below the red lines.'[71] The Palestinians in the Occupied Territories are also suffering from lack of food security,[72] with the majority of Palestinians in the Gaza Strip and the West Bank spending more than half their income on food.[73] In 2014 a third of households in Palestine were food insecure, with levels in the West Bank at 19 per cent and in Gaza (prior to Operation 'Protective Edge') at 57 per cent.[74] Food security includes both the availability of food and the ability to access and make use of food. The former depends on local production and imports. The latter depends on how people are able to grow and/or buy their own food.[75] Hilmi Salem notes that domestic food production within the Occupied Territories has 'rapidly declined due to the Israeli seizure of Palestinian farmland, the Israeli destruction of fertile agricultural land, and the Israeli closure of local and international markets. At this time, relief efforts have been unable to meet the growing levels of Palestinian poverty.'[76]

As a UN official has noted, 'Gaza is not a natural disaster. It is man-made, the result of deliberate political choices.'[77] Given the economic restrictions and their impact on the health and lives of the Palestinians (most acutely the Palestinians in Gaza), it is possible to consider this as 'genocide' under Lemkin's understanding of the term as well as under Article 2 (c) of the UN Genocide Convention.

## Water

Given that the most significant environmental effects of climate change for the people of the Occupied Territories over the course of this century are projected to be a decrease in precipitation and significant warming,[78] the question of who controls the water resources in the region is paramount. As well as the vital issue of land, 'demography ... and water were always at the heart of the conflict between the Zionist immigrants/settlers and the native Palestinians' (Masalha 1997: 16). The early Zionists understood the importance of water and intended to expand the supply for their planned state. Chaim Weizmann wrote to the British prime minister, David Lloyd George, stating, 'the whole economic future of Palestine is dependent upon its water supply for irrigation and for electric power'.[79] Years later Ariel Sharon was quoted saying: 'My view of Judea and Samaria is well known, the absolute necessity of protecting our water in this region is central to our security. It is a non-negotiable item.'[80]

The UN General Assembly and Human Rights Council have affirmed the right to water[81] as being a legally binding right recognized in several existing human rights treaties. Water is essential to human survival and the failure of the Palestinians in the Occupied Territories to realize this right affects Palestinians in 'every function that water plays in human life: drinking, bathing, cleaning, and watering of crops and animals',[82] and is thus closely linked to issues of health and economic survival. In the West Bank, water scarcity is a serious concern with access to, and control over, water resources a constant struggle. Israeli per capita water consumption is 'more than five times higher than that of West Bank Palestinians (350 litres per person per day in Israel compared to 60 litres per person per day in the West Bank, excluding East Jerusalem). West Bank Palestinian water consumption is 40 litres less than the minimum global standards set by the World Health Organization (WHO).'[83] The Applied Research Institute Jerusalem notes that of all the water sourced from the (Jordan) river, '92% is used by Israel, 8% by Jordan and 0% by Palestine … it is slowly shrinking … it [sic] pollution rate has also risen causing some of the water to be either useless or needing treatment'.[84] The Permanent Observer of Palestine to the United Nations, Riyad Mansour, has accused Israel of violating the Palestinian people's right to water and sanitation by exploiting 90 per cent of the shared water sources for its own use.[85] Furthermore, Israeli industrial plants based in the West Bank don't enforce any Israeli environmental laws regarding the discharge of untreated industrial waste (including hazardous waste) into the environment.[86]

In 2012, a UN report predicted that the main aquifer in Gaza may be 'unusable by 2016 and damage irreversible by 2020'[87] and around 90 per cent of the water in Gaza is currently undrinkable.[88] The ongoing blockade of the Gaza Strip has 'meant that the facilities for treating sewage are completely inadequate for the 1.4 million inhabitants. Most of the sewage either flows into the sea or builds up behind high walls of earth, threatening the adjacent homes.'[89] In recent years there have been several incidents of raw sewage flowing down streets in Gaza City largely as a consequence of Israeli control and limitation of fuel and supplies to Gaza.[90] In addition to the sanctions and blockade, over the last decade Israeli Defence Forces (IDF) 'have deliberately targeted water and sewage infrastructure throughout the Gaza Strip',[91] including during Operation Protective

Edge.[92] Restrictions on fuel and electricity, most of which is usually supplied by Israel, has led to the periodic paralysis of water and waste-water services, affecting water wells, sewage pumping stations, waste-water treatment plants and agricultural wells.[93]

The Amnesty International report *Thirsting for Justice* describes how the Israeli army has confiscated water tanks in the West Bank.[94] The lack of water means that villagers are unable to cultivate the land and many have had to leave their communities in the Jordan valley as the water situation is unsustainable. The report also details incidents when Israeli forces have demolished water cisterns that are used by rural Palestinian communities that are not served by water networks. Some of these cisterns are centuries old and have been destroyed so badly as to be irreparable. These tactics, according to Amnesty International, are used by the Israeli army as a means of expulsion to make way for Israeli settlements. Therefore, as well as potentially being 'devices considerably endangering life and health ... subordinated to the criminal intent to destroy or to cripple permanently a human group' (Lemkin 1944: 147), the control of the water supply in the Occupied Territories (specifically in the West Bank) is arguably an extension of the Zionist policy of expulsion, and a further extension of the settler colonial 'logic of elimination'.[95]

In the next section we will focus on what one scholar terms the 'environmental Nakba'[96] – ecocidal dimensions of the Israeli occupation and policies towards the Palestinians through a Lemkin-inspired genocide lens.

## The ecocidal method

The Israeli Occupation, in general, and the segregation wall in particular, have played, and continue to play, a major role in the degradation of agricultural and rangelands, deforestation, desertification, depletion of water resources and the degradation of water quality, leading to far-reaching social, economic and political implications in Palestine.[97]

Zionist colonisation of Palestine is a comprehensive system – comprising, among other things, commensurate economic, political, ideological, social, and ecological dimensions – that is responsible for the development of the two most serious and interrelated challenges, Palestinian Arab nationalism and

ecological sustainability ... this seemingly powerful venture is
neither economically profitable nor ecologically sustainable.
(Da'Na 2013: 67)

According to one commentator, the political and geopolitical
conflicts in the region 'have badly and severely contributed to, and
even accelerated the impacts of climate change'.[98] The destructive
effects of ongoing conflict and occupation are not surprising if we
understand that the Zionist colonial project in Palestine has long
attempted to:

> alter and forcefully refashion nature in its quest to establish a
> pure European colony in non-European terrain, which entailed a
> defiance of the nature of the landscape ... the Zionist movement
> colonised a country with a different rain pattern and volume,
> climate, soil fertility, and agricultural activities than Europe ... in
> order to establish a neo-European state. (Da'Na 2013: 50)

The impacts of this ideologically driven manipulation of the
environment are clearly demonstrated in the Occupied Palestinian
Territories (OPT). While historic forms of household and community
coping by Palestinians in the face of climate and other hazards 'offer
potential templates for adaptation to climate change in the Occupied
Palestinian Territories',[99] the UNDP describes how:

> the ongoing effects of the Israeli occupation undermine the
> conditions necessary to their operation, both economic – the
> free movement of goods and people – and political – national
> self-determination and democratic governance. Indeed, the
> continuing Israeli occupation fosters a wide range of maladaptive
> policies and practices (e.g. subsidised water-intensive livestock
> farming by settlers and the destruction of Palestinian olive
> groves) that need severely restrict the development of Palestinian
> resilience to climate hazards.[100]

The destructive impacts of the occupation on the environment
have been widely documented.[101] Tons of rubbish are taken daily
by lorry from Israel to the Occupied Territories, to avoid the strict
environmental laws that control operations within Israel. One

major dumping ground is Shuqbah, a village of 5,000, not far from Ramallah. According to the deputy director of the Palestinian Environmental Authority, Jamil Mtoor: 'For several years Israeli companies have been dumping solid and hazardous waste there.' He added: 'The subsequent burning of toxic waste including items such as x-ray films releases carcinogens into the environment, and this has affected the population, with many people developing asthma and related illnesses.'[102] Recall Curthoy's observation that within a settler colonial society the non-indigenous members often 'see themselves as *victims*, not oppressors' (Curthoys 2003, cited in Brantliger 2004). Similarly, Perugini and Gordon describe this inversion of the colonizer/colonized whereby ultimately 'the colonized native is transformed into a colonizer and a human rights violator ... in order for the colonizer to go native the historical and moral relationship between colonizer and colonized must be inverted' (Perugini and Gordon 2015: 123). For example, in relation to air pollution and its health impacts, a *Jerusalem Post* op-ed in 2012 referred to 'illegal unregulated production of charcoal ... causing severe health consequences for our children'.[103] Those producing the charcoal are Palestinians, and the writer is referring to the children living in a nearby Israeli settlement. It is interesting how the writer refers to the charcoal kilns as 'illegal' (but not the Israeli settlements), as is his assertion that the reason that they were not shut down is bias on the part of the Israeli Supreme Court in favour of the Palestinians: 'We can all imagine that had the polluters been Jews, the full force of the law would have been used to close down such nefarious and illegal behavior immediately. But when it comes to the enforcement of environmental laws against Arabs, it seems equal enforcement of the law is not to be assumed.'[104]

Thus reality is inverted, with the same language and arguments used by the colonized being appropriated by the colonizer, forming part of a bigger process of what Perugini and Gordon (2015) term 'the human right to dominate'.

Another example of environmental damage caused by the Israeli occupation is deforestation. Deforestation is a major contributor to climate change, and inherently ecocidal, causing as much as a fifth of global greenhouse gas emissions.[105] Around 1.5 million trees are estimated to have been uprooted by the Israeli occupation forces between 2000 and 2007 in the West Bank and Gaza Strip.[106] This will have a destructive effect on the OPT's climate, by 'disrupting the natural carbon sequestration process ... practices that increase carbon losses and decrease sequestration generally devastate the quality of soil, water, air, wildlife habitat, and the ecosystem in general'.[107] Furthermore, most of the trees were olive trees: a vital source of food, income and culture for the Palestinian people.[108] Olive trees are not just destroyed by the Israeli forces, but are also commonly burnt and destroyed by Israeli settlers, who have also reportedly poisoned livestock belonging to Palestinian farmers.[109] The destruction of olive trees has been likened to 'the erasure of communal memory'.[110]

Incorrect agricultural management practices enforced on Palestinians in the OPT have been described as a 'long-term ecocide'.[111] Such practices include:

> water scarcity, uncontrolled domestic and industrial dumping sites, and the heavy usage of fertilizers and pesticides ... [which] are partially causing in-situ soil deterioration (chemical and physical soil degradation) in the Occupied West Bank. Of course, the Israeli occupation exacerbates soil degradation, by consecrating and closing large swathes of Palestinian lands in the OPT. These practices and the Israeli strict control of the OPT have together increased pressure on the land that Palestinians retain access to, encouraging overgrazing and intensive farming practices, besides creating a highly disturbed environment, whereby planning and executing sustainable land management schemes have become extremely difficult and, in some cases, impossible.[112]

Biodiversity in the OPT is another casualty of the Israeli occupation.[113] According to a UNEP study, biodiversity 'can be interpreted as an indicator of environmental health' and is 'one of the pillars of future sustainable development in the Occupied Palestinian Territories'.[114] It states that biodiversity in the OPT is at risk owing to a number of factors, including direct degradation arising from military operations, the rapid growth of Israeli settlements and supporting roads in areas where land is already scarce, the construction of the separation fence and wall that effectively block movement of terrestrial fauna[115] and cut the natural ecological corridors, as well as Israel clearing land of vegetation for security purposes.[116] Others have expressed this same concern regarding the impact of land confiscation by Israeli authorities in the West Bank on the degradation of biodiversity in the region.[117] The UNEP study urges other parties including the Palestinian Authority, international agencies and civil society organizations to widen their data relating to agrobiodiversity beyond economic valuation, stating, 'any such valuation ... should consider not only the loss of livelihood, but also the historical, cultural and environmental losses, despite the fact that these costs are difficult to quantify, or may indeed be immeasurable'.[118]

> The impact of the conflict on ecosystems or individual species has not been evaluated. The exception to this is the recording of losses of natural forest, losses that are especially significant given that forests make up only a small proportion of the natural landscape. The impacts on natural systems and wild biodiversity may appear to be of low priority when compared to the parallel human suffering caused by the escalating conflict. However, the impacts on ecosystems should not be set aside, as these impacts can themselves have economic consequences, while there are also losses at the cultural level that may be irreplaceable.[119]

The Israeli government also conducts harmful environmental practices within Israel proper, which disproportionately affect the indigenous populations. The Palestinian Bedouin of the Negev – Israeli citizens – are described by the UK's Palestine Solidarity Campaign as being 'at the bottom of the environmental heap',[120] as 'their traditional grazing grounds and farmland have been either expropriated by the Israeli government or polluted by the highly toxic waste from the industrial zone of Beer Sheva'.[121] According to the Arab Association for Human Rights, between 2002 and 2004 Bedouin farmers in the Negev had their crops sprayed with herbicide by the Israeli Lands Administration as an extrajudicial tactic to force them to leave their land. Furthermore, they claim that the herbicide used is not suitable for aerial spraying owing to the toxic effects of the chemicals on humans and animals.[122]

While little has been written about the ecocidal impacts of the Israeli occupation in the West Bank and Gaza, this area has considerable relevance in relation to genocide studies. More research and analysis in this area is sorely needed.

**Cultural genocide**

*Fragmenting the genos: the Palestinian citizens of Israel*

> The Palestinians are still there – damaged, fragmented, occupied
> and oppressed, to be sure – but still there, both physically and
> politically. (Karmi 2007: 6)

> The imposition of the national pattern of the oppressor ... may
> be made upon the oppressed population which is allowed to
> remain ... (Lemkin 1944: 79)

The Balfour Declaration of 1917 indicated British support for the
Zionist project on the basis that 'nothing shall be done which may
prejudice the civil and religious rights of the existing non-Jewish
communities' in Palestine.[123] Thus, 'by the stroke of the British
colonial pen, the people of Palestine – 92 per cent of the population
– had been reclassified for the convenience of grand strategy as
"non- Jewish communities"' (Dimbleby 1979: 35). This expression
is still used today in official Israeli statistics relating to the Palestinian
population that remained in what became Israel – the Palestinians
with Israeli citizenship (Grossman 1993). This particular group
of Palestinians has been less studied than other groups.[124] Massad
suggests that 1948 should not be viewed as a finite episode but
rather an ongoing experience of colonization and occupation since
the 1880s, citing the Israeli–Palestinian 'struggle' which, 'according
to the Zionist narrative, is not a normal anti-colonial struggle or
one that demands national or ethnic or civil rights, but rather an
"abnormal" struggle to reverse the Nakba'.[125] The very fact that
Palestinians living in Israel are commonly referred to as 'Israeli
Arabs' as opposed to Israeli Palestinians or even just as Israeli citizens
raises the question of their identity and the group's self-identification
as opposed to an imposed identity. Certainly some would see the
'Israeli Arab' label as being 'designed to silence their Palestinian-
ness'. As Rogan explains:

> In 1948 the Jews of Palestine took on a national identity as
> Israelis, whereas the Palestinian Arabs remained just 'Arabs'
> – either 'Israeli Arabs' ... or 'Arab refugees' ... As far as Western
> public opinion was concerned, the displaced Arabs of Palestine

were no different than Arabs in Lebanon, Syria, Jordan or Egypt and would be absorbed by their host communities in due course. (Rogan 2009: 342)

Those with Israeli citizenship should theoretically have rights equal to those of any Israeli citizen. However, as Minority Rights Group International observes, 'Israel remains "the State of the Jewish people", not the state of its citizens, and Palestinian Arabs thus remain second-class citizens'.[126] As we are viewing this case from a settler colonial perspective, this is perhaps unsurprising. Settler societies are 'marked by pervasive inequalities, usually codified in law, between the settler and indigenous populations' (Elkins and Pederson 2005: 4). These inequalities have been evident since Israel's creation. For example, in 1948 the Palestinians who remained in the newly created state were subjected to military rule, not dissimilar to current practices in the Occupied Territories, for almost twenty years.[127] Despite consistently constituting almost 20 per cent of the Israeli population,[128] Israeli Palestinians have been discriminated against both officially and unofficially and are 'largely cut off from the geographical, cultural, economic and political mainstream'.[129] The discriminative policies affect what the International Crisis Group terms the 'three most fundamental assets of democratic society: resources, rights and representation'.[130] In terms of resources, there is quantitative evidence that the Israeli Palestinian community is allocated less funding than their Jewish Israeli counterparts. For example, in 2008 only 4 per cent of Israel's development budget was spent in Arab communities.[131]

Israeli politicians have regarded the number of Israeli Palestinians in the country as a threat to the Jewish nature of the state. Their presence was described by the current prime minister, Benjamin Netanyahu, as a 'demographic problem' in 2003.[132] The same year, the Nationality and Entry into Israel Law (temporary order) was created, which prevents Palestinians who marry Israelis from gaining residency or citizenship in Israel: a move that disproportionally affects Israeli Palestinians, preventing them from marrying a partner of their choice. Despite criticism from the Committee on the Elimination of Racial Discrimination, which claimed that Israel was violating international law,[133] the law has been repeatedly renewed. In September 2011, the Israeli government formulated the 'Bill on the Arrangement of Bedouin Settlement in the Negev' or 'Prawer Plan', which aimed to evacuate and dispossess all of the thirty-five unrecognized villages of the Naqab/Negev in southern Israel. Despite the presence of Palestinian Bedouins[134] in the Naqab/Negev for centuries, and the fact that today they are Israeli citizens, Bedouin villages are not connected to mains water or electricity as they are built on 'state land'. Discriminatory land and planning policies have made it virtually impossible for the Bedouin people to build legally.[135] Palestinian Bedouins in al-'Araqib, a village that has been demolished over fifty times in the last three years,[136] have termed recent events 'the new Nakba'.[137] The Israeli Knesset suspended the bill, though it remains to be seen what further efforts will be made. In September 2014 the Israeli agriculture minister even went so far as to suggest that he was considering ways to reduce the birth-rate of the Bedouin community,[138] which, as one Israeli commentator noted, could potentially be classed as a genocidal policy under Article 2 (d) of the UN Genocide Convention, 'imposing measures intended to prevent births within the group'.[139]

In the Israeli education system for Palestinian citizens, 'the development of identification with the Palestinian Arab peoples is suppressed'.[140] One such method of suppression is through Nakba denial – in 2009, the Israeli Ministry of Education ordered the term 'Nakba' to be removed from a textbook for Palestinian children.[141] The textbooks used by nearly one million Palestinian citizens of Israel are in Arabic but issued and written by the Israeli Ministry of Education. Abu-Saad argues that 'the on-going resistance of the Ministry of Education to making substantive changes in the history curriculum for Palestinian students parallels the approach other settler colonial states have taken toward teaching history to their majority and indigenous populations'.[142] The Nakba denial extends beyond the classroom – the 'Budget Foundation Law' or 'Nakba law' authorizes the finance minister to reduce or eliminate all state funding to any institute that offers an activity contradicting the definition of the State of Israel as a 'Jewish and democratic' state, or which marks the Israeli Day of Independence as a day of mourning.[143] This law violates the rights of Palestinians living in Israel to preserve their history, culture and identity.

Abaher el-Sakka, a professor of social sciences at Birzeit University, refers to the danger of 'erasing the memory of the place, connected to the original owners of the land, by using names that serve the interests of the colonisers, and this means the ultimate success of the colonial project'.[144] This is an issue in Israel, where in 2014 a group of Knesset members proposed a bill that would make Hebrew the only official language of Israel, annulling a requirement in existence since the British Mandate period that all official documents be published in Arabic as well as in Hebrew.[145] This is not the first time such a bill has been proposed[146] and the row over the languages used in Israeli street signage has also been ongoing,[147] with one Israeli scholar noting that:

> in multilingual societies, the question which languages appear on street signs is of political significance. The choice and placement of languages on street signs and the hierarchy of preference that this implies also demonstrate in visual terms how power relationships implicate the politics of language and identity into ordinary urban experiences.[148]

If we were not considering this section of Palestinians as part of a bigger whole, then the issues they face would be the same as those faced by any other minority group, and any discrimination they may experience would arguably be best understood within a minority rights framework. As Veracini notes (2006), there is a significant difficulty when attempting to compare the conditions of the different Palestinian groups – those that live within Israel having an entirely different relationship with the Israeli state than those in the Occupied Territories. However, the Israeli Palestinians form part of the Palestinian *genos* and are also seen as such by various Israeli politicians who have proposed 'transferring' Israeli Palestinians to a future Palestinian state in what they term a 'population exchange'.[149] This would indicate not only that the 'transfer' policy is ongoing, but also that Israeli Palestinians are susceptible to being 'transferred' or 'cleansed' from the land despite their current Israeli citizenship. As Ilan Pappé concludes, 'there are many Palestinians who are not under occupation, but none of them … are free from the potential danger of future ethnic cleansing' (Pappé 2006: 260).

*Potential legal implications* In 2014 Richard Falk recommended that the UN General Assembly request that the International Court of Justice provide an advisory opinion on the question of whether 'elements of the [Israeli] occupation constitute forms of colonialism and apartheid'.[150] More precisely, he recommended that the court 'be asked to assess the allegations that the prolonged occupation of the West Bank and East Jerusalem possess elements of "colonialism", "apartheid" and "ethnic cleansing" inconsistent with international humanitarian law in circumstances of belligerent occupation and unlawful abridgement of the right to self-determination of the Palestinian people'.[151] We would argue that there is also potentially a legal case to be made for genocide – particularly against the Palestinians of Gaza in recent ongoing military operations. International lawyer Francis Boyle has long contended that Israel has violated Article II a, b and c of the Genocide Convention,[152] describing how Israel has:

> ruthlessly implemented a systematic and comprehensive military, political, and economic campaign with the intent to destroy in substantial part the national, ethnic, racial and different religious (Muslim & Christian) group known as the Palestinian People.[153]

Recently, different citizens' initiatives and activist groups have been evaluating the Palestinian experience in relation to genocide.[154] Furthermore, two recent international 'citizens tribunals' have come to different conclusions about what term best depicts the Palestinian experience. As we have seen, the Russell Tribunal on Palestine concluded after Operation Protective Edge in Gaza that 'public incitement to genocide' had taken place, in breach of the Genocide Convention. Previously, when considering the broader Palestinian situation, the Russell Tribunal had concluded that 'sociocide' is taking place against the Palestinian people. It considered that 'the systematic destruction of the essence of a social group, i.e. of all the elements that make a group more than the sum of its members, will inevitably result in the destruction of the group itself even though its members are, for the most part, still physically unscathed.'[155] In our view, this 'social death'[156] is what makes the acts genocidal.[157] Whilst the narrow remit afforded to early genocide studies has led to journalists and scholars alike creating new concepts such as sociocide,[158] a Lemkin-inspired understanding of genocide would certainly consider the political and cultural destruction as techniques of genocide, not as a separate concept. Taking a different approach, the 2013 Kuala Lumpur War Crimes Tribunal found Israel guilty of genocide and concluded that acts committed by the State against the Palestinian people for the last 67 years amounted to genocide. The Tribunal agreed with the prosecution's argument that allegations in relation to the charge of genocide against Israel be placed in a more general historical context.[159] The prosecution ruled that:

> the destruction had cumulative effects of cultural and religious destruction, renaming villages and destruction of places of worship, troubled economic and physical effects, severe restricted freedom of movement, scarcity and control of water, adverse conditions of life and the impact of the 2006 attacks and the usage of White phosphorus ammunitions in 2009 on the reproductive health of the Gaza population. Basically, the harsh conditions of life were deliberately inflicted to destroy a group and the acts are equivalent to those of war with a genocidal intent.[160]

This conclusion encompasses both Lemkin's different techniques of genocide[161] and the fact that this destruction is part of a continual structural process – a settler colonial one in our view. Viewing the Zionist project as being of an ongoing settler colonial nature has implications for our understanding of how the Palestinian situation will ultimately be resolved. As Massad notes, 'as Zionism's colonization continues, so does Palestinian resistance. The Palestinian Question ... persists as long as Zionism's colonial venture persists.'[162]

## Conclusion

This chapter has considered the Palestinian case study through a Lemkin-inspired lens, which has highlighted the use of some key techniques of genocide he identified. In recent years some scholars and commentators have referred to specific incidences in Palestinian history (such as the Nakba of 1948 and Operation 'Protective Edge' in 2014) as being 'genocide'. Such inquiries are to be welcomed and it is hoped that further exploration and investigation through the genocide lens will be forthcoming as, unfortunately, there is considerable evidence to gather. Meanwhile, by considering this case through the lens of settler colonialism, this chapter has argued that 'genocidal' massacres have taken place within a wider context of a continuing 'Nakba'. The broader impacts of Israeli policies towards Palestinians – be they cultural, political or economic – are related to this inherently genocidal continuing process of colonization and dispossession – a recurring theme within all the case studies considered in this book. While respecting the differing contexts, it is also necessary to consider the effects of these techniques of genocide on the entire Palestinian *genos* – including Palestinians who are citizens of Israel and those living in the diaspora.

There is clearly scope for this case study to be explored in far more depth, particularly with regard to the potential ecocidal impacts of Israeli policies towards Palestinians, in the differing contexts of the Occupied West Bank and East Jerusalem, Gaza and within Israel itself. Ongoing deforestation, pollution and destruction of water resources and poor agricultural management of the land have impacted the capability of the environment to sustain life, which itself is a form of what Martin Crook and I have termed 'ecologically induced genocide' (Crook and Short 2014). Direct attacks on land inhabited by Palestinians in order to force them to relocate have a broader cultural, economic and environmental impact. More research and analysis in this area is sorely needed.

# 4 | SRI LANKA

*with Vinay Prakash*[1]

## Introduction

This chapter will explore the conflict between the Sinhalese and the Tamils in Sri Lanka through Lemkin's analytical lens. It will focus on questions of social identity, the creation of a *genos* and a range of key methods of genocide, from those identified by Lemkin, including physical, economic, biological and cultural, to the ecologically induced ecocidal method outlined in Chapter 2. Since its independence from the British in 1948 Sri Lanka, formerly Ceylon, has witnessed a gradual yet periodically rapid rise in animosity between the Sinhalese and the Tamils. What began as a move by the Sri Lankan government to politically alienate the Tamils resulted in severe marginalization, including the appropriation of Tamil lands in the north and the east, alongside brutal massacres, which ultimately culminated in one of Asia's longest civil wars. Both the Liberation Tigers of Tamil Eelam (LTTE) and the Sri Lankan government committed grotesque crimes. The number of people killed since the start of the civil war is staggering. Some estimates suggest that 338,000 people may have been killed since 1983 while others put the figure somewhere between 100,000 to 215,000.[2]

The LTTE exhibited extreme chauvinism towards Sinhalese and Muslims and vehemently quashed dissent among Tamils in pursuit of a homeland. However, many have viewed their struggle as that of a legitimate self-determination movement in response to years of state-sponsored suppression.[3] The end of the civil war not only resulted in the routing of the LTTE but also brought the Sri Lankan military's conduct during the last phase of the war to light. The military targeted hospitals in the no-fire zones and engaged in sexual violence and extrajudicial killings of suspected LTTE soldiers, including children.[4] Along with such massacres, there has been grotesque triumphalism, including the destruction of the graves of fallen LTTE fighters,[5] and the post-war functioning of government has witnessed extreme subjugation and subordination of the Tamil community in the north and east. All of this has alerted the attention of the Office of the Commissioner for Human Rights, which has argued for a hybridized court to bring justice to victims of war crimes and crimes against humanity.[6] Furthermore, post-war Sri Lanka has seen increased hostilities between the Sinhalese and the 'Moors', a Tamil-speaking Muslim community in the eastern part of the island; all of which is examined later in the chapter.

In order to understand the conflict between the Tamils and the Sinhalese, there is a need to explore the dominant narratives from one of Sri Lanka's national epics, the Mahavamsa, as it has been instrumental in shaping Sinhalese Buddhist nationalism and legitimizing genocidal practices on the Tamil community. The chapter will then move on to outline the development of a comprehensive identity, a *genos*, among the Tamils as a result of policy changes and alienation of minorities since independence and the creation of a vulnerable minority population susceptible to the peculiar harm of genocide. The final section of this chapter will interrogate key issues in post-war Sri Lanka, including environmental degradation in the wake of 'development' and its effect on the people in the former war zone and rebel-held territories in the north and east.

### Historical context

*The Mahavamsa* The Mahavamsa was written in Pali in the sixth century AD by the Venerable Mahanama Thera, a Buddhist monk and uncle of the Sinhala king Dathusena, who ruled Anuradhapura during the time of its conception. It has surpassed all other epics in shaping the Buddhist nationalist ideology since its translation into Sinhalese and English in 1839. Although explaining the Mahavamsa in its entirety is beyond the scope of this chapter, discussing the prominent ideological concepts is necessary to understanding the conflict. Many writers have established that a substantial section of radical Sinhalese Buddhists and politicians view the Mahavamsa as the undisputable truth and as a justification for atrocities against minorities (DeVotta 2007: 40).

The genesis of Sinhalese Buddhist nationalist ideology found in the Mahavamsa and to an extent in other manuscripts like the Culavamsa and Pujavalia is the notion of 'Sidhadipa' and 'Dhammadipa', which translates as 'island of the Sinhalese' and 'island where Buddhism [Dhamma] must be cherished and propagated' respectively (ibid.: 40). Moreover, the scriptures also highlight Buddha's prophecy regarding the deterioration of Buddhism in the land of its birth, i.e. throughout mainland South Asia, and foresees a sanctuary in Sri Lanka (Mahanama Thera 1912: ch. 1). It also explains the mythical origins of the Sinhalas as a colonizing people with the arrival of an 'Aryan' prince, Vijaya, on the island in 500 BC, coinciding with the death of Buddha (ibid.: ch. 1).

The Mahavamsa explains the arrival of Prince Vijaya on an island devoid of human civilization except for a race of demons known as the Yakkas, who were defeated by the prince and his entourage of 700 men with the assistance of a Yaka princess, Kuveni. However, in order to sanctify his claim on the island and establish a kingdom, the young prince was compelled to follow Vedic and caste customs and established matrimonial alliances with the Kshatriyas[7] from southern India. Thus, his search for worthy 'maidens of noble birth' resulted in the Pandyan king sending envoys and 'delivered up to the prince Vijaya the gifts and the maidens with the king's daughter at the head'; 'Vijaya ... bestowed the maidens, according to their ranks upon his ministers [fellow settlers] ... then the prince Vijaya consecrated the daughter of the Pandu [Pandyan] king with a solemn ceremony as his queen' (ibid.: 55).

There is no doubt that the matrimonial alliance between Vijaya and his consort from one of southern India's prominent Tamil kingdoms suggests the mixed heritage in the creation of a Sinhala state. This, however, is completely ignored by the Sinhalese nationalists in contemporary Sri Lanka. Prominent Sri Lankan intellectual Gananath Obeyesekere argues that the Sinhalese ignore the fact that the Tamils are not only 'kinfolk but also cofounders'[8] of the Sinhala nation.

The Mahavamsa's interpretation of the Aryan origin of Prince Vijaya from the Vanga kingdom (considered by Sinhalese to be in present-day Bengal) has been overtly emphasized to draw a distinction with the Dravidian Tamils. His birth and early life can be summarized briefly: Vijaya's grandmother, the daughter of the Vanga king, is abducted by a lion and forced to cohabit with it; she later conceives twins with the lion, a boy called Sihabahu and a girl called Sihasivali. Sihabahu eventually kills his father and escapes to

Vanga and is made king, with his twin sister his consort; the sibling couple eventually have twin sons of which Prince Vijaya was the eldest (ibid.: ch. 1). Obeyesekere states that this myth is entirely steeped in 'incest', 'patricide' and 'bestiality';[9] this, however, serves as a perfect 'mythomoteur' (which Anthony Smith (1986: 229) outlines as a constitutive myth that gives an ethnic group its sense of purpose) to conjure the passions of the Sinhalese claim to be a lion race and serves to legitimize their subordination of non-Sinhalese. Today, the myth of Vijaya and of the origins of the lion people is part of the Sri Lankan ethos and also institutionalized in state-run schools (DeVotta 2007: 7). Moreover, Neil DeVotta explains that the 'sword-carrying lion on the country's national flag' is disowned by some inhabitants of the island as it represents Prince Vijaya and Sinhalese hegemony over minorities (ibid.: 6). This is also used to explain the use of the tiger by the LTTE to counter the lion during the civil war.[10]

One particular event in the annals of the Mahavamsa that has been used to endorse animosity against Tamils is the battle between the Tamil Chola king Elara and the Sinhala king Duthagamini in the second century BC. According to the epic, Duthagamini, the son of the ruler of Ruhana in the extreme south-west of the island, was disgruntled with the Tamil Chola 'occupation' of Sri Lanka around the capital Anuradhapura under King Elara and successfully eliminated him in battle (Mahanama Thera 1912: 157). Authors like DeVotta claim that the ethnic distinction emphasized in the Mahavamsa is considered the most 'baneful to inter-ethnic harmony in the country' (De Votta 2007: 7); this can be attributed to the fact that the Mahavamsa exaggerates the ethnic distinction of the two rulers and dedicates an entire chapter to the one battle while only mentioning the dozens of other battles Duthagamini fought prior to the war against the Damila (Tamil) king Elara.

Leaving aside the exaggeration of the ethnic identities of the rulers, the Mahavamsa is contradictory in its portrayal of Elara as a just and secular king; this is evident from the support he garnered from among the Tamils and Sinhalese (Mahanama Thera 1912; DeVotta 2007). However, the Mahavamsa justifies the conflict solely on the basis of religion and the need to regain control over the island from the Damilas; this is evident in the ethno-symbolism in the Mahavamsa with claims that Duthagamini went to war adorned with the relic of the Buddha (possibly the tooth relic housed in Kandy) (DeVotta

2007: 8). Sinhalese nationalists not only use this battle to suppress the Tamils but also claim that the conflict between the Sinhalese and Tamils is more than two millennia old (ibid.: 8).

Moreover, Buddhist philosophers and radical thinkers claim that this battle was one of the first examples of Buddhist nationalism on the island and use the Mahamvamsa narrative to dehumanize non-Buddhists: Rahula Walpola, a radical monk and writer, states, 'The entire Sinhalese race was united under the banner of the young Gamini [Duthagamini]. This was the beginning of Nationalism among the Sinhalese ... A non-Buddhist was not regarded as a human being. Evidently all Sinhalese without exception were Buddhist' (Rahula 1956: 76; DeVotta 2007).

The Mahavamsa appears to be the key foundational myth for Sinhalese Buddhist ideology to establish the Buddha Dhamma throughout the island. Crucially, there seems to be a deep connection between the creation of the Mahavamsa and the threat to the *sanga* or Buddhist clergy with the growing influence of southern Indian Tamil non-Buddhist kings; Gunawardana argues that the Mahavamsa was created to serve as 'an inspiring model for contemporaries for future generations' (Gunawardana 1984 in Kapferer 1988: 81), i.e. a tool to rally the Sinhalese during times of great need, the latest being the threat from the LTTE. In terms of the political situation at the time the epic was conceived, Mahanama Thera's nephew-king, Dathusena, was instrumental in ending the rule of the 'six Pandyan [Tamil] kings' (Codrington 1927), which re-established Sinhalese hegemony on the island. This also explains the 'minority complex' (Tambiah 1986) endured by the Sinhalese, a majority in the state of Sri Lanka but a minority within a region with close to eighty million Tamils in mainland India.

*Social identities* Although a majority of Sinhalese and Tamils follow Buddhism and Shaivism respectively, the island is also home to a substantial population of Christians within the two groups; this is the legacy of more than four centuries of European influences.[11] However, while more or less objective distinctions exist between the Tamils and the Sinhalese – language and religion, for example – additional differences by virtue of caste, region and history have always played a significant role in creating schisms between the Sinhalese and the Tamils (Weiss 2011).

Commenting on the caste system among the Sinhalese, geographer Conrad Malte-Brun pointed out that '[the Sinhalese] are divided into castes, but they have not the ridiculous pride of caste which prevails in India, a Sinhala will not refuse to eat in the company of a respectable European' (in ibid.). Even so, geographical distinctions persisted among the Sinhalese, with many Sinhalese in the Kandyan highlands seemingly abhorring their western counterparts for harbouring and intermarrying with European Christians, and fearing domination by the southern peasants in an independent Sri Lanka, thus insisting on being classified as a distinct ethnic minority during the latter part of the colonial era (ibid.: 32).

While Malte-Brun was under the impression that Sri Lanka was immune to the rigid caste system dominant in southern India, Gunawardana, 31st Surveyor General of Sri Lanka, suggested that the Chola occupations influenced caste, not only among the Tamils of the island; immediately after the Chola occupation the 'distinctions become so rigid that they even affected the organization of Buddhist ritual' (Gunawardana 1990). However, while caste consciousness among the Sinhalese would alter and change over time, division among the Tamils, which endured throughout British rule on the island, persisted; the Jaffna Tamils of the northern peninsula, for example, were primarily from the warrior Vellala caste known for their 'chauvinistic dogma of superiority towards their mainland Indian brethren [in present-day Tamil Nadu, India], the Eastern and Plantation [Indian] Tamils' (Weiss 2011: n30). The dominant Vellalas claimed to be at the vanguard of the Tamil civilization under the Cholas and thrived in the Jaffna kingdom until the Portuguese conquest of 1619. Moreover, it was the Jaffna Tamils who benefited the most from British rule and were represented in the civil services.[12] Their intolerance and hegemonic tendencies were reflected in colonial attempts to enable 'equal seating' in Jaffna so that lower-caste Tamils might 'attend school' and met with resistance from upper-caste Tamils (ibid.: 287). Furthermore, post-independence moves for autonomy in the Tamil-speaking areas were not completely endorsed by the Tamils on the eastern coast, as they were concerned about the possibility of being dominated by the Jaffna Tamils.[13]

Despite the enduring prevalence of primordial ethno-linguistic Tamil and Sinhalese identities, constructed, reconstructed and reinforced through political use of the ethnocentric Mahavamsa and the period of colonization and civil war, some authors backed by anthropological and historical evidence suggest that the two communities have blended to form numerous hybridized communities within the island. Proof of cultural hybridity, or what Gunawardana calls the Tamil cultural influence on the Buddhist Sinhalese, is evidenced by the objectively similar caste system practised on the island; the worship or reverence of 'assimilated Hindu Gods' among Buddhists: one such example is the Sinhalese folk deity called 'Pattini', regarded as a guardian or protectress, which resembles the Tamil worship of 'Amman' (Eternal Mother/Shakthi), glorified in the *Vayantimalaya*, a poetical work translated from Tamil on the goddess Pattini which has been assigned to the period of the Sinhala Kotte kingdom.[14] Additionally the popular elephant-headed Hindu god Ganapati (Ganesha) has been revered in southern Sri Lanka through songs and renditions like the Parevi Sandesa, written by Sinhala Buddhist Totagamuve Rahula in the fifteenth century (Gunawardana 1990: 66).

Perhaps the most striking proof of cross-cultural hybridization is that the last king of Kandy, Vikrama Rajasinha, was a Tamil-speaking Buddhist from the royal court of Madurai; his dynasty inherited the throne in Kandy after the demise of the heirless Sinhalese king Vira Narendra Sinha, who named his consort's brother from Madurai, Vijaya Rajasinha, successor.[15] The evolution of what was considered Tamil and Sinhalese identity was under constant change and 'marked by contingency'.[16] However, Mahavamsa-based ethnocentrism was neutered by the British and proved politically useful in their expansion quest on the island.

The urgency to decipher the history of the island in order to facilitate a carving up of resources and subsequent development on the island prompted early officials to build a body of knowledge that used the Mahavamsa as the sole source. This process seemingly led to British prioritization of Sinhalese (the original colonists) interests over Tamil. James Tennent, the former colonial secretary of Ceylon, in his book *Ceylon: An account of the island*, writes that 'the exploits and escapes of the Malabars [Tamils] occupy a more prominent portion of the Singhalese annals than that which treats the policy of the native sovereigns'.[17] This statement shows that the British official on the island, like many during his time, clearly viewed the Sinhalese as the 'earliest colonists' (Tennent 1860: 401) of the island

and viewed the Tamils, with a significant population in southern India separated by a 22-mile shallow strait, as invaders who 'aspired not to beautify or enrich [the island], but to impoverish and deface it' (ibid.: 401). Anecdotes of an Aryan legacy and the degradation of their civilization, due to incursions from southern India, were later replicated to the masses by the Sinhalese elites in a democratic environment, which contributed significantly to Tamil alienation on the island.

For their part, Tamil intellectuals like Arunachalam Ponnambalam claimed that the Sinhalese people were a mixed race of Aryan, Dravidian, Vedda, Mongolian and Malay origins, while the Tamils were an 'old Dravidian race',[18] implying that the Tamils were racially pure. Another contemporary Tamil author and politician, Satchi Ponnambalam, stated that the Sinhalese were originally Tamils and it was Buddhism and the Pali language that created an 'ascriptive cleavage' among the 'Dravidians' of Lanka and divided them into Tamils and Buddhists (Satchi 1983: 20). However, during the nineteenth and twentieth centuries many Sinhalese elites exposed to the works of Hegel and Max Muller on Aryan race, who claimed to be Aryans, viewed the 'derogatory' statements made by Tamil politicians as a means to delegitimize the Sinhalese presence on the island. The Mahavamsa has helped classify the Tamils and the Sinhalese on the basis of religion and language, but does not dwell on issues beyond an ethnic and linguistic distinction. The recent government census for the year 2012 claims that the Sinhalese are a majority with 74 per cent, while the Sri Lankan Tamils, who are primarily followers of Shaivism,[19] form 12.70 per cent of the population, and the second-largest minority are the Sri Lankan Moors or Muslims who are primarily Tamil speakers with 9.2 per cent.[20] The Sri Lankan government has classified the Indian Tamil community under a different category and they form 4 per cent of the population and predominantly live in the Kandyan highlands.[21] They were brought in by the British from the mid-eighteenth century and served as labourers on the tea and rubber plantations, and many continue to do so.

The Citizenship Act of 1948 was the first of a series of anti-Tamil laws that targeted the Indian or Upcountry Tamils; this Act was a deliberate attempt to mitigate the apparent threat to Sinhalese hegemony in the Kandyan highlands. The process of democratization saw the rise in their political clout through the Ceylon Indian Congress and a check in their rise was considered necessary;[22] the implementation of the Act resulted in 'repatriation' of close to 350,000 Tamils to India over a period of three decades.[23] The elections of 1956 are considered a watershed moment in alienating Sri Lankan Tamils; they also saw the success of Sinhalese Buddhist nationalism as a tool for gerrymandering. That year was the 2,500th anniversary of Vesak, a celebration commemorating the birth, life and passing of Buddha (Arasaratnam 1964: 23). This, coupled with the Mahavamsa's narrative of Prince Vijaya's arrival coinciding with the passing of Buddha, gave the Sinhalese-oriented parties useful propaganda to exploit in the post-colonial era. In order to maximize Sinhalese votes, the Sri Lankan Freedom Party (SLFP) launched a Sinhala-only movement in conjunction with the mythomoteur and proposed making Sinhala the official language of the state if voted into power. This proposal, later replicated by other Sinhalese political parties, was subsequently passed in the parliament under a coalition led by the SLFP.[24] Tensions between the two communities escalated after non-violent protests by Tamil political parties were met with violence perpetrated by the police and Sinhalese militias.[25]

This event eventually led to *ethnic outbidding*, which is explained by Neil DeVotta as 'an insidious practice whereby parties representing the majority community [Sinhalese-oriented political parties] try to outdo each other to get the best deal for their ethnic kin, usually at the expense of minorities' (DeVotta 2007: 17).

A 'standardization policy' in the education system was introduced in 1971 and sought to promote Sinhalese enrolment into higher education by targeting Tamils, whereby students instructed in Tamil had a higher cut-off than their Sinhalese counterparts.[26] However, 1972 saw the introduction of a system of quotas to benefit underprivileged districts, i.e. districts that benefited the least from English education under the British. While enrolment from the 'underprivileged' Kandyan highlands increased, the real impact on the Tamil community is evidenced by the drop in Tamil enrolment from 1972 onwards.[27]

By curtailing the political ambitions of the Tamils through con-stitutional amendments in 1972 and by reducing the rate of uni-versity enrolment of Tamils according to their percentage in the population through the standardization process, the government of Sri Lanka not only reinforced racial stereotypes and prejudices between the two communities; it also concurrently reduced employment among Tamils, affecting the livelihood of millions of Tamils and directly contributing to radicalizing Tamil youth. These two incidents prompted the consortium of Tamil parties to propose the Vaddukoddai Resolution in 1976 and to seek complete independence of the Tamil areas in the north and east by all means necessary.[28]

The burning of the Jaffna library in 1981 by an organized group of Sinhalese 'thugs' and the anti-Tamil pogroms of 1983, both of which will be discussed in the next section, seemed to stratify the Sinhalese and Tamils beyond reconciliation. Such events contributed to ethnic solidarity among the Sri Lankan Tamils, breaking away from distinctions based on geography, caste and to a certain extent religion. The complete destruction of the library was a classic genocidal tactic and was viewed as an attack on the cultural roots of the Tamils, with old and irreplaceable documents lost; the Tamil legacy and heritage were attacked and much was destroyed.

The direct impact of the policies designed to alienate Tamils was the creation of the militant Tamil New Tigers, who began using guerrilla tactics against the Sri Lankan military; these attacks propelled them into the limelight. One such attack killed twelve Lankan soldiers and directly contributed to the anti-Tamil pogroms of July 1983, commonly referred to as Black July (discussed below). The genocidal atrocities witnessed during this time include Sinhalese mobs equipped with the electoral rolls targeting Tamil homes and businesses in urban centres and the plantation lands in the Central Province. The militarized Tamil areas in the east witnessed repeated revenge attacks on Tamil civilians and Hindu temples by military personnel and organized groups of thugs; one such incident in 2006 involved attacks by air force personnel on Tamil civilians in the village of Kappalthurai, in retaliation for claymore mine attacks that killed two airmen.[29]

## Occupation, settler colonial genocide and the cultural method

'Sinhalization' is a term that has been used to describe Sinhalese expansion into areas traditionally inhabited by Tamils in the north and the east. The instrument of expansion has been colonization through strategically planned demographic alteration in the north and east through 'irrigation and resettlement' propagated by successive Sri

Lankan governments. It also includes changes to names of villages and streets from Tamil to Sinhala and the construction of Buddha statues,[30] which can also be associated with the cultural method of genocide.

Sinhalization has its roots in British Ceylon, where Universal Adult Suffrage in 1931 led to the Sinhalese majority in the State Council creating a framework for settlement of Sinhalese farmers from the densely populated south-west to the Dry Zone,[31] a region in the north and east inhabited by Tamils. While the initial justification for development projects was to alleviate population pressures in the south-west and to increase agricultural productivity in the water-deficient Dry Zone through irrigation, the ulterior motive was to revive the honour of the Sinhalese peasantry destroyed by the British introduction of 'ancillary service industries and trade and the spread of commercial crop production (tea, rubber) within the native economy'.[32] This initiative was aimed at popularizing the policy among the landless Sinhalese but invariably affected already established Tamil agriculturists in the Dry Zone.

In 1949, D. S. Senanayake inaugurated the Gal Oya Multi-Purpose Project in Paddipalai (renamed in Sinhala as 'Inginiyagala') in the east. While the initial rhetoric could have been passed off as the post-colonial nationalism of a nascent state, it is, however, clear that this laid the foundation for Sinhala Buddhist nationalist ideology, 'Sidhadipa' and 'Dhammadipa', which translates as 'island of the Sinhalese' and 'island where Buddhism [Dhamma] must be cherished and propagated' respectively (DeVotta 2007: 40). These two concepts are engrained in the Mahavamsa, Sri Lanka's national epic, as we saw earlier, penned in Pali in the sixth century AD by the Venerable Mahanama Thera, a Buddhist monk and uncle of the Sinhala king Dathusena, who ruled Anuradhapura during the time of its conception.

D. S. Senanayake considered the Sinhalese settlers as pioneers in re-establishing Sinhalese glory on the island, and in his address to Sinhalese settlers in the Padaviya settlement stated:

> Today you are brought here and given a plot of land. You have been uprooted from your village. You are like a piece of driftwood in the ocean; but remember that one day the whole country will look up to you. The final battle for the Sinhala people will be fought on the plains of Padaviya. You are

men and women who will carry this island's destiny on your shoulders. Those who are attempting to divide this country will have to reckon with you. The country may forget you for a few years, but one day very soon they will look up to you as the last bastion of the Sinhala.[33]

The statement suggests that the will of the government was to supersede established Tamil culture with Sinhalese, what Lemkin called 'supplanting'. Although this statement, along with previous statements, drives a rhetorical wedge between the Sinhalese and Tamils and thus safeguards a strong block of votes among the Sinhalese peasantry, it also epitomizes the fact that land was not merely a tool for economic development but the basis for creating an ideological plan for colonization, which was reiterated in the elite's rhetorical appropriation of Sinhalese kings to serve their political agenda: 'The early political advocates of irrigation projects, United National Party leaders D. S. Senanayake and his son Dudley, claimed descent from ancient Dry Zone kings like King Parakramabahu; their successor, President J. R. Jayawardane, posed as the Boddhisattva (an Enlightened being), claiming that like "the kings of old" he would bring "water prosperity, and justice to the people"' (Deckard 2010: 44).

Alarmed by the influx of Sinhalese into the Tamil east, the Tamil Federal Party issued a statement in 1956: 'the colonisation policy pursued by successive Governments since 1947 of planting a Sinhalese population in the traditional homelands of the Tamil speaking peoples is calculated to overwhelm and crush the Tamil speaking people in their own national areas'.[34] The statement also sought the 'immediate cessation of colonising the traditionally Tamil speaking areas with Sinhalese people'.[35] Nevertheless, the settlement/colonization policy continued and over time Tamil concerns grew. Indeed, they were reiterated twenty years later in the Vaddukoddai Resolution, where they accused the government of 'Making serious inroads into the territories of the former Tamil [Jaffna] Kingdom by a system of planned and state-aided Sinhalese colonization and large scale regularization of recently encouraged Sinhalese encroachments, calculated to make the Tamils a minority in their own homeland'.[36] However, their protests and apprehensions came at the time of the National Language Act, whereby Sinhala superseded English and Tamil as the national language, and their non-violent protests were viewed as the 'reactionary cause' of a minority that had fallen from privilege, and regardless of the 'caste, class or place of origin' were considered a privileged community that deserved no guarantee or protection within the constitutional framework.[37]

Moreover, the agitations and non-violent *satyagraha* protests against the Language Act and the settlements were met with the first anti-Tamil pogrom, which engulfed the entire country, including the Gal-Oya settlement, where indoctrinated Sinhalese settlers in cahoots with the military and police actively committed crimes of rape, massacre and other forms of violence, and 150 Tamil civilians were massacred within a matter of five days.[38]

The elites in power firmly believed in 'infusing Sinhalese nationalism with the vision that the colonisation of the Dry Zone was a return to the heartland of the ancient irrigation civilization of the Sinhalese', thus by 1960 nearly 300,000 acres of land in the Dry Zone had been allotted to 67,000 settlers.[39] From 1946 to 1959 the Sinhalese population in the Dry Zone increased from 19 per cent to 54 per cent. In 1976 they constituted 83 per cent of the population, increasing tenfold in the thirty years between 1946 and 1976 (Peebles 1990: 37). The Dry Zone has been transformed since independence from a plural yet largely Tamil-dominated area to a homogeneous Sinhalese Buddhist one. The government of Sri Lanka was implementing the 'millennial visions' of the Sinhalese nationalists (ibid.: 40).

Following the United National Party's victory in the 1977 elections, Junius Jayawardene proposed completing the Mahaweli Development Programme in six years as opposed to the thirty years envisaged in the 1960s. The 'Accelerated' Mahaweli Programme, later sanctioned by the World Bank, planned to settle 700,000 mostly Sinhalese individuals in thirteen different settlements scattered around the Dry Zone and the east. Furthermore, areas within the settlements were given Sinhalese names; for example, the region locally known as Manal Aru in Tamil was renamed Weli Oya in Sinhala, a move that sought to culturally dilute Tamil influence on the island.

Implementation of this project brought displacement and environmental degradation, while unprecedented monsoon rains inundated the areas adjoining the partially built Victoria Dam in Kandy, displacing thousands and destroying forests and plantations in the hill country. However, it is important to note that the government evacuated 5,825 families numbering 35,000 people (approximately 85 per cent were Sinhala Buddhist, 6 per cent were Tamil Hindus and another 7 per cent were Muslim) and resettled most of the Sinhalese in the Mahaweli zones while all the non-Sinhalese (Tamils and Muslims) were resettled in Kandy.[40]

Additionally, in order to spiritually guide the new settlers the Ministry of Maheweli Development focused on the government's intention to protect the traditions and culture of Sinhalese Buddhist society as the core aim of the entire project:

> The Mahaweli authorities ... will not only lead the settlers towards material prosperity, but also provide them with spiritual guidance to make them morally upright ... On Poya [full moon] days every family has been advised to go to temple, offer flowers, perform other rites, listen to sermons and observe sil [Buddhist precepts] ... Their engagement in rituals, ceremonies and reciting of Pali stanzas is only the first step in their spiritual ascent, as this only attunes the minds for higher and more important religious exercises.[41]

### Physical genocide

*'Black July'*

> I am not worried about the opinion of the Tamil people ... now we cannot think of them, not about their lives or their opinion ... the more you put pressure in the north, the happier the Sinhala people will be here ... Really if I starve the Tamils out, the Sinhala people will be happy.[42]

The anti-Tamil pogroms of 1983, commonly referred to as Black July, were triggered after the bodies of twelve soldiers and one officer, all Sinhalese, from the 1st Battalion of the Sri Lanka Light Infantry arrived in Colombo. The soldiers were killed in an ambush by the Tamil New Tigers in Thinevely in Jaffna.[43] The resulting crisis would directly contribute to the commencement of the Eelam Wars, or more commonly the Sri Lankan civil war.

While violence against Tamils has been a mainstay of 'post-colonial' Sri Lanka, Black July was a breaking point in Tamil–Sinhalese relations on the island and consolidated a Tamil identity that surpassed geographical, religious and caste distinctions that would otherwise have defined Tamil culture and lifestyle. While the ruling UNP party at the time defended the actions of Sinhalese mobs as a 'spontaneous backlash' to the killing of Sri Lankan soldiers in Jaffna, many Tamils and scholars consider the violence during this time 'as a genocide or holocaust of Tamils'.[44] There is sufficient evidence to suggest that mobs (*goondas*) on the government payroll and the armed forces engaged in acts of genocide against the Tamil people. *The Review*, a publication issued by the International Commission of Jurists, stated that the evidence from 1983 'points clearly to the conclusion that the violence of the Sinhala rioters on the Tamils amounted to acts of genocide'.[45] These acts included mobs torching buses ferrying Tamil civilians, killing civilians in their homes and burning Tamil homes and businesses.

According to eyewitnesses and reports at the time, prior to alcohol and violence taking hold of the mobs, attacks on Tamil homes were systematic: 'only those who resisted or chose to stay in their homes were killed. Those who chose to flee were more often than not permitted to leave, provided they did not take any valuables with them.'[46] Within days Colombo resembled a war zone, with supplies of essential commodities, such as milk, flour and sugar, hit by the elimination of Tamil establishments. Additionally, with the spread of violence to other cities and towns such as Nuwara Eliya, Kandy, Matale, Gampaha, Kalutara and Trincomalee, the numbers of casualties and Tamil refugees began to grow. One of the most chilling examples of blatant massacres under the supervision of authorities was the murder of fifty-three Tamil political prisoners in two separate massacres in Colombo's Welikada prison. An Amnesty International report stated that prison authorities assisted Sinhalese prisoners in killing the Tamil inmates; there were also reports of cell doors being deliberately left open.[47] On the streets of Colombo and other towns and cities mobs went on a killing and looting spree; Norwegian tourist Eli Skarstein and her fifteen-year-old daughter witnessed a Sinhalese mob pour petrol onto a minibus with twenty Tamil occupants inside and set it alight, killing the passengers inside.[48]

Paul Steighart, in a key International Commission of Jurists (ICJ) report, uncovered evidence of custodial killings of Tamil 'political detainees' by the military stationed in the north and east. Steighart also found that state apparatuses like the police and armed forces were routinely complicit in anti-Tamil violence.[49] As S. J. Tambiah writes in his book *Ethnic Fratricide and the Dismantling of Democracy*, 'in Trincomalee, the beautiful, coveted harbor on the east coast, where Tamils and Sinhalese (the majority of whom are considered by the Tamils as intruders/settlers) were poised in equal numbers, sailors from the Sri Lankan navy ran amok, themselves setting a bad example for the civilians to follow. The sailors, later assisted and accompanied by civilians, ran riot, killing and looting and setting houses and shops ablaze. Moreover, a district of Tamil residential concentration was reduced to ashes' (Tambiah 1986: 25). The *New York Times* reported similar military behaviour in Jaffna, where 'Sri Lankan Army troops pulled 20 civilians off a bus and executed them in retaliation for a Tamil guerilla attack that killed 13 soldiers'.[50] The government rhetoric at the time was that these events were 'Sinhala mob' rampages and not state-sanctioned or encouraged; however, Seighart argued that the incidents were:

> not a spontaneous upsurge of communal hatred among the
> Sinhala people – nor was it, as has been suggested in some
> quarters, a popular response to the killing of 13 soldiers in an
> ambush by Tamil Tigers on the previous day, which was not
> even reported in the newspapers until after the riots began. It
> was a series of deliberate acts, executed in accordance with a
> concerted plan, conceived and organized well done in advance.[51]

Rioters carried out attacks with systematic precision, which included 'the use of electoral lists to identify Tamil homes, the commandeering of state-owned vehicles to transport the goons and the direct participation by the armed forces'.[52]

There were numerous reports that highlighted the acquiescence of the army and police, who actively encouraged the looting. Eyewitnesses reported 'that army men travelling in lorries waved merrily to the looters, who waved back [while] no action whatsoever was taken to disperse the mobs. Not even tear-gas was used. The criminal gangs gained in confidence.'[53]

Eyewitnesses at the time apportioned responsibility for the violence and looting to key members of the ruling UNP party with allegiance to two prominent cabinet ministers, one of whom, Cyril Mathew, was the president of the pro-UNP trade union. According to one Tamil survivor from Colombo:

> The goon squads were organised in two ways. There was the first group under the command of UNP youth leaders and well-known local thugs often used by UNP politicians as their local militia. Then there were the more organised squads drawn from the pro-government trade union called the JSS – Jathika Seveya Sangaya. These squads had come into existence early during the UNP regime and were under the control and command of Minister Cyril Mathew who was a cabinet minister in the Jayewardene Government.[54]

Cyril Mathew had been complicit in an unofficial vendetta against the Tamils for decades. He was responsible for the propagation of several extremely chauvinistic pamphlets and published a booklet in Sinhala entitled 'Protect the Buddhist religion'. He advocated the '*bhumi putra*' and saw the Sinhalese as the only 'true sons of the soil', deserving of the lion share of Sri Lanka's wealth and resources, and the Tamils as a privileged race. In parliament he stated that the pogroms of 1983 against the Tamils were 'long overdue and only a spark was needed to make it happen and that the spark fell on 24th July'.[55]

During this time there were growing rumours of an Indian military invasion to safeguard Tamil interests, which further added to the tense situation. In September 1983, just a few weeks after the pogroms, Gamini Dissanayake, a cabinet minister in the government, addressed besieged Indian Tamil estate workers in the Central Highlands area and threatened the annihilation of all Tamils in Sri Lanka in the event of an intervention from India:

> Who attacked you? Sinhalese. Who protected you? Sinhalese. It is we who can attack and protect you. They are bringing an army from India. It will take 14 hours to come from India. In 14 minutes, the blood of every Tamil in this country can be sacrificed by us [Sinhalese]. It is not written on anyone's

forehead he is an Indian or Jaffna Tamil, a Batticalao Tamil
or Upcountry Tamil. Hindu Tamil or Christian Tamil. All are
Tamils.[56]

In addition to their direct participation in the pogroms of 1983,
both Gamini Dissanayake and Cyril Mathew were directly involved
in the riots of 1981, a prequel to the horrors of 1983 that saw the
destruction of the Jaffna public library, which had a repository
of 100,000 books, manuscripts and palm leaf inscriptions from
antiquity. The two cabinet ministers, incumbent at the time of the
riots, were in Jaffna specifically to disrupt an election rally organized
by the Tamil United Liberation Front (TULF).

In a classic bout of 'vandalism' as described by Lemkin in his
early thinking on genocide's cultural methods, with the presence of
the two instigators in the city coinciding with the TULF election
rally, uniformed security men and plain-clothed thugs took part
in a destruction spree that included complete devastation of the
library, a thriving symbol of Tamil cultural identity on the island,
'a Hindu Temple, the office and machinery of the independent
Tamil daily newspaper *Eelanadu*, the house of the MP of Jaffna,
the headquarters of the TULF, and more than 100 shops and
markets'.[57] Discrete genocidal methods rarely, if ever, result in
narrow corresponding impacts, but rather have considerable knock-
on effects and are often accompanied by complementary methods.
In this case, in addition to the destruction of the library, four people
were killed in the violence and dozens more wounded.[58] Although
the library has been rebuilt and has regained some of its cultural
significance, it has unfortunately always been used by the Sinhalese
to exercise dominance over the Tamils, with repeated vandalism
and desecration, the most recent example being vandalism by
Sinhalese tourists, who were most likely part of the triumphalism
tour in November 2010.[59]

The number of people killed in the last week of July alone is
staggering; Tamil estimates suggest 2,000 dead, while official
government estimates are 371 Tamil lives lost. A further 100,000
Tamils were rendered homeless, creating at least 130,000 refugees;
the government shipped nearly 70,000 refugees to the north and east,
while a considerable number migrated to India, western Europe,
Canada and Australia, thus establishing a diaspora (Tambiah 1986:

22). As of 1995, anywhere between 350,000 and 950,000 Tamils are believed to have migrated to India and the West.[60]

*The Mullivaikal massacre* The horrors of 1983 gave the LTTE the necessary impetus to bolster their guerrilla war against the Sri Lankan government, and although throughout their existence they engaged in a perpetual struggle, they were successful in creating a de facto Tamil state in most of the Tamil-dominated areas of the north and east. However, the twenty-first century saw a series of dramatic events, including a call for a military solution to the separatist struggle from among the Buddhist nationalists and the sudden defection of the LTTE's eastern command under 'Karuna' to the government side, leading to annihilation of the LTTE in 2009.[61]

As we saw in Chapter 2, for Lemkin both 'colonial expansion' and 'military conquests' often involve genocide Lemkin n.d., quoted in Docker 2004: 7); both these factors have made the Tamils a subjugated minority at risk of genocide. The number of civilians killed by the military in the last phase of the war is tantamount to ethnic cleansing, which again is akin to genocide. Interestingly, the Sri Lankan military is known to have been killing an average of 233 Tamil civilians every month, or seven a day, in 1986.[62] However, the People's Tribunal on Sri Lanka notes that in 2009 the military was killing thirty-three people a day at the end of January; unfortunately, however, UN agents have been quoted as stating that by May 2009 the number of Tamil civilians killed by the military was up to 1,000 a day, around 20,000 in total, although further investigation has revealed that the number could have been as high as 40,000.[63] Furthermore, according to experts and the UN, owing to the lack of government willingness to address growing grievances over the loss of Tamil lives in the war and its unwillingness to listen to the recommendation from the Lessons Learnt and Reconciliation Commission, the world will never know the real number of lives lost and must just depend on estimates. Furthermore, the UN report has claimed that there is sufficient evidence implicating the security forces in war crimes/crimes against humanity; the report also claims that the security forces' actions against the Tamil civilian population were committed on 'discriminatory grounds'.[64] Furthermore, the UNHCR strongly believes that the limitation of humanitarian relief supplies to the war zone 'may amount to the use of starvation of the civilian population as a method of warfare, which is prohibited under international humanitarian law'.[65] In addition to this there have been discrepancies in accounts of the number of people currently missing; for example, a senior public official, Ms Imelda Sukumaran, based in Jaffna, stated that 'in January 2009 there were nearly 350,000 people [Tamils] from the districts of Kilinochchi, Mannar, Vavuniya and Mullaittivu'.[66] However, after the war in May 2009, the entire Tamil population in this region was put into internment camps; official figures for the numbers of Tamils in internment were 280,000,[67] which leaves at least 70,000 people either deceased or missing. This is further exacerbated by government-enforced disappearances of those constituting perceived threats, including alleged LTTE cadres, politicians and Tamil activists, a disturbing claim supported in the UN Human Rights Council's report on Sri Lanka.[68]

*Sexual exploitation of Tamil women* The LTTE were pioneers in women's empowerment; the role of women greatly evolved in all facets of life under their rule. According to one source, 'the police force, as well as the lawyers and the judges, had nearly 50 percent female members'.[69] Women's representation in the rebel units was high too; many Tamil women joined the LTTE to escape poverty and a strict family environment but a large number enlisted in the militia either to avoid or avenge molestation at the hands of the Sri Lankan military.

The military occupation in the north and east has put Tamil women at risk of sexual exploitation. Rape and disappearances are common in the north and east, and many refrain from complaining for fear of further harassment or confiscation of land and property; a woman from Kilinochchi, Jaffna, told the International Crisis Group that many Tamils live in minimalistic dwellings that lack doors and windows and have visitors who are 'mostly from the armed forces side. People do hear screams at times, but there are also instances where nothing is heard. I've asked why they keep quiet [and don't report to the authorities]. They say "these are our own lands, property, etc. We have to protect them, otherwise the military will take over".'[70] Moreover, according to Human Rights Watch, people in the north refrain from complaining to the authorities, 'be it about rape, murder, trafficking, disappearance as it only opens the victim to further abuse and gives the military access to people's lives'.[71] The

UN Commission on Human Rights and Human Rights Watch have also documented the use of rape and murder as a tool for retribution in the north, especially towards Tamil women with the 'audacity' to complain against the security forces. In one case at the height of the civil war, Muruguesupillai Koneswary from Batticaloa was harassed by the police after she complained that officers had stolen timber from her home; according to Human Rights Watch, 'on May 17, 1997 alleged police officers entered her home and raped her, then detonated a grenade at her genitals that caused her death. No one was convicted for the crime.'[72]

Unfortunately, and more alarmingly, Tamil women, particularly widows and those in female-led households, are vulnerable to sexual coercion at the hands of security forces and government officials; according to interviews conducted by the Crisis Group women and young girls in internment camps just after the war were expected to offer sex in exchange for using a soldier's phone or cell phone charging points; in addition to this women have to barter sex in exchange for documents or other entitlements.[73] In a survey conducted by the Sri Lanka Supporting Regional Governance programme (SuRG), 65 per cent of the women respondents said that women without husbands face 'pressures to have sexual relationships to get work done'.[74] The recently released UN report also corroborates this sentiment and states, 'In the militarised context in the conflict-affected areas, women headed households are extremely vulnerable to sexual harassment, exploitation and violence.'[75]

The stigma associated with rape prevents many women from seeking justice; many more commit suicide, are deserted by husbands and families or are forced to become sex workers in towns and cities like Jaffna and Kilinochchi, or are duped and trafficked into brothels in Colombo.[76]

Overall, the enduring trauma due to the war, especially the events during the last phase in 2009, has adversely affected the social fabric of the Tamil people in the north and east; increasing alcohol abuse among men and an omnipresent military have fuelled domestic violence within Tamil families and have also led to deteriorating societal norms among Tamils, which are essential for a healthy balanced life. A resident in Kilinochchi told the Crisis Group that '[I]n one village, there are four girls under the age of fourteen – all of whom are pregnant by men from within the community. This happened while their mothers were away working in the paddy field. The fathers and the men in the community are visibly drunk.' Thus, notwithstanding the massacres of Tamils civilians, there is considerable evidence that the effect of the civil war and its immediate aftermath have resulted in collective trauma and a deterioration of the social fabric of Tamil society.

## Land grabs and the economic method

The anti-Tamil pogroms of the 1970s and 1980s brought many Tamils from the highlands and Colombo closer to their brethren in the north and east. Many of the displaced Tamils were housed on the Kent and Dollar Farms close to Vavuniya, properties owned by Tamils; however, their presence was resented by the local authorities owing to the 'alleged' rise of insurgency among the Tamils. Therefore, in 1984, citing law and order problems in the wake of the insurgency from the LTTE, the authorities utilized the controversial Land Acquisition Act, which was designed to 'expropriate land free of encumbrance' and was an instrument used to settle 'the dry zone by providing governments the means of expropriating private lands [mainly Tamil properties] for public purpose' (Muggah 2008: 80). Additionally Article 42 of the law allowed authorities to expropriate land within forty-eight hours; this was invoked with the help of the police and Sinhalese settlers, as seen previously in Vavuniya during anti-Tamil riots in 1984.[77] Furthermore, guerrilla attacks by the nascent LTTE forces (Tamil New Tigers) on police and Sinhalese settlements in the Kent and Dollar Farm areas saw the government and military establish High Security Zones throughout the north and east; the stated aim being to end the insurgency, although in reality it seemed more geared towards perpetuating the settlements and protecting settlers; however, with the broader goal of a nationalistic state being the establishment of Sidhadipa, it was essential to end Tamil numerical and political hegemony in the north and east.

Over the course of the Eelam Wars (1983–2009) and given the military success of the LTTE, there was an evolution of government rhetoric and apparent prioritization of 'self-preservation' in the face of a brutal insurgency and the violence perpetrated by the LTTE. The war gave rise to radical Sinhalese parties like the Jatika Hela Urumaya (JHU) led by monks that steered the government towards the elimination of the LTTE militarily and gave no quarter for peace discussions.[78] It is a standard tactic of the genocidal perpetrator to repeatedly claim to be in some way victimized by the groups targeted for removal, and the Sinhalese were no exception. Furthermore, to boost the potency of such rhetoric, another standard tactic was invoked – the construction of fear within the civilian population. Indeed, the general Sinhalese population were targeted with classic threat propaganda – suggesting that he Sinhalese, and even Buddhism itself, were at risk of extinction at the hands of the Tamil minority. In the following statement, Champika Ranawaka, the incumbent cabinet minister at the time in Mahinda Rajapaksha's government, stoked flames of fear in an interview with Juliana Rufus from Al Jazeera: 'They [Tamils] have totally chased out the Sinhalese out of the Northern Province and some parts of the Eastern province and they are trying to link these areas together [the Central Highlands and the East]. Also since 600,000 Tamils live in the Western Province [around Colombo] as well, they will link here too, so that the Sinhalese are trapped. That is our fear.'[79]

Tambiah argues that the Sinhalese majority embraced this fear to the extent that the populace developed a distinct 'minority complex' (Tambiah 1986). Horowitz suggested that 'the Sinhalese, like the Khmers, Fijians or Malays fear extermination at the hands of contrastive ethnic communities' (in Peebles 1990: 32). The threat was of course given more weight with consistent linkage to the mere presence of 70 million Tamils in the state of Tamil Nadu in southern India – both of which have provided the rhetorical impetus and justification for policies that have produced a genocidal impact.

After the defection of LTTE's Eastern Command led by Colonel Karuna in 2004, reports surfaced of renewed escalation in settlements and colonization in the east through the process termed 'Nagenahira Navodaya', Sinhala for Eastern Revival, in the Ampara district. The residents, mainly Tamil-speaking Muslims,[80] expressed apprehension over the government's apathy and felt vulnerable given the presence of the Sri Lankan armed forces, particularly the Special Task Force (STF).[81] There was also increased violence against Muslims; on 18 September 2006, ten Muslim labourers who had gone to repair a portion of the Radella irrigation tank the day before were found murdered; while the Muslims suspected STF of being responsible for the murders, the government blamed the LTTE even before investigations.[82] Protests against the STF were met with force, with some observers believing that this was a warning to 'Muslims to get out of the area'.[83] In 2007 the government incorporated the Sinhala lion in the flag of the Eastern Province, which contributed to a fear of 'cultural colonization' among many Tamils and Muslims.[84] Creeping Sinhalese settler colonization was perhaps most successful in the Eastern Province, where government-stimulated demographic change eventually managed to break Tamil numerical dominance, particularly in the district of Trincomalee, where the population percentage of Sinhalese was 3 per cent in 1901, with the Tamils at 58 per cent; fast-forward to 2007 and we see a dramatic increase in the percentage of Sinhalese to 25 per cent and a decline in the percentage of Tamils to just 29 per cent.[85]

Since the end of the civil war in 2009 one of the key sources of the conflict, settler colonial-style land grabs, has not only continued but also accelerated.[86] Post-war, such land grabs are now bolstered by even more potent propaganda. Indeed, they are currently taking place under the unquestionable social and political 'goods' of 'security and development', a tried and tested global political tactic for justifying human rights abuses. The land grabs, which involve the confiscation of private and public land, are sanctioned by the government and primarily carried out by the military, facilitated by the occupation of former Tamil areas. During the war land designated as 'high security zones' (HSZs) was confiscated and since then there has been a distinct reluctance to return it to the thousands who were displaced. Moreover, although a minority of HSZs have lost such designation, considerable areas of arable agricultural land are still administered under the HSZ designation with only military personnel allowed in. During the war the legality of the HSZs rested on emergency regulations, which have now been repealed. Five years after the end of conflict, there is no clear legal basis for the remaining HSZs.

Recently, the United Nations Human Rights Council passed a resolution calling for an international inquiry into allegations of war crimes during the last stages of the war in Sri Lanka. Reports indicate that the military have made concerted efforts to identify and destroy mass burial sites and that the increased militarization and land grabs greatly aid this endeavour. Since the armed conflict ended, the military has continued to confiscate public and private land largely under the pretext of security. While many military camps have been created for the army and navy, the government has also resettled thousands of Sinhalese soldiers and civilians from the south in Tamil areas with incentives of free land and permanent housing. Meanwhile the UNHCR reports that 57 per cent of 138,651 households residing in the north remain in transitional or emergency shelters while only 32 per cent have permanent homes.[87]

Land grabs reignited fears of a concerted effort by the government to change the demographics of Tamil areas in the north and east. Land grabs were also brazenly justified under the pretext of building Buddhist temples and statues in Tamil areas – in Lemkin's terms, imposing the national pattern of the oppressor on the oppressed. In addition to changing place names from Tamil to Sinhalese, the creation of monuments and war museums that celebrate the Sinhalese victory created additional grievances. Many of these war museums and monuments commemorating the government victory over the LTTE built in Tamil areas are open only to the Sinhalese and have been built over destroyed Hindu temples or on private land without permission. The continued promotion of Sinhala nationalism and triumphalism through land grabs, five years after the war, has done little to promote any meaningful kind of 'reconciliation'.

Given that they lived under an equally nationalistic LTTE for around thirty years, there is no doubt that the current presence of a military force speaking a different tongue and professing a different faith would make for a feeling of occupation among the Tamils of the north and east. One can get a sense of the scale of occupation by considering the ratio of 'security personnel' to civilians in northern areas. Since the end of the war the ratio of soldiers to civilians in Tamil areas has increased from 1 soldier for every 16.6 civilians to 1 for every 5.04 civilians in 2012.[88] Moreover, the military is almost entirely composed of Sinhalese from the south and includes at least fifteen army divisions and personnel from the navy, air force, civil defence force, intelligence, police and Special Task Force. This conservative estimate roughly translates into 198,000 soldiers or 70 per cent of the security personnel in 14 per cent of the country. The trend towards militarization has only increased, with Sri Lanka's defence budget for 2014 reported to be the highest allocation of funds thus far, at $1.95 billion or 12 per cent of the country's total spending.[89]

The ecstatic government-led triumphalism since the war is a clear indication of a concerted aim to subjugate the Tamil population;

alongside the destruction of graves and cemeteries of fallen LTTE fighters can be seen the confiscation of properties including houses and agricultural lands from Tamils and their redistribution among families of Sri Lankan military soldiers. While direct physical killing as part of a military conquest can produce genocidal impacts on a targeted '*genos*', other actions that also produce genocidal conditions, often through occupation and control policies, deserve attention in a Lemkin-inspired analysis. Indeed, in this case it should be noted that the Sri Lankan military has also been responsible for 'militarizing the economy' by controlling/monopolizing not only tourism in the north and east but also the sale of agricultural produce, which renders the traditional farmers redundant and dependent on state aid.

The Sri Lankan military's influence extends over almost every aspect of the former mainstays of the Tamil economy, which are agriculture and fishing, both primarily subsistent. Problems with competition over resources are a recurring theme in a landmark International Crisis Group (ICG) report, especially when it comes to fishing, as one interviewee highlighted:

> there is a group of [Sinhalese] fishermen and divers belonging to a company from the south who are now operating in Selvanagar beach. They say the owner is related to Rajapaksa and connected to the army. They are doing illegal activity by using oxygen cylinders and focus lights to dive in the ocean for kadal attai [sea cucumber] ... It affects the small fishermen who are fishing near the shores – the fish catch gets greatly affected and it is not a good practice. The army allows this to happen; when we complain to the army they say that they cannot do anything about it. They claim they are Rajapaksa's friends.[90]

Such illegal and unsustainable methods by such fishermen, in close collaboration with the military and government, are clearly detrimental to the livelihoods of the poorer, usually Tamil, fishermen in post-war Sri Lanka. Moreover, the military has confiscated large tracts of land on which it has set up farms and other business ventures, such as hotels, shops, restaurants, energy infrastructure, airline services and tourism. Worse still is the fact that such ventures rarely employ Tamil people. A telling example is the 'Thalsevena resort' in Kankesanthurai High Security Zone,

Jaffna, which is almost entirely staffed by the army, right from the receptionists to the waiters and bartenders – position here reflecting the rank one holds in the army.[91] These commercial endeavours are greatly aided by favourable government tax breaks, incentives and subsidies, which means that they can outcompete any remaining Tamil business with ease. In a recent United Nations survey only 9 per cent of 138,651 resettled families in the north have found permanent employment.[92]

Tamil communities which have relied on fishing for their livelihood have reported that in their areas 'land seizures have also occurred by scrupulously removing the names of the residents from government documents such as the voters' registry, abusing legal ownership regulations ... ignoring provisions in the customary law [and] using coercive means upon the residents who are unable to produce titles to the land they have been occupying'. The Tamil National Alliance's situation report noted:

> [b]y appropriating the limited economic opportunities that might otherwise be used by local residents to bring income and revenue to the fragile local communities, the military is sustaining and reinforcing the cycle of poverty. With the access and advertising support of corporate entities in the South and the unfair benefits of highly subsidized cost structure through the use of state infrastructure the military is distorting and suppressing any attempt at economic recovery in the North.[93]

In the village of Odhiyamalai, in Mullaitivu, Tamil farmers returning after the war, despite having valid permits covering most of their land, were not allowed to work it for over two seasons. Sinhalese from the nearby Padiviya area, working with the assistance and the protection of the army, have cultivated former Tamil land since the end of the war in 2009. The area of Weli Oya is almost entirely militarized, with a network of army camps and checkpoints limiting access for outsiders, controlling and closely monitoring movements. As a farmer from Odhiyamalai explains: 'This season [September 2011], I went to plough ... I took my tractor. First day they allowed, I went and marked out the area, but when I went on the second day, the army said that they cannot allow me. There were some Sinhalese who were working in the field.'[94]

In addition to the occupation the army is responsible for controlling the prices of vegetables and other agricultural produce in the militarized areas and spend next to nothing on the agriculural production, thus reducing the selling price of their produce and invariably placing the Tamil farmers, who spend considerable amounts of money on fertilizers, nutrients and pesticides, close to destitution. The International Crisis Group reported that the same process was under way in other nearby villages, including Maruthodai, Pattikudiyiruppu, Thanikkallu, Oonjalkatti and Vedivachchakal. It is not just the dispossession of farmers that is the problem; those who are allowed to continue cultivating are being priced out of the market. As another ICG interviewee put it:

> The [Sinhalese forces] involving themselves in agriculture is a problem. They get things for free. Their labour is paid for by the government, whereas all the expenses like seeds, fertiliser, weedicide, harvesting for a farmer are all expenditures that one has to pay for from one's own pocket. So the forces are easily able to sell their produce for a lower price than the farmers. It is creating a problem. But of course the consumers are benefiting. If we sell a product for twelve rupees, they are able to sell for eight.[95]

It is clear that the livelihoods of Tamils are being destroyed. According to a government official based in the same area:

> A farmer who had cultivated ocra was devastated by the low prices at which the civil defence forces were able to dump their produce. The farmer had a skirmish with the camp officers, and when I intervened, I found out it was about ocra. I said as a consumer I am happy to buy at a lower price. The farmer replied, 'I am living with my only child, a daughter, and if this continues I may have to take poison [and commit suicide]'. For them [the military] there is no cost for labour.[96]

Another official explains the causative factors that place the Tamil farmers in this predicament and explains how military commanders help themselves to fertilizers: 'The military commander [from Kaeppapulavu] asked the agrarian services and took the fertilisers for free. Twice. These were earmarked for farmers of the village. I think they also took water pumps and other inputs from the department … When the army comes and asks, what can a government department official do?'[97]

The military also raid Tamil farmers' water sources on a regular basis for their own cultivation projects, as one farmer explained: 'the army is also doing cultivation. Mahaweli authority constructed wells for them. But they had also used our water sources. It created a problem and the Brigade commander had to intervene. Then they took the water pumps away from our water source.'[98]

The military occupation, and its control over the land base and 'development' policy, has effectively sidelined the Tamil civil administration, suppressing any attempts to address the fundamental needs of internally displaced persons. Additionally the TNA situation report tabled in the parliament in 2011 showcases major Tamil grievances, including military control and intrusion in the private lives of the Tamils. Every village in the north and east has a Civilian Affairs Counter managed by the armed forces, where Tamils entering a village are required to register themselves. Additionally, Tamil families 'must inform the army of the guests they receive, their relationship, and the reason and duration of their visit. Any family gathering to celebrate the birth or naming of a child, attainment of puberty of a girl, a wedding or even a death, requires prior permission from the nearest police post.'[99] These factors have adversely affected the traditional practices of the Tamils, with many avoiding, as far as possible, any bureaucratic engagement with the state for fear of harassment.

*Suppression of memory and protest* The families of LTTE fighters killed during the civil war have been prohibited from commemorating or mourning their dead, a policy which also functionally extends to much of the civilian Tamil population.

The end of the war signifies two different realities for the Sinhalese government and the Tamils. While Victory Day or Remembrance Day, observed by the government on 18 May, commemorates fallen war heroes and the commencement of 'peace' on the island, the TNA and other Tamil groups unofficially celebrate it as a day of 'National Mourning and Prayer', as for them it represents a series of violent massacres of Tamil militants and civilians (even if the language of genocide is rarely invoked for fear of further persecution) and the perpetuation of militarization, settlements and incarceration of Tamils. These two contrasting realities have resulted in the government's drive to contain Tamil mourning and memorialization through the process of cultural suppression and supplanting, or in other words the cultural method of genocide.

In the latter stages of the war, the LTTE depended on forced conscription to fill their ranks, which inevitably meant that all families in the LTTE-administered areas had someone among the LTTE cadre. The military destruction of LTTE graves and prevention of Tamils from mourning their dead seek to obliterate a large part of Tamil history since the end of British rule. Every year, in the run-up to 18 May, the military is beefed up and Tamils are barred from holding memorial activities, especially in Vellamullivaikal, in Mullaithivu district, which saw the worst massacres in 2009 and was where LTTE leader Vellupillai Prabakaran was killed.[100] Additionally, Tamil devotees are prevented from visiting Hindu temples to offer prayers to the departed during Victory Day/Remembrance Day celebrations.[101]

Alongside all this, there is a continuing denial of fundamental rights, including freedom of religion and non-violent protests.[102] During the run-up to the 2013 provincial elections, the military and STF were accused of intimidating Tamil activists protesting against military occupation, threatening them with death.[103] However, despite a heavy military presence, blatant violations of civil and political rights, voter intimidation and violence against (Tamil) candidates, the Tamil National Assembly (TNA) secured a significant victory in the 2013 Northern Provincial Elections, winning 30 out of 38 seats.[104] Although it is clear that the Tamil population in the north and east resent the government's model for development of the north, the Sinhalese elites have a very clear view on post-war reconciliation. Indeed, in their view, any meaningful reconciliation process must aim at defeating Tamil nationalism and any positive approach towards the political demands of Tamil nationalism is to be categorically rejected (Nirmal 2013: 19). It is also believed that in order to prevent a resurgence of Tamil nationalism the government must reinstate a 'pre-Tamil Nationalist order' and facilitate the 'resettlement of non-Tamil people, especially Sinhala people, who were forced to leave during the war ... and ensure sufficient military presence in the region to prevent any threat to this [Sinhalese] hegemonic order' (ibid.: 19).

This move represents a concentrated and coordinated attack upon all elements of nationhood among the Tamils and is a form of colonial genocide. Today this includes changing the names of villages and streets 'to honour fallen "war heroes" of the victorious [Sri Lankan] army'.[105] Furthermore, 'Kokachankulam village in Vavuniya district is now Kolbaswewa'[106] and 165 Sinhalese families have now settled in the same village. In addition to this, statues of Buddha have been constructed without permission on 'private land' and eyewitness accounts suggest construction of Buddhists icons and statues has taken place over destroyed Hindu temples.[107]

It is clear that the these programmes have the potential of perpetuating the conflict, as opposed to government claims of bringing peace between the two communities through integration and reconstruction, where talk of 'civil and political rights is seen as irrelevant at best'.[108] Furthermore, post-conflict reconstruction in the north clearly ignores the core issues faced by the Tamils in Sri Lanka, who seem to be paying for the crimes of the LTTE, and if current trends continue we will see renewed ethnic tensions; as Paikiasothy Saravanamuttu notes, 'if the economic development is seen as mega development projects by people in these areas, which do not answer to their [immediate] needs with regard to land … farming … fishing, we [the state of Sri Lanka] are only sustaining the sources of conflict'.[109] The process of Sinhalization through 'economic development' ensures that the dividends of 'peace' are not shared with those most in need.

Although the former president Mahinda Rajapaksa's political fortunes have taken a beating since 2015, his unequivocal use of Sinhalese nationalism and his promise to rid the island of the LTTE have given him an immense baseline of popular support. In the immediate aftermath of the war posters in Colombo and the south exalted the new Sinhalese hero with statements like 'Our President, Our Leader, He is next to King Dutugamunu' (DeVotta 2007: 9) – King Dutugamunu slayed the Tamil Chola emperor Elara more than two thousand years ago, thus the circle of establishing Sri Lanka as a sanctuary for Sinhalese and Buddhism through a programme of subjugation and colonization is completed. Another episode that highlights the easy combination of Buddhist ethno-symbolism and the present political environment took place in August 2006, when numerous Buddhists flocked to temples in the south claiming that the Buddha statues were emanating light. The 'phenomenon' was later interpreted by a political Buddhist monk, Medananda Thera: 'Sri Lanka was being blessed through President Mahinda Rajapaksa, who was a modern day Dutugamunu'.[110] It was subsequently explained by some as a political tactic to mobilize support from the Sinhalese masses for the government's bid to begin their last assault on the LTTE, but even if this explanation was incorrect the frequent use of mythomoteurs and the subsequent victory made Rajapaksa an autocratic ruler.[111]

### Ecocide and deforestation: war and neoliberalism

From 1983 onwards the war took an enormous human toll; deaths, displacements and genocide. There was also a significant ecological toll, as is usual with armed conflicts, from bombing to land clearance and the like. Indeed, in the words of Ranil Senanayake, an ecologist and chairman of Rainforest Rescue International in Sri Lanka: 'There has been destruction of much forest and mangrove areas to provide less cover for the antagonistic parties.'[112] During the latter half of the war, between 1990 and 2005, Sri Lanka suffered one of the highest rates of deforestation in the world, losing about 35 per cent of its old-growth forest and almost 18 per cent of its total forest cover. Over 2.5 million palmyra trees, for example, were felled for construction purposes alone. Reconstruction efforts in the wake of the 2004 tsunami also increased the pressure on the country's forests. However, some parts remain relatively unscathed. Indeed, it is arguable that in the north of Sri Lanka the more gradual human population movements, rather than modern warfare, have proved more destructive of the environment and ecosystems. Ranil Senanayake argues that 'many wetlands and other critical ecosystems in the "war zone" have been spared the pillaging that follows the "economic development" agents, who treat all land as a commodity to be exploited for instant economic gain'.[113]

The government of Sri Lanka is continuing to implement a rigorous neoliberal, non-sustainable development model that has no regard for the environment and has displaced and impoverished thousands of Tamil people. Already ravaged by the longest civil war in Asia and by natural catastrophes such as the 2004 tsunami, Sri Lanka in general, and the north in particular, currently faces severe environmental issues, with the worst of them being appalling levels of deforestation and biodiversity loss. Sri Lanka is featured in several lists of 'biodiversity hotspots' – meaning regions both biologically rich and endangered – along the Indian Western Ghats,[114] but a Conservation International report states that only 1.5 per cent of the island's original forests remain.[115]

Over time the huge population transfers to the Dry Zone have produced the usual wealth of human-induced environmental 'externalities'. Where once many Tamil people in the rural population were able, at least in part, to sustain themselves on what the previously vast forest could provide, owing to population growth and the amount of available forestland, forest-based sustenance has gradually declined in favour of permanent cultivation by private owners. Deforestation of the Dry Zone has been caused by a range of human activities throughout the conflict, from agriculture and resettlements to logging. Since the end of the war there has been further encroachment into the region's protected areas, largely located in the remaining Dry Zone evergreen forest. The government is using the area to continue to redistribute Sinhalese from other regions, which has resulted, over time, in large volumes of people moving into the Dry Zone. This population boom has caused severe negative impacts to the environment. Whereas Dry Zone scrub forest ecology has adapted over the years to its dry conditions, from 1961 large-scale irrigation projects were developed to ensure the Dry Zone could be cultivated and by 1978 it was estimated that nearly one third of the country's Dry Zone area was permanently cultivated.[116] Consequently, the proportion of forestland declined and was estimated at less than 40 per cent in 1987.[117] This is the direct result of population redistribution. The government argues that irrigation is needed to sustain the large, new populations that have moved into the Dry Zone districts. Large irrigation projects such as the Gal Oya Irrigation Project (1948–52) and the Mahaweli Development and Irrigation Programme (MIDP) (1970–2000) were spawned by a modernization ideology that fused capital-intensive interventions with centralized national planning (Muggah 2008: 82–3). The Mahaweli Ganga project to bring more farming into the Dry Zone plans to irrigate 593,000 hectares. One of the main causes of deforestation now is rice production, which the government is backing to increase employment in the Dry Zone and ease the burden on the densely populated Wet Zone.

The neoliberal[118] 'development' agenda promoted by the government in Sri Lanka is the preferred rationale for contemporary population relocations and the cause of considerable displacement of Tamil people from their lands and their livelihoods. From around 1996 onwards the government began moving rural agriculture from 'low-value' crops, i.e. subsistence farming for local populations, to 'high-value' cash crops for foreign export markets.[119] Farmers were encouraged to sell their land plots and move out of the villages to seek non-farm employment. A subsequent policy document stated that the government expected migration from the countryside to make rural/urban proportions 50:50 by 2010.[120]

Neoliberal agendas frequently espouse expanding exports through attracting foreign direct investment (FDI) and promoting a regulation-free private sector that will spew out 'externalities' such as environmental degradation, bolstered by suitable infrastructure and cheap non-unionized labour. For Sri Lanka this has resulted in chronic economic disparities; the richest 10 per cent of the people hold nearly 40 per cent of the wealth and the poorest 10 per cent hold just 1 per cent,[121] with the majority of Tamil people firmly in the bottom 10 per cent.

## Conclusion

This chapter has reviewed the key aspects of the conflict between the Sinhalese and the Tamils in Sri Lanka, invoking Lemkin's colonial territorial connection and his key methods of genocide, from physical killing to the economic and cultural, supplemented by the ecologically induced ecocidal method Martin Crook and I have outlined. Despite the LTTE defeat, today the Tamil minority in Sri Lanka still challenge the state's notion of social cohesion, homogeneity and purity. Neoliberal 'democratization' and the process of ethnic outbidding have resulted in further stratification, marginalization and subjugation of the Tamil minority, seemingly with no possibility of reconciliation as the racist paradigm has spiralled out of control. The current empty rhetoric of post-war 'reconciliation' is little more than a veneer that glosses over a long-term genocidal process. Indeed, the military's occupation and dominion over the population coupled with systematic land grabs are the latest elements of a genocidal process that is destroying the land-based political, economic, social, cultural and environmental foundations of the Tamil population.

# 5 | AUSTRALIA

## Introduction

This chapter is the first of two to focus on indigenous peoples and settler colonial societies.[1] The major difference between the two well-known sites of conflict, Palestine and Sri Lanka, and the Australian and Canadian (Alberta) case studies is that the latter are not generally considered to be sites of conflict, since widespread *violent* conflict has long ceased and their current political form is generally considered to be democratic. Nevertheless, despite these differences, we shall see that at a core fundamental level there are key structural similarities between all of the case studies in this book – principally concerning broad, and continuing, colonization policies and practices that dispossess, control, dominate and subjugate social groups while inflicting considerable social, cultural and environmental harms.

Most of the scholarly works that consider the question of genocide in Australia focus on the 'dispersal' extermination campaigns of the 1800s and/or the issue of the 'Stolen Generations'.[2] Such studies often dwell on the seemingly ubiquitous problem of genocide scholarship – a preoccupation with positive and provable genocidal intent. In the Australian case this is perhaps understandable since many indigenous fatalities were not the direct consequence of an intended policy of extermination. Unknown illnesses such as smallpox accounted for the greatest number, while alcohol, malnutrition, demoralization and despair played their fatal part. Moreover, it could be argued that the intent was to take over a land, not to eradicate an ethnic or religious group. In this sense we could say that territoriality is settler colonialism's specific, irreducible element (Wolfe 2006: 388). Yet the British desire to plant colonies in Australia meant *supplanting* (Barta 2008a: 115), and, as previously noted, Patrick Wolfe observes, 'land is life – or, at least, land is necessary for life [and] thus contests for land can be – indeed, often are – contests for life' (Wolfe 2006: 387). The ensuing land grab involved such significant amounts of violence and what some now term 'ethnic cleansing' directed against indigenous groups; when considered alongside the effects of illness and malnutrition, it seemed 'inevitable' that the indigenous peoples of Australia would die out and disappear (Barta 2008b). In a seminal essay which takes issue with an overly intentionalist take on the question of genocide in Australian history, Tony Barta suggests that 'it is not too simplistic to see in this dominant opinion the most comfortable ideological reflection of a relationship which could only be recognised in good conscience for what it was – a relationship of genocide' (Barta 2000).

While writers like Barta and Wolfe imply that genocidal structuring dynamics are still at work in Australia,[3] theirs is a distinct minority opinion in genocide scholarship and certainly in popular consciousness. Present-day indigenous/non-indigenous social and political relations, and the colonial structures in which they operate, are rarely discussed through the analytical lens of genocide. Yet while direct physical killing and genocidal child removal practices may have ceased, some indigenous people contend that genocide is a continuing process in an Australia that has failed to decolonize and continues to assimilate.[4] Such a contention, I suggest, is predicated on a victim's understanding of the culturally genocidal dimensions of settler colonialism and the central importance of land to the survival of many indigenous peoples *as peoples*.

When discussing and ultimately supporting the above claim the argument developed herein is primarily concerned with those indigenous peoples in Australia who retain a cultural connection to land and who still live, or wish to live, primarily in accordance with indigenous laws and customs. There are at least 250 such groups in Australia today who have proved this form of indigeneity to the satisfaction of the settler colonial authorities in order to receive recognition of their rights to their land.[5] Of course, there are many indigenous peoples who no longer have a meaningful connection to land, live in cities and live primarily 'Western' lifestyles. Their indigenous identity is based around a culture *that is already lost* to them and consequently their present-day lived experience is not one that can be accurately described as genocidal; rather it is, to a certain extent, *the product of* a settler colonial genocidal process that has rendered them 'natally alienated' (Card 2003: 73) from their indigenous ancestral culture.[6]

### 'Cultural genocide' in Australia

Unlike in the USA, Canada and New Zealand, the colonization of Australia did not entail any formal settlements, involving dialogue and treaties, between the European invaders and the indigenous people. Throughout the last 200 years, the indigenous peoples of Australia have been the victims of appalling injustice and racism that was legitimized by the lack of negotiated treaties and recognition of rights to land. It was this historical lack of a negotiated treaty or treaties that led the National Aboriginal Conference in April 1979 to instigate a concerted campaign for a treaty. The campaign was not well received at first, but it subsequently gained legitimacy when it was adopted by the Aboriginal Treaty Committee (ATC), a respectable 'think tank' of white academics (see Harris 1979; Attwood and Markus 1999). With their support, the campaign gained significant press coverage to the extent that favourable editorials became increasingly common. The ATC hoped to secure a treaty that would recognize and restore Aboriginal rights to land and self-determination, compensate for the loss of and damage to traditional lands and way of life, while protecting Aboriginal identity, languages, law and culture (Harris 1979: 12). The principle of self-determination imposes requirements of *participation and consent*, and comprises a world order standard at odds with colonialism (Anaya 2004: 104). Indeed, the substantive content of the principle inheres in the precepts by which the international community has held colonialism illegitimate (ibid.: 104). By granting genuine self-determination[7] and meaningful land rights to indigenous peoples across Australia a treaty or set of treaties of this nature had the potential to break the colonial 'relationship of genocide' (Barta 2000).

The term 'treaty', however, elicited strong opposition from prominent politicians who were concerned that it implied an agreement between two 'sovereign nations', and from the time of conquest up to the present Aboriginal people have never officially been regarded as possessing either nationhood or sovereignty (see Reynolds 1996). The settler state constituted itself as the only sovereign nation within the territory, a situation that acted as a bar to meaningful dialogue on the notion of a treaty. John Howard, the then opposition leader, suggested that 'it is an absurd proposition that a nation should make a treaty with some of its own citizens' (1988: 16). Such forthright criticism eventually resulted in the treaty idea undergoing political dilution into a 'reconciliation' initiative that made no commitments to address any of the treaty campaign's key priorities, and certainly made no commitment to granting indigenous peoples self-determination or land rights. Instead, the official reconciliation process, which began with the enactment of the Council for Aboriginal Reconciliation Act 1991, exhibited an overt assimilationist nation-building agenda (see Short 2003: 294; Moran 1999) that was not the product of consultations with indigenous peoples and which had two major functions. First, via the full incorporation of indigenous people, it aimed to enrich a historically immature settler culture with symbols of Aboriginal spirituality, which highlighted their deep cultural and historical connection with the land (Moran 1999). Secondly, by incorporating Aboriginality into the cultural fabric of the nation, it inherently weakened the claims of those indigenous peoples whose identity is constructed around a sense of '*separateness*' from settler culture.[8]

While the dilution of the treaty idea into reconciliation ensured that return of land to indigenous peoples was not promised as part of the process, the issue was thrust to the fore of political debate by the High Court shortly after the instigation of the official reconciliation process. In 1992, the High Court handed down its landmark *Mabo* judgement (*Mabo and Others* v. *Queensland* (No. 2) 1992), which held that in certain situations indigenous groups *might* have rights to land or 'native title' that had survived colonization. The content of such rights derived from currently observable *and provable* indigenous laws and customs, but the inherent colonial 'trick' here was that the continuance of such 'traditional' laws and customs would not give rise to any concomitant political right such as self-determination. These vital institutions of indigenous culture would not be accorded the equal recognition and status of settler institutions. White law would continue to trump indigenous law even where native title could be proved. Even if indigenous groups can prove 'traditional connection' they are required still to be in occupation. Dispossessed indigenous groups stand no chance of regaining lost land and revitalizing their culture.

At this point, it is useful to note that Australia has the world's largest reserves of uranium, lead, silver, zinc, titanium and tantalum, while there are large quantities of uranium on Northern Territory indigenous lands (approximately 30 per cent of the world's currently identified uranium reserves). Australia is among the world's top six countries in its reserves of coal, iron, aluminium, copper, nickel and diamonds (see Diamond 2006: 396). Consequently, soon after the High Court had handed down its judgement in *Mabo*, the Commonwealth came under immense pressure from powerful vested interests, and the extractive industries lobby in particular, to 'limit' the application of native title, with some industry commentators advocating outright 'extinguishment' – a modern-day example of what Patrick Wolfe (2006) has termed the 'logic of elimination'.

A mining lobby campaign of misinformation was particularly successful, and in no small part influenced the government's legislative response to *Mabo* (see Short 2007: 857), ensuring that only a right to negotiate, rather than veto, was granted native title holders over future developments on their land. Indigenous groups would not be able to resist development or develop on their own terms. The right of veto was an integral part of the Northern Territory Land Rights legislation back in 1976, the absence of which, as Mr Justice Woodward suggests, renders indigenous land rights largely meaningless (Woodward 1974) – which is why the veto was a key indigenous demand after *Mabo*. The 1993 Native Title Act's primary purpose was the *validation* of existing commercial titles and the provision of guarantees that future land negotiations would be conducted within the parameters set by existing colonial power inequalities – thus ensuring that the native title regime would offer indigenous peoples no protection from settler colonial expansionist pressures powered by the engine of global capitalism.

Nevertheless, in 1996, responding to another High Court case, the Howard government amended the Native Title Act to detail a host of white property interests that would automatically extinguish native title (Short 2008: ch. 4). This modern-day act of dispossession has been described, quite rightly, by the United Nations monitoring Committee on the Elimination of all forms of Racial Discrimination as a racially discriminatory piece of legislation.[9] The Committee subsequently recommended that the government enter into genuine negotiations with indigenous peoples to find an alternative. This has not been done; instead the Commonwealth Government began a process of erosion (termed 'reform') of the only land rights Act in Australia that contained a de facto right of veto over development on indigenous lands: the Aboriginal Land Rights (Northern Territory) Act (ALRA) 1976.

Significant erosion of the veto had already begun in 1987 with amendments restricting the veto to the exploration stage, whereas previously there was a right to veto at both the exploration *and mining* stages. During 2004/05, the Commonwealth Government developed a new package of reforms to the ALRA, with particular attention paid to changing arrangements for leasing of indigenous land, followed in September 2006 by a review of the permit system (which hitherto allowed a degree of indigenous control over access to their land). Of key importance are the new sections 19A–19E, which provided options for ninety-nine-year head leases of Aboriginal land to a Commonwealth or Northern Territory government entity. The provision for long-term leases over townships on Aboriginal land was allegedly to 'make it easier for Aboriginal people to own homes and businesses on land in townships',[10] but while the leases were still subject to the provision of free, prior, informed consent by traditional owners, if a head lease were signed, then the permit system would be relaxed to allow in a sublease holder or anyone with 'legitimate business' in the lease area. The overriding rationale of the amendments appears to be less about individual home ownership and more about promoting 'economic development on Aboriginal land by providing for expedited and more certain processes related to exploration and mining on Aboriginal land'.[11]

Following the now familiar settler state tactic when dealing with indigenous interests, *none of these amendments was produced via consultations with those indigenous peoples likely to be affected by them*. It is unsurprising, then, that few indigenous communities have opted to go down this road to 'economic development' with very little incentive being offered to forgo the available exercise of authority over the land they own.[12] These amendments, however, were only the start of a far more sinister attack on indigenous land rights, autonomy and cultural integrity that has led some indigenous peoples to describe their present-day lived experiences as tantamount to genocide.

### The 'Intervention'

The benign use of government language – mainstream services, practical reconciliation, mutual obligations, responsibilities and participation in the real economy – cloaks a sinister destination. … The extinguishing of indigenous culture by attrition.[13]

This is about the beginning of the end of Aboriginal culture; it is in some ways genocide.[14]

In 2007, the Howard government introduced the Northern Territory National Emergency Response Act (often referred to as the Intervention). The Intervention was a discriminatory package of changes to indigenous welfare provision, law enforcement, land tenure and basic freedoms. The Howard government justified the legislation on the basis of the *Little Children Are Sacred* report,[15] commissioned by the Northern Territory (NT) government and written by former NT Director of Public Prosecutions Rex Wild, QC, and senior Aboriginal health worker Pat Anderson. *Little Children Are Sacred* found that the sexual abuse of Aboriginal children in the NT is seriously widespread and quite often goes unreported. According to the inquiry, sexual abuse of indigenous children was happening largely because of the breakdown of indigenous culture and society, as a consequence of colonial dispossession and the combined effects of poor health, alcohol and drug abuse, unemployment and poor education and housing. The inquiry made ninety-seven recommendations, which included suggestions to: improve school attendance; provide education campaigns on child sexual abuse and how to stop it; reduce alcohol consumption in Aboriginal communities; build greater trust between government departments, the police and Aboriginal communities; strengthen family support services; and, *most importantly, to empower Aboriginal communities to take more control and make their own decisions about their future* – a common conclusion to reports on Aboriginal problems that actually sought indigenous input, but one which never seems to penetrate the colonial mind-set.

The Howard government's 'Intervention' was designed without consulting the affected indigenous peoples, took little notice of the breadth of the *Little Children Are Sacred* recommendations, and 'suspended' the operation of the Racial Discrimination Act 1975 so as to include what the United Nations has since denounced as racially discriminatory[16] measures, such as: bans on alcohol consumption, the compulsory acquisition of Aboriginal townships through five-year leases, the removal of customary law and cultural practice considerations from bail applications and sentencing within criminal proceedings, the suspension of the permit system on indigenous land, retaining a proportion of welfare benefits to all recipients in the designated communities and of all benefits to those who 'neglect' their children, and the abolition of the Community Development Employment Projects, which had previously acted as an alternative to welfare.

Beyond the government rhetoric the compulsory land acquisition measure seemed to have little to do with preventing child abuse as it was simply a further development of a policy of land tenure reform first started back in 2004 – well before the *Little Children Are Sacred* report. As discussed above, during 2004/05 the Commonwealth Government developed a new package of reforms to the ALRA which altered leasing arrangements for indigenous land. The Intervention's five-year lease compulsory acquisition provisions were a response to the poor uptake of the 2006 ALRA amendments' ninety-nine-year voluntary leases options. If indigenous peoples did not wish to relinquish control of their land, it appears the Commonwealth would take it from them for at least five years, during which time it would continue to negotiate for ninety-nine-year township leases with traditional owners, pursuant to Section 19A of the ALRA. So having stripped traditional owners of the use of, rights to and responsibility for their land, the Commonwealth would seek to 'negotiate' ninety-nine-year leases under grossly asymmetric colonial power relations, which would leave indigenous owners extremely vulnerable to 'sweeteners' from the Commonwealth (Altman 2007) – such as the promise of better housing and infrastructure in return.

Despite all this a few high-profile indigenous spokespersons, most notably Noel Pearson and Marcia Langton, welcomed much of the Intervention's measures, accepting the alleged overarching rationale of protecting the rights of women and children.[17] Nevertheless, from a human rights perspective there was a need for 'free prior and informed consent' of those affected by policies such as these and the production of a 'rights balancing act'. Within international law, interpreting a state party's obligations under a human rights treaty is possible only by reading all of the human rights treaties to which a state is party as a whole. Australia's obligations under the Convention on the Rights of the Child must therefore be understood in conjunction with the country's obligations under other human rights agreements, such as the International Convention on the Elimination of All Forms of Racial Discrimination (Vivian and Schokman 2009: 97) and the

United Nations Declaration on the Rights of Indigenous Peoples – which the Australian government has now belatedly endorsed. Even so, Langton argues (2007) that 'to expect that people who reel from one traumatic event to another can enjoy the much lauded Aboriginal "rights to self-determination" while their own community and the larger society repeatedly fail them is an indulgent fantasy. It is also an indulgent fantasy to require "consultation" before intervening to prevent crimes being committed.'

While one would not expect a police officer to seek community agreement before making an arrest *to stop* a crime such as child abuse, seeking *to prevent* such crimes is a far more complex issue, especially when far-reaching control measures are *imposed* on communities that have suffered a history of colonization and political and social subordination. In this sense, Langton's prescriptive position is seriously at odds with the findings of the *Little Children Are Sacred* report, which emphasized the importance of empowering indigenous communities to take control of decisions that affect them. It is also unclear where compulsory land acquisition fits into Langton's child protection 'crime prevention' analysis. Finally, the right of Aboriginal people to enjoy their rights free from discrimination on the basis of race cannot be abrogated on the basis of promoting the rights of women and children as 'more important'.

At this juncture it is worth bearing in mind a crucial point made earlier: the social death that is central to the concept of genocide may result from forcible, and ultimately misguided, attempts 'to do good'. Notwithstanding the views of Langton and Pearson, the overwhelming majority of indigenous peoples actually affected by the Intervention were strongly opposed and spoke of losing control, of losing land and of losing their culture. The combination of such factors, as we shall see, caused some to talk in terms of *genocide*.

The following are just a few examples of the voices of protest, which, unlike those of Pearson and Langton, were rarely given space in the mass media. On 27 October 2008, Harry Nelson of the Yuendumu peoples presented the minister for indigenous affairs with a statement signed by 236 residents in a meeting at the community, which stated:

This is our land. We want the Government to give it back to us. We want the Government to stop blackmailing us. We want houses, but we will not sign any leases over our land, because we want to keep control of our country, our houses, and our property. ... We want the *Racial Discrimination Act* 1975 reinstated now ... We want community control ... Everything is coming from the outside, from the top down ... We want to be re-empowered to make our own decisions and control our own affairs. We want self-determination.[18]

The Prescribed Area Peoples' Alliance (PAPA) represented Aboriginal people from communities affected by the NT Intervention. More than 130 people joined the Alliance over two meetings in Mparntwe, Alice Springs, on 29 September and 7 November 2008. After the latter meeting, they released a statement, from which the following is an indicative extract:

These assimilation policies destroy our culture and our lives. It is the Stolen Generation all over again. ... The government is refusing to build us any housing unless we sign over control of our land for 40 years or more. We say NO LEASES. We will not sign. ... The government having this control is no good. Our lives depend on our land. It is connected to our songlines, our culture and our dreaming.[19]

Following this statement, PAPA travelled to Canberra to lobby the government. In February 2009, they held a day of meetings at the Aboriginal Tent Embassy – a long-standing protest site – to drum up support for their campaign against the Intervention. They brought with them a host of signed statements from Arnhem Land and set about drafting an open letter for the media and key players and MPs likely to be supportive. Once again the key issue was the forcible assimilationist nature of the Intervention and its consequences:

You talk about 'closing the gap' between Indigenous and non-Indigenous people. But we want to close the Gap our way, on our terms – not like past assimilation policies. Self-determination has been shattered and abused by the government. ... Compulsory land acquisition is a gateway to longer leases. 5 years, 40 years, 99 years. Now you are threatening to not build houses until we sign your leases. But we will not sign. The vision of our old people comes with responsibility to maintain our land and culture. Development of our communities must support our dreams and aspirations, with our land and resources in our hands.[20]

Along with the immediate repeal of the Intervention laws, territory-wide consultations and the implementation of the UN Declaration on the Rights of Indigenous Peoples, a key demand in the PAPA letter was to: 'Stop the promotion of genocide. By the UN Genocide Convention, one definition of genocide is; Conditions of life set to destroy the group in whole or in part.'[21]

In March 2010, the Australian Indigenous Doctors' Association (AIDA), in collaboration with a University of New South Wales research centre, launched a comprehensive health impact assessment of the Intervention.[22] The research utilized a methodology which invoked an Aboriginal interpretation of health that includes five dimensions – cultural, spiritual, social, emotional and physical – and which involved interviews with over 250 affected people.[23] The report unequivocally concluded that 'the intervention does more harm than good' and predicted that 'that the intervention will cause *profound long-term damage to our Indigenous communities* ... with any possible benefits to physical health largely outweighed by negative impacts on psychological health, social health and wellbeing, and *cultural integrity*'.[24] Such a conclusion is entirely at odds with the claims of the then Rudd government, and those supporters of the Intervention like Langton and Pearson, who saw the Intervention as key to indigenous survival. On the contrary, in the context of an ongoing colonial relationship and the culturally genocidal effects of the denial of self-determination, such a far-reaching policy of control measures imposed on indigenous groups, especially compulsory land acquisition, would inevitably produce yet more culturally genocidal effects. The AIDA report ended with the now familiar conclusion that negative impacts may be minimized '*only if governments commit to working in respectful partnerships with Indigenous people*'.[25]

Returning to the crucial issue of land, given that the 2006 ALRA reforms were promoted to open up Aboriginal land to mineral exploration and development, the Intervention's compulsory acquisition of townships has created a dangerous precedent for other Aboriginal lands (Altman 2007: 9). In late 2007, the Howard government signed up to the US-led Global Nuclear Energy Partnership initiative (GNEP),[26] which committed Australia to mine and enrich its uranium, export it to other countries, then reimport the resultant radioactive waste to be stored for evermore in the Australian desert. Approximately 30 per cent of the world's currently identified uranium reserves are to be found on NT indigenous lands, and since 2014 the number of exploration licences for uranium in the NT has doubled, with nearly eighty companies either actively exploring or having applied to explore. With the ALRA amendments and the Intervention's compulsory acquisition measures Indigenous peoples will have no effective means to resist the now 'inevitable' increase in uranium mining in Australia,[27] resulting in yet further culturally genocidal pressures on some indigenous groups, alongside the inevitable ecocidal impacts of uranium mining on their local environment.[28] This may seem to be conflating *forcible* settler appropriation and exploitation of land with the issue of cultural genocide, but if the relationship to land of many indigenous peoples is properly understood this is entirely correct. Indeed, when the *genos* in question is an indigenous social figuration with a relationship to land at its identity core, and where the settler exploitation involves *intentional forcible* dispossession, then the effect is quite simply culturally genocidal even where the primary *motive* is economic expansion.[29]

*Rebranding the Intervention* In the usual fashion with racially discriminatory government policies, which ultimately fail even on their own terms and prove to be somewhat embarrassing, a rebrand is required. Such a move usually follows an 'independent review' of some sort which focuses on micro-issues laden with managerial jargon and talk of 'outcomes' and 'capacity building' at the expense of fundamental change and the language of human rights, self-determination, cultural revitalization and the like. In other words the broad policy continues with minor changes and a new name. In late 2008, following just such a review of the Intervention, the Australian government pledged to form a legitimate relationship with the indigenous people based on 'consultation', acknowledge Australian human rights responsibilities and reinstate the Racial Discrimination Act of 1975. Following these consultations, on 23 November 2011 the government introduced legislation[30] to parliament and released the

'Stronger Futures' policy statement, which stated that the Australian government was committed to providing voluntary five-year leases and would not extend the measure for compulsory five-year leases in the Northern Territory Emergency Response Act. In addition, 'the Australian Government and Northern Territory Government would continue to negotiate leases with Aboriginal landowners to "manage social housing in remote areas"'. However, the legislation would continue the policy of opening up indigenous land for commercial use by designing regulations that 'ease leasing on town camp and community living area land' in the Northern Territory in order 'to encourage Aboriginal landowners to use their land for a wider range of functions such as economic development and private land ownership'.

The new legislation has attracted almost as much criticism as its predecessor as it fails in many similar areas. First, we again saw the ubiquitous issue of consultative 'box ticking' and the state's preference for a narrow consultative net. Pertaining to this, Mick Gooda, the Aboriginal and Torres Strait Islander Social Justice Commissioner, discussed the 'inadequacy' of the Aboriginal consultations within a report by the Australian Human Rights Commission, which identified the lack of cultural competency and attention paid to the competency and ability of Aboriginal governments.[31] The Yolŋu Nations Assembly, meanwhile, which represents 8,000 Aboriginal people in the western, central and east Arnhem Land in the Northern Territory,[32] argued that the federal government has not only continued with many Intervention powers but also awarded themselves new ones. The Yolŋu Nations consequently called on all traditional owners across the Northern Territory to refuse participation in land lease negotiations with the Australian federal government, and approval for any exploration licences.

In a widely supported statement[33] the Yolŋu Nations argued that 'the traditional owners of prescribed community lands have been placed under extreme pressure from the Australian federal government to grant them head leases over these communities. The Land Councils are increasingly being pressured by government to act outside their roles and become agencies of government ... We want our Land Councils to advocate for our needs and not have their independence curtailed by government funding arrangements and political interference.' The Yolŋu Nations further called on both the Australian federal and Northern Territory governments to end their interventionist policies and agendas, end the Working Futures policy, and for 'Homelands' to be considered equal to communities that were former mission and government settlements (more on this below). Finally, in terms of cultural maintenance, the Yolŋu Nations called for an end to the Northern Territory government's compulsory policy of teaching in English for the first four hours of each school day. To be successful, they argued, they needed education with instruction in their own Yolŋu languages through all levels of schooling.

A statement by twenty-seven 'leading Australians',[34] including Professor of Anthropology Jon Altman, the Hon. Ian Viner and the Hon. Malcolm Fraser, criticized the 'new' policy for not sufficiently involving Aboriginal people or elders and for its failure to obtain affected communities' informed consent. They called on the government to abandon the legislation and set up appropriate mechanisms to involve Aboriginal leaders and elders of the Northern Territory in the decision-making processes that define their future. Amnesty International concurred with this critique, calling on the Australian government to collaborate with the indigenous communities of the Northern Territory and construct appropriate approaches that 'respect the rights of those affected' and comply with 'the minimum standards set out in the UN Declaration on the Rights of Indigenous Peoples and grounded in the free, prior and informed consent of Aboriginal people living in the Northern Territory'. The requirement of neoliberal capitalism to secure more and more ever scarcer resources, and the process of extreme energy, is a guarantee that the issue of land rights and opening up of indigenous lands to development will never go away. Indeed, since the Stronger Futures policy was initiated the government has reiterated its push for ninety-nine-year leases over Aboriginal townships, once again on the back of a number of 'review reports'.

On 1 August 2014 a report into 'Indigenous training and employment' programmes, called 'Creating Parity – the Forrest Review',[35] was launched. With a classic colonial mind-set, the review into indigenous training and employment was chaired by a West Australian billionaire miner by the name of Andrew Forrest, the chairman of Fortescue Metals Group.[36] He was commissioned by an Australian government apparently hungry to 'hear breakthrough ideas that will end the disparity in employment for Indigenous Australians' and consequently opined that 'seismic, not incremental, change is required and the time for action is now'. Such a remit was not, of course, referring to genuine decolonizing self-determination and meaningful land rights, but rather was characterized by the rhetorical lip-service to self-determination found in the report's final chapter: 'Empowering people in remote communities to end the disparity themselves'; so long, of course, that it involves neoliberal market-based solutions combined with the usual dose of deregulation. Indeed, the report vociferously supported the Commonwealth's continued drive for ninety-nine-year leases over Aboriginal communities (under Section 19A of the Aboriginal Land Rights Act) and its plans to devolve the powers of land councils in the Northern Territory (under Section 28A). Furthermore, the report singles out the Northern Land Council as an impediment to long-term leasing for private investment and urges the Commonwealth to consider how it will 'ensure' that land councils 'participate in and support the new arrangements', and in a throwback to the Lockean logic of 'mixing labour with land'[37] to acquire property rights, the report recommended 'unlocking ... chronically under-utilised' Indigenous lands to achieve 'significant sustainable economic advantages to first Australians' – with absolutely no appreciation of resource extraction being anything but a sustainable solution. Worse still, it recommended that the Commonwealth exercise the 'significant leverage' it holds in the Northern Territory, to favour spending on housing and infrastructure within those communities, but only those which agree to surrender control of their land under a Commonwealth lease.

Following the Forrest report, on 4 September 2014 the Federal Parliament's Joint Select Committee on Northern Australia tabled its final report: 'Pivot North', which also argued that Aboriginal Land Rights in the Northern Territory and the Native Title Acts were an impediment to 'development' in the north, despite the fact that it admitted that the committee heard no evidence that Aboriginal people themselves wanted to alter the current tenure system of inalienable freehold title in the NT. Indeed, the report stated that 'evidence from the land councils in the Territory was that Traditional Owners were happy to use the current provisions of the [Land Rights] Act for both commercial and private development proposals'.[38] During the review process the NT government noted that under the current system governments now pay rent to Traditional Owners for the use of Aboriginal land and in its submission observed that 'paying rent for Indigenous land is a major step in seeing land owners derive economic benefits from their land'.[39] Even so, their submission went on to lament the 'near total absence of private investment and development', which is no doubt due to the corporate need to maximize profits, combined with an inherent aversion to paying fair rent and dealing with indigenous peoples on anything like an equal footing. Given such an impediment to the privatization of indigenous lands, in a draft of the NT government submission, mistakenly sent to ABC News, the primary recommendation read: 'at the very least there needs to be capacity to compulsorily acquire ALRA land for government/strategic purposes'.

But of course, in the time-honoured colonial rhetorical tradition, this had nothing to do with a desire to 'unlock' indigenous lands for private corporate gain and resource exploitation but was rather, so it was claimed, motivated by a desire to help indigenous people develop for their own sake. Following a meeting in Canberra of the Council of Australian Governments (COAG) on 10 October 2014, NT chief minister Adam Giles announced that his government, together with those of the Commonwealth and Queensland, would urgently investigate indigenous land administration and land use, 'to enable Traditional Owners to attract private sector investment and finance for development'.[40]

The Hon. Ian Viner, Aboriginal Affairs minister responsible for the Aboriginal Land Rights (NT) Act in 1976, wrote a scathing critique of these developments[41] in which he argued:

> The whole framework and security of traditional Aboriginal land, protected by the Land Rights Act, is in danger of being subverted by Governments, bureaucracies and people who have no real understanding or sympathy for traditional communal land ownership. 99-year town leases turn traditional ownership upside down. In reality they put the Commonwealth back into ownership and control of traditional Aboriginal land like it was before the Land Rights Act was passed ... A Commonwealth Head Lease is a device by the Commonwealth to take control of Aboriginal land away from traditional owners. It is thoroughly

misleading for the Commonwealth to suggest giving the Office of Township Leasing a 99-year lease of Aboriginal land is the same as 99-year leases in the Australian Capital Territory (ACT). The ACT leases Crown land to people instead of granting freehold ownership. Aboriginal traditional owners already have freehold title, the best form of ownership in Australia. There is good reason to think the Commonwealth devised 99-year leases and the Office of Township Leasing as the head lessee as a way to avoid having to compensate Aboriginal people on just terms under the Constitution for taking control of their traditional lands. The Commonwealth objective is the permanent alienation of traditional land from Land Trusts.

The culturally genocidal practice of alienating indigenous people from their lands shows no signs of abating; indeed, as we shall see later in this chapter, the indigenous peoples of Australia, like those of North America, are now having to deal with the genocidal and ecocidal process of extreme energy.

**Cultural genocide through urbanization**

In the early 1970s, an indigenous 'post-colonial' initiative[42] saw Aboriginal peoples in the Northern Territory migrate out of government settlements and missions, returning to live once again on their traditional lands. This process of migration and decentralization was termed the 'outstations movement', and today there are an estimated 560 communities with populations of fewer than one hundred people dotted across the Territory. Almost all are located on Aboriginal-owned land that covers 500,000 square kilometres – nearly half of the NT.[43] While there is significant diversity in outstation activities, some with vibrant local economies built on arts production, employment as rangers and wildlife harvesting, with others highly dependent on welfare income, their key commonality is the determined *choice* they have made to actively engage with their land, based on a desire to protect sacred sites, to retain connections to ancestral lands and ancestors, to live off the land, or to escape social dysfunction that might be prevalent in larger townships.[44] Despite this the 'viability' of outstations/homelands has been under review in policy circles since the late 1990s and a public debate began in earnest in 2005 when the indigenous affairs minister

Amanda Vanstone described remote Aboriginal communities as 'cultural museums'.[45] A neoliberal commentary ensued, largely championed by the Bennelong Society, including the 'Leaving Remote Communities' conference in Sydney in September 2006,[46] which appears to have had significant influence on policy.

Indeed, in 2009 the Intervention was renamed 'Closing the Gap in the Northern Territory' under the National Indigenous Reform Agreement plan, purportedly to 'address Indigenous disadvantage in Australia'.[47] 'Closing the Gap' is implemented through a series of 'National Partnership Agreements', which commit state and territory governments to a common framework of outcomes, progress measures, policy directions and, crucially, funding. A key agreement for people living in remote communities is the agreement on 'Remote Service Delivery'. This agreement establishes the priority or 'hub' town model, which effectively transfers funding to selected, larger economic centres, relying on them to act as 'servicing hubs' for outlying areas where many Aboriginal peoples live.

The Northern Territory government sought to implement this agreement under the so-called 'Working Future' initiative, which seemed designed to produce urbanizing pressure on those remaining indigenous peoples living in remote communities by moving financial support away from outstations to twenty larger Aboriginal communities it called 'Territory Growth Towns'(now expanded to twenty-one and rebranded as 'Major Remote Towns'),[48] alongside which it committed to building *no more new homes outside these centres*, and *no new homelands* would be established in the Northern Territory. The 'Working Future' policy statement anticipated that these towns would become robust nodes for vibrant and sustainable economic development. Underpinning such an approach is the neoliberal paradigm that seeks to meet the labour and resource needs of mature capitalism while eliminating non-state spaces.[49] But, as Altman points out:

> During the past 30 years, a growing body of research has indicated that life at outstations is better – in health outcomes, livelihood options, and social cohesion, even housing conditions – than at larger townships, despite neglect. … Many Aboriginal people remain determined to live on their ancestral lands, pursuing a way of life that is informed by fundamentally different

value systems. *Working Future* envisages only a conventional mainstream future for remote-living Aboriginal people.[50]

In a protest press release at the time the Gumatj clan nation from the MataMata Homeland in north-east Arnhem Land wrote:

> the Northern territory Government is 'proposing to stop all funding to small remote communities, called Homelands or Outstations. These communities – like that we live in here at MataMata – is the cultural source of identity, pride and indigenous religion and law. These are sacred Homelands that the people WILL NOT leave.[51]

In 2011, an Amnesty International report undertook a rights-based critique of the initiative, stating: 'Aboriginal Peoples have the right to live on their traditional homelands without being effectively denied access to services like public housing and related infrastructure'. While Patrick Dodson argued that the government has ignored the positive attributes of outstations, including the health benefits of people living on their lands, and 'to ignore that, in a manner to force people, ultimately, to come to these designated major centres, is really, slowly but surely, a way of *killing people's culture and extinguishing the strength of Aboriginal life*'.[52]

Echoing a similar concern with cultural erosion, after it was revealed that the Laynhapuy Homelands Association, which looks after around one thousand people living in remote north-east Arnhem Land, was in financial trouble, Luke Morrish, head of the Bawinanga Aboriginal Corporation, argued that: 'there has to be a recognition of the culture, and the value of the culture, and the value of maintaining that culture from an overall benefit of Australia … By seeing people move off their homelands, removing those links to their land, language and culture and seeing that drift away, is a loss that we really need to ask ourselves a question as a country, do we want to bear that loss?'[53]

Unfortunately, preliminary census-based indications are that the urbanization these commentators feared has already started to happen. Indeed, a report on population shifts in the NT outlined a significant redistribution of people: 'the Indigenous population of the NT is redistributing internally over time with progressive urbanisation (lower proportions living in remote parts of the NT) being the main pattern'. Perhaps most worrying for cultural sustainability was the finding that 'overall, in comparison to the Indigenous population of the NT as a whole, there was substantially higher growth in the young and youth cohorts (aged zero to 20 years) at Territory Growth Towns (TGTs). There was a striking absolute increase in the Indigenous male population aged 10–14 years and 25–29 years at TGTs from 2006 to 2011.' The report concluded that 'the Indigenous population of TGTs grew at double the rate of the NT as a whole'.[54]

## Ecocide and extreme energy

Indigenous peoples in Australia have had a difficult relationship with extractive industries to date (Short 2008: chs 3 and 4), and in recent years it has become even more problematic as the process of extreme energy has driven the development of new technologies to open up previously untapped resources such as natural gas (mostly methane), which is locked within coal seams under high pressure. It is an extreme energy technology which requires large numbers of wells across a landscape (as opposed to conventional gas, which requires fewer wells that tap into large gas pockets that are thousands of metres below the surface). Suitable coal seam gas (CSG) seams are typically nearer the surface – usually no more than 400 metres below – and are often less than a metre thick and clustered over large areas.[55] The process is considerably more intense than with conventional wells. Indeed, before gas can be produced the balance in the coal structure needs to be significantly altered through dewatering and hydraulic fracturing.[56] The well must be drilled, the coal seam dewatered (sometimes at a rate of 400,000 litres of water per day, as happened with one of the first wells in the Surat Basin), primed with potassium chloride and then hydraulically fractured with water, sand and chemicals that are pumped into the seam at high pressure. Once the process is complete all the surface area of the coal is theoretically propped open and gas flows.[57] There are around 40,000 square kilometres of Queensland that have CSG leases currently being developed.[58] As with other fracking processes, what goes on below the surface is just part of the picture. Indeed, fracking's associated activities and infrastructure usually require the construction of roads and pipelines for the gas and saline water, building of water treatment facilities, gas compression stations, high-tension power lines and well pad and pipe route rehabilitation.[59] Even though the environmentally destructive impact on the surface affects only around two hectares during drilling and a half hectare thereafter, cumulatively CSG production is a landscape-altering phenomenon of some magnitude. In common with shale gas production, CSG wells do not produce large amounts of gas per well and production declines very quickly, and thus every gas field requires a multitude of interlinked wells, some clustered on 'pads', but which can extend thousands of square kilometres.

Much like shale gas fracking, CSG production has produced a range of negative environmental and social impacts, which include methane migration, toxic water contamination, air pollution, increased carbon emissions and a general industrialization of the countryside; whereas CSG-specific impacts include depletion of the water table and potential subsidence.[60] Despite this CSG is expanding rapidly in Queensland and is moving into northern New South Wales, and the industry anticipates development in other parts of Australia. The rapid expansion of CSG has made it even more difficult than with conventional mining for Aboriginal people to have any kind of say in how it develops and where it develops. In a recent study, Trigger et al.[61] found that 'issues raised by Aboriginal people in relation to agreements arising from CSG and broader development aspirations' were largely concerned with 'links to land (or 'country'), membership of groups of beneficiaries, cultural identity negotiations, representation of collective Aboriginal interests and related governance of groups, and leverage required to negotiate with and extract real outcomes from resource companies'. They further note that 'these challenges appear to reflect the scale and speed of CSG development, relative to the time taken for making collective decisions by Aboriginal groups and for resolving native title claims in the courts'.[62] The study noted 'a diverse range of views within and across Aboriginal populations about CSG developments', with some in favour of CSG development, while many others objected to it 'as a form of land use'. For many indigenous peoples CSG development is but the latest example of the colonial dilemma – whether or not to accept environmental destruction, and its cultural corollary, for some degree of involvement (be it a negotiated land use agreement with some fiscal benefits, or short-term employment opportunities) with the 'development' process. Three recent cases highlight the problems.

Determined in 2007, and covering some 1,120 square kilometres of Queensland and northern New South Wales, the Githabul Native Title determination (granting a non-exclusive right), which includes nine national parks and thirteen state forests,[63] has been the source of significant conflict regarding the CSG issue of late.[64] Following an application by the New South Wales Aboriginal Land Council for gas prospecting in the Tweed and Byron Shires – areas covered by Githabul Native Title – some elders and representatives decided to distance themselves from both the land council and the Native Title registrar.[65] Githabul spokeswoman Gloria Williams argued that the Native Title agreement was being wrongly used to allow coal seam gas interests into the region: 'because we signed off on a consent determination agreement ... and when we sign off on a consent determination agreement we are literally giving them consent to come and do what they want ... [via] Native Title ... they are coming through our country mining the hell out of it'.[66]

Commenting on this statement, Trigger et al. argue that it 'glosses over underlying factors in the dispute about CSG; namely, intra-Indigenous contestation about representation and authority among Githabul people', when it seems to actually highlight such intra-indigenous contestation.

Sentiments like that of Gloria Williams are no doubt fuelled, at least in part, by the fact that the NSW Aboriginal Land Council (NSWALC) lodged their application without prior consultation with NSW Aboriginal people. In January 2013, Githabul opponents of CSG were reported to be 'planning a legal challenge in an international court if necessary against their own, to dissolve the Githabul Nation Aboriginal Corporation (GNAC), which approved mining on their country without their consent or approval'.[67] However, NSWALC CEO Geoff Scott accused a reluctant NSW government of 'pandering'[68] to opponents in the environmental movement who are fighting its plan to become a player in the coal seam gas industry. The land council's board decided to become involved in resource extraction apparently in order to generate long-term income and job opportunities for Aboriginal people. In Geoff Scott's words: 'it's employment opportunities and long-term income streams we are after from this.[69] Do you want to get benefit from it or do you want to continue to get the scraps off the table? Do you want to continue to rely on government for your livelihood? I think we owe our children better than that.'[70]

For many indigenous peoples the rapid rise of CSG poses yet another stark choice between a settler colonial rock and a hard place; a native title system devoid of a veto power and extreme energy 'solutions' being presented, counterfactually, as environmentally 'safe' and the only realistic lifeline for economically disadvantaged indigenous communities. The economic reality of CSG production, however, is far more complicated. For example, a recent study[71] has highlighted how Aboriginal people are not as able to access employment opportunities as they had expected from CSG projects. CSG-impacted Aboriginal people identified a range of barriers to such access, including:

- the rapid development of the industry outpacing a group's ability to establish or expand a business interest;
- a lack of access to contracts/contractors, because contracts are too large for local or fledgling businesses to take on;
- a lack of requirements for indigenous business development in major contracts;
- balancing work and cultural responsibilities;
- lack of appropriate formal qualifications;
- limited ability to hold companies and contractors accountable for poor performance and failing to achieve commitments related to Aboriginal employment;
- and frustration with continued training without resulting employment.

As is the case with extreme energy projects around the world, the rhetoric doesn't square with the empirical reality. Despite disagreements between community groups and their elected representatives, such as can be seen with the Githabul example above, other potential CSG development areas are seeing more consistent resistance born out of a greater awareness of the ecocidal externalities of extreme energy technologies, the usual flow of economic benefits and the potential for long-term ecologically induced genocidal impacts. For example, Gomeroi country extends from the QLD/

NSW border region to Tamworth, Aberdeen/Muswellbrook, Coonabarabran and Walgett, all areas rich in subsurface resources. In January 2012 representatives of the Gomeroi people filed an application in the National Native Title Tribunal. The following year the Gomeroi Native Title claimants lodged an injunction on mining.[72] Claimant Alf Priestley said the:

> Aboriginal people are the land. We are connected to the land, trees, rocks and waters ... Aboriginal people have been forced to sit on the fence about this. Either way our land is being taken away from us. There is only 17 per cent of vegetation left in Australia and that's because these farmers and cities have cleared the land to put crops in and to build big towers. We aren't benefiting out of CSG and neither out of stopping CSG.

Fellow claimant Anthony Munroe stated: 'Mining is coming to our country but we are going to fight them every step of the way through the courts, through the protests, and through the support of the Gomeroi people. The Gomeroi people will not be lying down.'

While Michael Anderson, the last remaining member of the original Tent Embassy activists alive, and fellow Gomeroi claimant, argued that: 'native title has not been extinguished on water, and Native Title has never been extinguished over our trees, plants, animals and everything else. We don't care what title you've got, but we're not going to allow you to destroy our connection with all those things.'

Running through Gomeroi perspectives on coal mining and CSG is an appreciation of the ecocidal impact it will have on their land and a hope that their decision to fight mining will inspire others in the country to do the same.[73] There was considerable support for the Gomeroi stance from the anti-fracking movement's Lock the Gate Alliance,[74] which is a national grassroots organization made up of over 30,000 supporters and more than 230 local groups who are concerned about unsafe coal and gas mining. These groups are located in all parts of Australia and include farmers, traditional custodians, conservationists and urban residents. Many such groups use the influential 'CSG-Free Community Strategy' launched by CSG-Free Northern Rivers, which goes beyond the idea of locking individual gates to take resistance to the community level;

with communities being trained in non-violent civil resistance and encouraged to form local committees to block local roads against CSG activity, the idea being that as local networks link up then whole valleys and communities will become CSG-free areas.[75] North West Alliance representative Anne Kennedy said: 'I am delighted to support the stand of the Gomeroi people ... In our area, Wun-Gali representatives have resolved to declare a moratorium on all coal seam gas activities on their traditional lands and in the Coonamble Shire.' Tambar Springs farmer David Quince stated: 'I have the greatest respect for the stand made by the Gomeroi people, working to make sure this magnificent land remains healthy and capable of supporting humans, and also fauna and flora.'[76]

Indigenous resistance to CSG looks to be spreading. The Mithaka People, traditional owners of Queensland's Channel Country, have written to the UN's Special Rapporteur on the Rights of Indigenous Peoples arguing that the government has ignored international law by failing to consult with them over planned coal seam gas activity on their land.[77] Mithaka representative Scott Gorringe was particularly concerned about CSG's effect on water:

> Most of our stories start and end around water ... Our main significant sites are around water. Not only culturally, environmentally I think it's critical for that country especially ... You start mucking around with rivers out our way and damaging underground water, it's sitting on the Great Artesian Basin. And we don't know what potentially can happen. You know, mining companies are telling us one thing and they're tainted with a brush. And Government's telling us another and I think they're tainted with the same brush. There's a whole lot of other opportunities that would present themselves out there if people would be strong enough to hold back and have a look at this stuff and have a talk to us about the opportunities we see. But we're not getting that opportunity. The Queensland Government's not talking to us.[78]

Following a tour of Australia's gas-field regions, international lawyer and prominent End Ecocide advocate Polly Higgins wrote: 'The stories I heard over the last two weeks about CSG, the fracking I saw and the extreme levels of community concern I experienced led to the question: is this not an Ecocide? Surely it cannot be right to subject our people and planet to gasfield processes that cause significant harm.'[79]

For indigenous peoples in Australia, many of whom are struggling to survive as distinct peoples in the face of the relentless culturally genocidal pressures we have just discussed, to feel that they have little option but to become involved with an ecocidal industry is a searing indictment of modern Australia and where it is heading. Jared Diamond has argued that Australia may well be the First World's 'miners' canary: a developed country facing a rapid decline in living standards as its burgeoning population outstrips its rapidly degrading natural resource base' (Diamond 2006: ch. 13). Indeed, for all the corporate and political talk of extreme energy technologies providing 'sustainable' energy, it is a gross misunderstanding at best and a barefaced lie at worst. There is nothing sustainable about scraping the bottom of the fossil fuel barrel. Indeed, as I mentioned earlier, it is testament to the fact that most conventional sources of energy have peaked. In a holistic analysis Diamond goes farther than detailing unsustainable ecocidal energy extraction to discuss Australia's profound ecological crisis. He highlights acute problems of soil fertility and salinization, land degradation, diminishing freshwater resources, distance costs, over-exploitation of forests and fisheries, importation of inappropriate European agricultural values and methods and alien species, alongside related problems of trade and immigration policies. Diamond concludes that the 'mining' of Australia's natural resources, i.e. their unsustainable exploitation at rates faster than their renewal rates since European settlement began, means that:

> Australia illustrates in extreme form the exponentially accelerating horse race in which the world now finds itself. ('Accelerating' means going faster and faster; 'exponentially accelerating' means accelerating in the manner of a nuclear chain reaction, twice as fast and then 4, 8, 16, 32 ... times faster after equal time intervals.) On the one hand, the development of environmental problems in Australia, as in the whole world, is accelerating exponentially. On the other hand, the development of public environmental concern, and of private and governmental countermeasures, is also accelerating exponentially. Which horse will win the race? (Ibid.: 425)

The environmental picture for Australia is even worse if we consider the wider impact of this 'mining' of a continent – its impact on global emissions. Much like recent studies of shale gas in North America, recent studies concerning fugitive emissions from CSG fields in Australia are reporting disturbing results regarding potential methane emissions. One report[80] found consistently elevated methane and carbon dioxide concentrations within the CSG fields of the Darling Downs. The study clearly showed that there is something going on in these areas leading to increased atmospheric greenhouse gas concentrations, but of course the negligent, arguably criminal, lack of baseline studies makes it very difficult to prove the chain of causation. However, the study's lead author, Dr Damien Maher, said there were clues as to where the methane and carbon dioxide was coming from: 'The technology we used gives us additional information about the methane and carbon dioxide, and the methane in the atmosphere of the Darling Downs gasfield has a very similar fingerprint to methane in the CSG of the region.'

National coordinator for Lock the Gate, Phil Laird, welcomed the report:

> This study takes a landscape approach to fugitive emissions. It suggests that, not only do wells, pipes and other infrastructure leak, but the ground may also be leaking through cracks and fissures after the coal seams are depressurized and the gas is mobilized. It is devastating for human health and the environment. Fugitive methane emissions are strong indicators of the presence of toxic gasses such as sulphur oxide, nitrogen oxide and volatile organic compounds. Gases that likely contributed to health impacts to the residents of Tara ... This study shows that people and gasfields should not mix ... The research clearly shows that unconventional gas is far from a 'transition fuel' and is in fact a dirty, emissions heavy energy source that neither community health nor the planet can afford. It is reckless in the extreme that both state and federal governments allowed drilling to commence without strong baseline studies in place.[81]

It is not hard to see why Australia has recently been named the worst-performing industrial country on climate change.[82] This report states: 'The new conservative Australian government has apparently made good on last year's announcement and reversed the climate policies previously in effect. As a result, the country lost a further 21 positions in the policy evaluation compared to last year, thus replacing Canada as the worst-performing industrial country.'[83] The report, produced by the think tank Germanwatch and Climate Action Network Europe, covers the top fifty-eight emitters of greenhouse gases in the world and about 90 per cent of all energy-related emissions. Jan Burck, one of the report authors, stated: 'It is interesting that the bottom six countries in the ranking – Russia, Iran, Canada, Kazakhstan, Australia and Saudi Arabia – all have a lot of fossil fuel resources. It is a curse. The fossil fuel lobbies in the countries are strong. In Australia they stopped what were some very good carbon laws.'[84] While Erwin Jackson, of the Australian charity the Climate Institute, argued that: 'Australia has been heading backwards by undertaking actions such as attempting to kneecap the renewable energy industry through regressive policy changes.'[85]

Such a direction for Australia is particularly disturbing for its indigenous populations, who frequently bear the brunt of environmental destruction, often experiencing it as ecologically induced genocide, but it is also deeply troubling for the settler population given the world's need to drastically reduce greenhouse gas emissions to avert runaway climate change. Moreover, it is positively irrational if you consider that much of Australia's environment is currently a very harsh and inhospitable place; combine that with the ecological crisis Jared Diamond has highlighted, and the recent Commonwealth Scientific and Industrial Research Organization (CSIRO) and Bureau of Meteorology report that predicts climate change will hit Australia harder than the rest of the world,[86] and the current irrational preference for a 'business-as-usual' approach to burning fossil fuels will likely hit Australia with a catastrophic temperature rise of more than 5°C by the end of the century, outstripping the rate of warming experienced by the rest of the world.

Here we can see another dimension of the nexus between genocide and ecocide; the possibility of viable human adaptation and survival in an even harsher environment is currently being undermined by the continuing culturally genocidal policies inflicted on indigenous peoples by the settler colonial authorities. If we consider how we have responded as a species to environmental changes in the past, unlike other creatures that adjusted to change in their environment through gradual biological adaptation, humans generally created innovative ways to live and communicate, and passed such knowledge down to their children (Johnston 2000: 96). Cultural diversity – the multitude of ways of living and communicating knowledge – gave humans an adaptive edge; developing analytical tools to identify and assess change in their environment to search out or devise new strategies, and to communicate and incorporate these strategies throughout their group (ibid.). As anthropologist Barbara Rose Johnston points out, 'for the human species, culture is our primary adaptive mechanism'. The continued cultural and ecological genocidal pressures on indigenous people in Australia endanger not just their own survival as distinct peoples but also the adaptation potential for the settler nation more broadly.

## A series of continuing genocides and ecocides

> Use of the term 'genocide' to describe the colonial experience has been met with scepticism from some quarters ... Yet the political posturing and semantic debates do nothing to dispel the feeling Indigenous people have that this is the word that adequately describes our experience as colonised peoples. (Behrendt 2001: 132)

Many indigenous societies have evolved spiritual beliefs, ceremonial traditions, sacred designations and worldviews based on their own lands (Pilgrim et al. 2009). Both the personal and cultural identity of such groups is intertwined with the physical landscape and nature as a whole, such that when land is taken away from peoples they become disconnected from nature, leading to significant mental and physical health repercussions as well as significant cultural erosion. For such groups, land truly is life (see Wolfe 2006).

In the Secretariat's Draft of the Convention, which Lemkin penned, genocide was defined as 'a criminal act directed against any one of the aforesaid groups of human beings, with the purpose of destroying it in whole or in part or *of preventing its preservation or development*'.[87] In its colonial relationship with indigenous peoples, the Australian state has had a history of preventing the *preservation* of indigenous peoples as culturally distinct peoples through continued dispossession of land and thinly veiled cultural assimilation drives. In recent times, dispossession continues, somewhat perversely, through land 'rights', which were shaped by commercial interest groups – the usual culprits and beneficiaries being mining corporations and the pastoral industry – to ensure that indigenous groups cannot resist 'development', while official reconciliation[88] and, more recently, the current drive to urbanize indigenous peoples in 'Territory Growth Towns' are coercively assimilationist.

The bulk of these policies breach international laws against racial discrimination[89] and are completely at odds with a number of key articles in the UN Declaration on the Rights of Indigenous Peoples, especially the right to self-determination. Given Lemkin's enthusiasm for international law[90] and his view that 'genocide as a concept provides for a protection of a *minimum of basic human rights* of members of those groups which are under a constant attack throughout history',[91] it is interesting to ponder what he would have made of such persistent contraventions of human rights norms by a colonial settler state that has failed to decolonize and which had a violently genocidal past. Would he have viewed these policies as but the latest cultural dimension of a singular genocidal process first set in motion in 1788? There is an important temporal issue to consider here: given that Lemkin viewed genocide as a function of colonization, the singular genocidal process could occur over a long period of time and may well start with direct physical killing on the frontier – which of course ultimately ended – while Lemkin's second stage of 'imposing the national pattern of the oppressor' continues into the present. As Patrick Wolfe observes, 'settler colonialism persists over an extended period of time', and so it seems does its 'structural genocide' (Wolfe 2006: 122).

Whatever Lemkin may have thought of the current situation of indigenous nations in Australia, I would argue that such policies of the colonial state forcefully alter the cultural trajectory of indigenous peoples' social figurations to the extent that vital cultural continuity is impossible to maintain. Commenting on the urbanization drive discussed above, indigenous activist Michael Anderson states, 'the creation of the hub centres is a way of removing the people from their traditional lands, blackmailing the people into signing over their lands for infra-structure development. Not to sign over the land means nothing will be done for them. Forcing indigenous people from their lands in this way is cultural genocide.'[92] Such policies are a direct attack on the four intrinsic components of cultural continuity identified by

Pretty et al., and in this sense they are producing something more sinister than mere cultural change: the level of forceful coercion involved makes *genocide* a more appropriate description. Indeed, we can now dispense with the 'cultural' descriptor since, as we have seen, it is simply a method of genocidal practice – one way in which a group can be destroyed or crippled. We then also avoid the problem that Wolfe warns of whereby *only* physical genocide is seen as 'the real thing' (Wolfe 2006: 118).

To be clear, it may be that the Australian case is not a continuing genocide as such but *a series of continuing genocides* in which possibly hundreds of distinct indigenous social figurations are suffering dispossession, loss of autonomy, significant mental and physical harm, cultural erosion and ecocidal damage to their environment. Even though genocidal social death can be produced without specific 'intent to destroy', I would argue that there is reasonably foreseeable intent here. Whatever the underlying *motives*, certainly the forcible dispossessions are *intentional*, the exertion of *forcible* control over peoples' lives *is intentional*, and the moves to *forcibly* coerce people off their sacred homelands *are intentional*. Although the resulting physical, cultural and mental harm may be the opposite of the alleged motivation and hence not prima facie intentional as such, in traditional British legal parlance 'foresight and recklessness' as to the consequences of action are 'evidence from which intent may be inferred' (see Fieldhouse 1981): how else should we interpret the repeated reckless disregard for the views of those indigenous peoples affected by policies like the Intervention in its various guises *and* the repeated failure of successive governments to learn the 'great lesson' articulated by the Royal Commission into Aboriginal Deaths in Custody back in 1991?

> The great lesson that stands out is that non-Aboriginals, who currently hold all the power in dealing with Aboriginals, have to give up the usually well intentioned efforts to do things for or to Aboriginals, to give up the assumption that they know what is best for Aboriginals ... who have to be led, educated, manipulated, and re-shaped into the image of the dominant community. Instead Aboriginals must be recognised for what they are, peoples in their own right with their own culture, history and values.[93]

Along with this emphasis on self-determination, a central conclusion of the Royal Commission was that the root cause of current structurally entrenched social inequality was the dispossession of land. Over the last few decades, numerous other official reports have reached the same conclusions and yet 'Aboriginal Affairs' policy continues to move ever farther away from measures that could halt the genocides – genuine decolonizing self-determination, meaningful land rights and respect for the principle of 'free prior and informed consent' towards further dispossession, disempowerment and assimilation. This is genocidal, although of course not in international law since the cultural methods of genocide were largely removed from the final Convention.

## Conclusion

By invoking a broader understanding of genocide in keeping with Lemkin's ideas, this chapter has sought to highlight the *continuing* genocidal context in which many, but not all, indigenous peoples in Australia live, the seriousness of *present-day* culturally and environmentally destructive state policies and a potentially decolonizing pathway out of the 'relationship of genocide' (Barta 2000). This case study has also highlighted important dimensions of the nexus between genocide and ecocide; from the settler colonial land grabs that fuel the continued 'mining' of Australia (Diamond 2006: ch. 13) – most notably through the capitalist-driven process of extreme energy and CSG production – to the question of viable human adaptation and survival in an even harsher Australian environment, which is arguably acutely threatened by the continuing cultural and ecological genocidal pressures on indigenous peoples, their traditional knowledge systems, cultural diversity and ecological sustainability.

# 6 | TAR SANDS AND THE INDIGENOUS PEOPLES OF NORTHERN ALBERTA

*with Jennifer Huseman*[1]

## Introduction: 'the Tar Sands are killing us'[2]

Our message to both levels of government, to Albertans, to Canadians and to the world who may depend on oil sands for their energy solutions, is that we can no longer be sacrificed. (Chief Roxanne Marcel, Mikisew Cree First Nation, quoted in Waller 2008)

This final case study chapter focuses on a second liberal democratic settler context, Canada, and more specifically the province of Alberta. The case study is instructive on a number of levels: once again we see a historical colonial relationship that continues into the present, involving dominion, dispossession, pervasive control, subjugation and subordination, all of which conspire to produce genocidal effects. Moreover, a relationship that is driven by the resource thirst of global neoliberal capitalism is necessarily going to produce ecocidal externalities that can, over time, ecologically induce genocide. The Alberta tar sands are also the poster child of extreme energy, the epitome of scraping the bottom of the barrel, and, as we shall see, are so energy intensive to extract that their continued production threatens the very survival of us all. The chapter begins with a discussion of genocide and the right to exist as it pertains to the indigenous peoples of the area and their current plight. It then moves on to explore the historical and legal context that has ultimately facilitated and justified this situation, before exploring the nature of the tar sands and the ecological, cultural and physical destruction that their extraction and production brings.

The concept of genocide, and the narrow legal understanding to a lesser extent, seeks to protect and uphold the right to exist of entire human social groups, and when it comes to culturally distinct indigenous peoples it is vital to appreciate the basis of their culture, for it is that which gives them their distinctiveness and is the root of their '*genos*'. As Native author and activist Andrea Smith noted (Smith 2005: 121), 'when Native peoples fight for cultural/spiritual preservation, they are ultimately fighting for the landbase which grounds their spirituality and culture'. That is, the land or 'specific geographical setting' (Churchill 2005: 168) with which many[3] indigenous nations/communities identify themselves fundamentally embodies their 'historical narrative' (Abed 2006: 326) and who they are as peoples; with both their 'practices, rituals, and traditions' (ibid.: 327), *and* their political and socio-economic cohesion as a group, inextricably bound to the surrounding landscape. Alienation from that landscape, therefore, inevitably results in the dissolution of an indigenous people's 'network of practical social relations' (Powell 2007: 538), for they will no longer be able to carry out, develop and preserve their 'cultural heritage and traditions', or 'pass these traditions on to subsequent generations' – thereby rendering them 'socially dead'.[4] It is Native peoples' recognition of this point that has led some to refer to the concept of genocide to describe their past and present-day experiences at the hands of the colonial states in which they live (see Short 2010a, 2010b). This understanding is in keeping with the understanding of Lemkin, who, as we have seen, viewed physical genocide and cultural genocide, not as two distinct phenomena, but rather as *one process that could be accomplished through a variety of methods and means*. This position, based on a functional understanding of national/group structure, whereby the physical and cultural aspects are seen as interdependent and indivisible, appreciates that the destruction of a nation/group could occur when *any* structural element is destroyed. Even if the national group's sovereignty is not recognized by the state, Lemkin thought it had *an inherent right to exist*, just like the sovereign individual – and that such groups provided the essential basis of human culture as a whole. He thus *specifically* designed his concept of 'genocide' to protect that life (Powell 2007: 534).

In other words, Lemkin defined genocide in terms of the violation of a nation's right to its *collective existence* – and so genocide in this sense is quite simply the destruction of a nation. Such destruction can be achieved through the 'mass killings of all members of a nation'; *or* through 'a coordinated plan of different actions aiming at the destruction of essential foundations of the life of national groups'. As we have seen, it is this latter point that is missed or ignored by those genocide scholars who insist on the centrality of mass killing to the concept of genocide.[5] It is a focus on *social death* (as opposed to mass killing) which allows us to distinguish the peculiar evil of genocide from crimes against humanity and mass murder (on this points see Short 2010a and Abed 2006). Genocidal murders are but an extreme means to achieve social death, which *can* be produced without specific 'intent to destroy' – occurring, for instance, through sporadic and uncoordinated action or as a by-product of an incompatible expansionist economic system (see Wolfe 2006). They might even result from attempts to do good: to enlighten, to modernize, to evangelize (Powell 2007: 538).

Up until the end of the frontier era in the late nineteenth century, genocidal processes in North America were largely geared towards, and derived from, expansionist policies opening up Indian land for a seemingly limitless influx of settlers. In the post-frontier period, settlement has unquestionably continued to be a pressing factor – however, following the Industrial Revolution, the Euro-North American genocidal logic became increasingly focused on the elimination of Indian peoples in order to gain access to their territory for the purpose of *resource extraction.*

This compulsion intensified dramatically during the 'Cold War' era,[6] spurred on by an escalating 'need' for both energy resources and nuclear weapons production[7] in the face of mounting fears (fabricated or otherwise) regarding aggression/subterfuge emanating from the 'Communist Bloc'. Given that it would be impossible to sustain 'popular enthusiasm' for this military/technological build-up if mainstream North American society were exposed to the brunt of the carcinogenic and mutogenic contamination resulting from such extraction – 'thereby suffering the endemic health consequences' (Churchill 1997: 304) – and given that the majority of the required energy resources were to be found on Indian land anyway, the literal sacrifice of Native North American peoples was yet again 'deemed necessary, useful, or at least acceptable' (ibid.: 324) in the interests of furthering Euro-North American expansionist/economic endeavours.[8]

Canada and the United States entered this energy race with one of the world's largest pools of oil and natural gas, and the exploitation of these valuable and versatile commodities has long contributed to their economic and political power, as well as to the profitability of large transnational energy corporations (TNECs) like BP and Exxon

(Klare 2010). In the process, however, most of North America's easily accessible onshore oil and gas reservoirs have been all but exhausted. And so to guarantee a continuous supply of oil and gas, and the continued profitability of the large TNECs, successive governments have promoted the exploitation of extreme energy options seemingly without a care for the resulting dangers (ibid.). In recent years, the demand for plentiful and 'secure' energy resources has become greater than ever with the governments of the USA *and* Canada engaged in their 'war on terror'[9] – resulting in 'the single largest energy policy shift in North America since ... production peaked in 1971'[10] As Macdonald Stainsby argues (2007: 89), having failed to pacify Iraq and having engendered new regional opposition in Africa, South America and the Middle East, the US empire has driven oil prices up to new heights – a trend which will continue into the future. Though peak oil has profound implications for the US dollar and the militarized global economy, these prices have, in the short term, been masterfully recast as US imperialism's latest and greatest asset: *the creation of massive new oil 'reserves' in a politically friendly region which can feed the US domestic oil market.* Namely, the tar sands in Northern Alberta, Canada,[11] where, once again, the desired energy resource lies almost entirely within the traditional territories of Native North Americans.

In the next section the history of the area is explained to achieve a better understanding of how we have arrived at a situation whereby a liberal democratic settler society engages in extreme energy resource extraction and exploitation, on lands which were once controlled and sustainably 'exploited' by the indigenous peoples who currently describe their modern-day lived experience as tantamount to a 'slow industrial genocide'.

## The tar sands and the Indians of Treaty 8: 'taking without grabbing'

The end of the Seven Years War and the signing of the Treaty of Paris in 1763 resulted in the British acquiring most of the French-claimed territory in North America. In the same year there followed the Royal Proclamation, which organized Great Britain's new North American empire and sought to soothe relations between the British Crown and the Indians through strict regulation of trade, settlement and land acquisition on the western frontier. The Proclamation also established a frontier between the colonies and 'Indian Country' and determined that only the Crown could acquire further territory, and only then with the *full consent* of the affected populations; and further stated that any 'lands whatever, which, not having been ceded to, or purchased by Us, are reserved to them' (Samson 2003). While many colonists at the time dismissed the Proclamation – in the manner of George Washington – as little more than 'a temporary expedient to quiet the minds of the Indians', it became the theoretical cornerstone for subsequent 'Indian policy' and the treaty was its instrument in both Canada and the United States (ibid.: 42).

Underpinning the Proclamation of 1763 was the colonial assertion of Crown sovereignty over all Indian lands. Within such a framework the rights of indigenous peoples existed only on sufferance from the Crown. Even so, the fact of prior aboriginal occupation was eventually deemed to result in an underlying 'aboriginal title' – a so-called 'burden on the Crown'.[12] During the nineteenth century this burden was supposedly discharged by the signing of a succession of numbered treaties, which were 'negotiated' between Treaty Commissioners – appointed by the Dominion of Canada – and a variety of designated aboriginal 'bands' created by the Euro-North American colonizers.[13] In essence, the treaties involved the natives extinguishing their 'underlying title' to their land, usually in return for a variety of economic and material benefits such as cash payments, hunting and fishing equipment, ammunition and the like. Treaties were most often deemed necessary when settlement had begun, or was about to begin, and when there was a desire to open up the land for development. As the people affected by the issues examined in this chapter predominantly fall within the boundaries of the Treaty 8 region, we will now briefly examine the construction and content of that particular treaty.

In 1899, when Treaty 8 was signed, the Cree and Anthapaskans (or Dene) peoples – including Beavers, Chipewyans, Dogribs, Slaveys and Yellowknives – were the two major language groups in the region. The lives of these groups in the north – with its harsh climate and cyclical fluctuations of animal and plant life – differed dramatically from the Plains Indians in the more hospitable south (Fisher 1973). The fur trade apart, the Indians of the north led a subsistence lifestyle based on hunting, fishing and gathering with regional variations depending on available resources; the Chipewyans relied principally on caribou and fish and the Slavey on moose, but both groups gathered birds' eggs and berries and hunted small game (Daniel 1999: 49). Each grouping had its own territory but the boundaries were flexible and there was significant sharing of resources between them, as well as with non-Indians – so long as the latter behaved respectfully and did not endanger the Native peoples' way of life (ibid.).

A fur trade, principally between the Indians and British and French traders, allowed the Indians to develop their material culture while retaining substantial control over the terms and relations of the exchanges, and their access to natural resources. The levels of dependence on such economic relations varied between local indigenous groups, but at this stage none of them had lost the ability to subsist on their natural resources alone, which meant there was only a limited incentive to trade. Thus, the material basis for their traditional cultures remained largely intact despite the availability of economic development and outside cultural influences – for in the early stages of trade between indigenous and non-indigenous people, the social and cultural relations were essentially characterized by an interdependence based on equality and reciprocity rather than domination (ibid.: 53). While the fur trade gave the Indians an understanding of European concepts of the right to control, buy and sell animals, prior to the treaty they had no experience of land as a commodity.

From 1870 until the treaty was eventually signed in 1899 the Canadian government received advice, from missionaries, traders, geologists and geographers, on the potential suitability of the proposed Treaty 8 area for settlement, resource extraction and economic development, and on the condition of the Indian population (ibid.: 55). At various points in this period, reports of significant Indian hardship and pleas for aid were received by the government, but it invariably declined to offer assistance to Indian peoples with whom it had not signed a treaty. In lean years, such pleas sometimes came from the Indian 'bands' themselves, but in 1897 the Indian Commissioner of the Northwest Territories reported that appeals for assistance from *non-treaty* areas were infrequent – as the Indians were still 'in an independent condition'.[14]

Seemingly more important to the government than reports of Indian hardships were the reports from field personnel of the Department of the Interior and the Geological Survey Department, which indicated that parts of these territories might be richer in mineral resources than previously thought (Daniel 1999: 58). As Daniel writes:

> As early as 1793, the explorer Sir Alexander Mackenzie had mentioned that tar and oil could be found oozing from the banks of the Athabasca. Since that time, few explorers of the area failed to mention the tar sands or to speculate on its future potential ... In 1875–76 A.R.C. Selwyn and Professor Macoun of the Geological Survey of Canada reported that petroleum existed in the Athabasca region in almost inexhaustible supplies ... and in 1890 and 1891 R.G. McConnell 'estimated that there were 4,700 million tons of tar in the region, as well as natural gas, bitumen, oil and pitch'. (Ibid.)

Such reports of plentiful northern mineral resources convinced the government of the need for a treaty to be agreed with the Indians of the region in order to extinguish their aforementioned 'aboriginal title'. Furthermore, advances in transportation were opening up the territory to frontiersmen, a process which accelerated sharply in 1896 when gold was discovered in the Klondike region of north-western Canada. The resultant invasion of miners on a massive scale produced many conflicts with local Indian populations, as their acceptance of strangers was stretched to the limit and their way of life seriously endangered.

The relatively slow pace of settlement and resource exploration, combined with the prairie treaties ultimately costing more than the government envisaged, meant that there was no rush to enter treaty negotiations in the north. Furthermore, reports from missionaries and Mounted Police suggested that the Indians were not well disposed to the idea of a treaty as they feared the loss of the ability to hunt, fish and trap (Fumoleau 2004: 65–6). However, the reports of huge mineral wealth, and the relatively unregulated expansion of prospecting and settler mining, pressurized the government to 'treat with the natives'. A report for the government by former North West Mounted Police officer James Walker, in 1897 made the point: 'They [Indians] will be more easily dealt with now than they would be when their country is overrun with prospectors and valuable mines discovered' (ibid.: 65).

Finally, on 27 June 1898, Cabinet granted approval for treaty negotiations to commence. The expense of the preceding numbered treaties was ultimately not considered a pressing concern since the government anticipated that Treaty 8 would be significantly cheaper; a 'slimmed down' treaty based on the prior treaties but taking account of the particular conditions of the north. The Indians, the government thought, would still be able to subsist adequately on the unoccupied lands of the north such that a governmental welfare safety net would not be needed as it was in the prairie regions. Treaty 8 would also give less money to the Indians by way of compensation since they were not required to give up most of their land – unlike in the prairie treaties.

The Treaty 8 Commission opened negotiations with the Indians at Lesser Slave Lake on 20 June 1899. The records of the negotiations are incomplete and partial – largely deriving from the federal government side. However, there is some record in Indian oral history and testimony that offers an alternative view which is vital to understanding the *spirit* of the negotiations. In order to gain the extinguishment of aboriginal title they wanted, the primary task of the government negotiators was to reassure the Indians that their way of life would remain intact, that they would not be confined to reserves and that they would be protected from the settlers. Commissioner Laird gave the opening speech, which set the tone for the proceedings, combining harsh realities with contradictory promises:

> As white people are coming in to your country, we thought it well to tell you what is required of you. The Queen wants all white, half-breeds and Indians to be at peace with one another, and to shake hands when they meet. ... We understand stories have been told you, that if you made a treaty with us you would become servants and slaves; but we wish you to understand that such is not the case, but that you will be just as free after signing the a treaty as you are now ... One thing Indians must understand, that if they do not make a treaty they must obey the laws of the land – that will be just the same whether you make a treaty or not: the laws must be obeyed. (Daniel 1999: 75)

Despite the last sentence above (which would apply to government-imposed hunting and fishing controls) Laird went on to say that

'Indians who take treaty will be just as free to hunt and fish all over as they now are' (ibid.: 76). Bishop Breynat conveyed the corollary to the Indian desire to continue hunting and fishing: 'the Crees and Chipewyans refused to be treated like Prairie Indians, and to be parked on reserves ... It was essential to them to retain complete freedom to move around' (Fumoleau 2004: 78). The report of the commissioners refers to these Indian concerns and the difficulties they had in overcoming them:

> Our chief difficulty was the apprehension that the hunting and fishing privileges were to be curtailed. The provision in the treaty under which ammunition and twine is to be furnished went far in the direction of quieting the fears of the Indians, for they admitted that it would be unreasonable to furnish the means of hunting and fishing if laws were to be enacted which would make hunting and fishing so restricted as to render it impossible to make a livelihood by such pursuits ... they would be as free to hunt and fish after the treaty as they would be if they never entered into it ... the Indians were generally adverse to being placed on reserves. It would have been impossible to make a treaty if we had not assured them that there was no intention of confining them to reserves. We had to very clearly explain to them that the provision for reserves and allotments of land were made for their protection and to secure to them in perpetuity a fair portion of the land ceded, in the event of settlement advancing.[15]

And yet, despite such assurances, in the same meetings Commissioner Ross talked about the inevitability of the country being 'opened up' for development by the white man (Daniel 1999: 77). Ross was also aware that Parliament was intending to extend, in duration and scope, an existing prohibition on killing buffalo (which was causing real concern among the Indians) but chose not to discuss this during the negotiations since 'our mission would likely have been a failure if we had opened up the question'.[16]

Such manipulative contradictions and intentional avoidance certainly secured Indian agreement, but the Indians took the assurances at face value as guarantees of freedom to hunt, fish and trap throughout the area and as guaranteeing primary rights over fish and wildlife.[17] Thus, today Indian elders of the Fort Chipewyan area still maintain that the treaty guaranteed their rights to hunt, fish and trap without restriction (Fumoleau 2004: 78). That this understanding endures is unsurprising since at the time it was repeatedly bolstered by the interventions of several missionaries who accompanied the Commissioners – allegedly to act as translators and intermediaries but behaving more like salesmen. For example, Father Lacombe (speaking in Cree) stated: 'Your forest and river life will not be changed by the Treaty, and you will have your annuities, as well, year by year, as long as the sun shines and the earth remains. Therefore I finish my speaking by saying, Accept.' The missionaries undoubtedly played a vital role in convincing the Indians that the treaty was in their own interests (Daniel 1999: 84). Some missionaries, such as Constant Falher – who was present at the negotiations – subsequently reflected on this role. In a letter to Bishop Breynat he wrote: 'if Bishop Grouard had not advised the chiefs to sign the treaty, telling them that there was nothing which was not to their advantage; the treaty would still be waiting to be signed today' (Fumoleau 2004: 67).

Ultimately, for a specified list of gifts and reserved land, the 'bands' that were signatories to Treaty 8 at Lesser Slave Lake in 1899 had to 'CEDE, RELEASE, SURRENDER AND YIELD UP to the Government of the Dominion of Canada, for Her Majesty the Queen and Her successors for ever, all their rights, titles and privileges whatsoever, to the lands included within the following limits ...' (ibid.: 71, capitalization in original). 'Reserves' were included for the Cree, Beaver and Chipewyan Indians but the treaty simultaneously demanded that 'such portions of the reserves and lands ... as may at any time be required for public works, buildings, railways, or roads of whatsoever nature may be *appropriated* by Her Majesty's Government of the Dominion of Canada ...' subject to 'due compensation'.[18]

The great difficulty with seeing such a treaty as a legitimate surrender of rights, of course, derives from the fact that native peoples did not know what the treaties signified to the whites, especially seeing as so many had no concept of private, let alone state, property, so could only guess at what the agreement meant (Samson 2003: 43). As Brody writes: '[T]here is a world of difference between the terms of [Treaty 8] and the understanding the Indian signatories had of it ... Indians did not understand Treaty 8 to be a surrender of rights' (Brody 2002: 68). Moreover, as Fumoleau writes:

> Most treaties and land surrenders were signed after the Indians had lost control of their territory. Their only choice was to lose their land with a treaty, or to lose it without one. Usually they were guaranteed official use of a 'reserve', which was held in Trust by the Crown. This was a measure to protect the Indians from further encroachments, and to offer them security against the aggressiveness of their white neighbours. Other treaty gifts: free education, free medical care, cash annuities, groceries etc., also helped to win the Indian people's good will. Protecting the Indian was not the main reason for treaties, however. Overriding all other considerations was the land: the Indians owned it and the white people wanted it. Even when the Indians posed no threat, treaties were still signed, as a moral or ethical gesture: a gentleman's way to take without grabbing. (Fumoleau 2004: 18)

Today Canada plays a colonial trick, arguing that via treaties the British Crown extinguished 'aboriginal title', and when it is challenged over its failure to honour the range of obligations specified in the treaties it argues that it was the British Crown and not Canada that negotiated the agreements (Samson 2003: 44). This colonial trick, combined with the treaty extinguishment provisions and the ability to encroach upon reserved land, paved the way for modern industrial development on Treaty 8 Indian lands.

### What exactly are the 'tar sands'?

Exploitation of Canada's tar sands is widely considered to be the most destructive industrial project on earth by environmental and human rights groups and indigenous activists alike.[19] The expression 'tar sands' is a colloquial term used to describe sands that are perhaps more accurately described as bituminous sands. They constitute a naturally occurring mixture of sand, clay, water and bitumen – an exceptionally viscous and dense form of petroleum – which has, since the late nineteenth and early twentieth centuries, been referred to as 'tar' owing to its similar viscosity, odour and colour. However, naturally occurring bitumen is chemically more similar to asphalt than to tar, and the term *oil sands* is now more commonly used by industry and in the producing areas than *tar sands* since synthetic oil is what is manufactured from the bitumen. Even so, the term *oil sands* fails to convey the constituent complexity of the sands, and moreover serves to sanitize the environmentally destructive industrial processes intrinsic to this particular form of oil production. Indeed, the environmental costs (externalities) of this form of unconventional oil production are enormous.

Tar-sands-derived oil must be extracted by strip mining or the oil made to flow into wells by 'in situ' techniques, which reduce the viscosity by injecting steam, solvents and/or hot air into the sands. These processes use much more water than conventional oil extraction – three barrels of water are used to process one barrel of oil[20] – and produce huge 'tailings ponds' ('tailings lakes' would be more accurate) into which over 480 million gallons of contaminated toxic waste water are dumped daily. Some of these tailings ponds are so toxic that the energy companies employ people to scoop dead birds off the surface; and most are unlined.[21] Taken together, these waste lakes 'cover more than 50 square kilometres (12,000 acres) and are so extensive that they can be seen from space'.[22] In addition, producing liquid fuels from such sands requires huge amounts of energy for steam injection and refining processes, which its seems generate considerably higher levels of greenhouse gases per barrel of final product than the production of conventional oil.[23] However, owing to a lack of impartial data and an over-reliance on industry figures there is no scientific agreement on exact figures for the GHG emissions comparisons, but there is broad agreement in all studies that tar sands GHG emissions are certainly higher than those of conventional oil. Given the industry's desire to present tar sands production as hardly worse than conventional oil production it is prudent to look to non-industry sources for such data; for example, the United States National Energy Technology Laboratory concluded in 2009 that 'unconventional crude oil sources including Canadian oil sands ... require energy intensive extraction processes and pre-processing that result in GHG emissions several times greater than that for extraction of conventional crude oil'.[24]

Furthermore, most statistics on the carbon intensity of bitumen mining don't include the destruction of the boreal forest. Yet as Andrew Nikiforuk (2010: 132) writes: 'the region's hardworking trees and peat bogs now sequester or bank twice as much carbon as a tropical forest. Both open-pit mining and steam assisted gravity drainage (SAGD) projects subvert that function by cutting down trees and draining peat bogs ... excavating one of Canada's best carbon sinks and weather stabilizers to produce a product with three times the carbon footprint of conventional oil may be an example of global freak economics.' These observations bring us to the larger climate change point that respected climate scientists make when discussing such extreme energy 'solutions'; we should be using what little easily available conventional reserves we have left to invest in renewables, not carbon-intensive unsustainable extreme energy projects like the tar sands. As NASA climate scientist James Hansen puts it:

> exploitation of tar sands would make it implausible to stabilize climate and avoid disastrous global climate impacts. The tar sands are estimated to contain at least 400 GtC (equivalent to about 200 ppm $CO_2$). Easily available reserves of conventional oil and gas are enough to take atmospheric $CO_2$ well above 400 ppm ... if the tar sands are thrown into the mix it is essentially game over.[25]

Thus, if one is not seeking to minimize the impact of these externalities the term 'tar sands' is preferable: it suggests the sand has a more complex constitution and that usable oil must be *extracted* from the sticky, heavy, viscous base material (bitumen) through industrial processes which have huge environmental and human costs. It is to these costs, and the nature of their lethal ramifications on the indigenous peoples of North America, that this chapter now turns.

### Ecologically induced genocide

It is worth noting that the tar sands 'reserve' is not exactly *new*. Canada initiated oil production in the tar sands in 1967 – 'after decades of research and development that began in the early 1900s'[26] – with Suncor Energy Inc. generating roughly 12,000 barrels per day. Even so, the tar sands were not regarded as a significant player in North America's bid to prolong the life of its petroleum-based economy until 2003 – around the time of the American invasion of Iraq.

Before this period the extremely difficult extraction and production processes involved in developing tar sands were considered too expensive to be economically viable, but with oil prices heading towards $150 per barrel, the tar sands not only became viable but the basis for a sudden American reliance on North American petroleum as a source of fuel.[27] We can therefore see how, as during the Cold War, the rhetoric of 'national security' is being used in this situation 'as a pretext to increase energy resource extraction' (Smith 2005: 180) in North America, and, in turn, as a justification to once again 'sacrifice' the lives and lands of Native peoples to the 'needs' of the dominant Euro-North American capitalist society; making it clear that, then as now, 'consolidating [the North American] empire abroad is predicated on consolidating the [North American] empire *within* [North American] borders'.[28] Furthermore, it illustrates how what Wolfe has called 'the logic of elimination' (Wolfe 2006: 388) that informed frontier massacres, and the formulation of the assimilationist agenda in the mid to late nineteenth century, have, over the last hundred years or so, transmuted into perhaps history's *subtlest* (Churchill 1997: 319) form of physical, biological, and cultural extermination yet: 'invasive industrial interventions' (LaDuke 1999: 2).

As previously stated, many, if not most, indigenous peoples indefatigably avow that their relationship with their traditional land bases is vital to their physical and cultural survival as discrete, autonomous groups – that it is 'constitutive of the Indian cultural identity and designative of the boundaries of the Indian cultural universe'[29] – and that, consequently, they cannot be forcibly alienated from their land *without* genocide being committed.[30] Large-scale resource extraction processes alienate Native peoples from their land not only by driving them off it in order to make room for industrial activities, but also by way of the concomitant toxic by-products that put water supplies, land cover and wildlife at serious risk; thereby gravely jeopardizing the lives, cultures and health of indigenous communities who depend on these resources for their continued existence. As such, these processes both embody the driving *purpose behind* the North American genocide (i.e. the appropriation and pilfering of Indian land), and also in and of themselves *beget* and *require* further *acts* of genocide.

This has been corroborated by testimony from indigenous peoples around the world which indicates that they perceive themselves as having been 'pushed to the edge of a cliff' by the environmental problems caused by industrialism (Zinn 1995: 1). As Davis and

Zannis note, 'after 1945 traditional colonial terror was transformed into a "genocide machine" as the nature of capitalist domination became less overtly racist and more attuned to American corporate imperatives' (Davis and Zannis 1973). The ongoing tar sands mining 'project' in northern Alberta is, without a doubt, the most disastrous instance of this specifically contemporary (Churchill 1997: 9) genocidal phenomenon in North America to date, producing a 'virtual catalogue of environmental destruction' (Zinn 1995: 3) and an attendant litany of social ills.[31]

This process creates chronic pollution of the lower Athabasca river and adjacent western Lake Athabasca emanating 'from licensed discharges; from above-ground and below-ground pipeline leaks and breaks; and from tailings pond leaks' (Timoney 2007: 54). These leaks and breaks date back to the initial stages of production in 1967, and finding information to document them is an arduous task (ibid.: 50). One of the largest early spills occurred in February 1982 (ibid.: 52), with oil and contaminant discharged into the Athabasca river from tar sands company Suncor's 'wastewater pond'[32] as a result of a series of upgrader refinery explosions and a major fire. Federal contaminant expert Otto Langer stated at the time, 'a 20-tonne spill could be "extremely catastrophic" to the river system'. In this case a minimum of 42 tonnes were spilled (ibid.: 53). The present situation is difficult to determine accurately owing to 'the veil that has been drawn down over provincial river monitoring activities' (ibid.: 53). However, an indication of the true gravity of the situation can be found in an admission from Suncor in 1997, in which they stated that their Tar Island Pond 'leaks approximately 1,600 cubic metres of toxic fluid into the Athabasca River every day'.[33] 'That volume is 1,600 tonnes, roughly 38 times the size of the big spill in 1982 described above. If that statement is even remotely accurate, the Athabasca River is in trouble' (ibid.: 53).

This poisoning of the watershed and land base is matched only by their *depletion*, for simply making room for tar sands mining activities involves the draining of rivers, lakes and wetlands to subsidize the 'enormous quantities of water needed to force the bitumen from the ground;[34] the diversion of rivers; and stripping of all trees and vegetation from the forest'.[35] Over the last forty years of production, tar sands mining has changed northern Alberta 'from a pristine environment rich in cultural and biological diversity to a landscape resembling a war zone marked with 200-foot-deep pits and thousands of acres of destroyed boreal forests' (Thomas-Muller 2007: 13) – and now that Canada is the USA's largest source of 'foreign' oil',[36] and production has correspondingly intensified, this destruction is accelerating at a startling rate.

Indigenous peoples living close to and in the midst of tar sand deposits[37] have been expressing concern over the lethal impacts that these industrial events have had on their communities for years, with elders citing caustic changes to river water quality, meat quality and to the availability of wild fish and game.[38] Concern is growing recently as health professionals and community members witness more and more friends and family fall ill with a variety of serious illnesses, and local fish populations are inflicted with ever more severe deformities.[39]

In 2006, local doctor John O'Connor was the first medical professional to publicly call attention to these issues. In his own downstream community of Fort Chipewyan, he cited disturbingly disproportionate levels of deadly diseases such as leukaemia, lymphoma, lupus, colon cancer and Graves' disease. He also noted five cases of an extremely rare cancer of the bile duct – cholangiocarcinoma – occurring in the past five years within Fort Chip's population of 1,200; normally, only one in 100,000 people contract it.[40] He concluded that these abnormally elevated levels of disease were the direct consequence of steadily rising carcinogens in the sediments and waterways emanating from industrial activities associated with tar sands mining.

After Dr O'Connor made his findings public the government of Canada not only ignored and dismissed his report,[41] but went on to attack his credibility – even going so far as to have a formal complaint brought against him in tandem with the Alberta College of Physicians and Surgeons (ACPS) for 'causing undue alarm'.[42] However, these charges were subsequently dismissed in 2009 when, after years of lobbying by health officials and community members in Fort Chipewyan,[43] Alberta Health Services finally reviewed cancer rates in Fort Chipewyan with a new study. This confirmed many of O'Connor's original medical findings, showing that the number of cancer cases observed in Fort Chipewyan was in fact 'higher than expected for all cancers combined and for specific types of cancer, such as biliary tract cancer and cancers in the blood and lymphatic system'.[44]

Even so, the study declined to make any pronouncements as to the cause,[45] claiming that 'an increase in observed cancers over expected rates could be due to chance, to increased detection, or to increased risk (lifestyle, environmental or occupational) in the community'. They went on to again assure Fort Chipewyan residents that 'there is no cause for alarm', and therefore no need for immediate action, yet indicated that 'continued monitoring and analysis are warranted'.[46] While community members felt vindicated by the confirmation of elevated cancer rates, they still roundly rejected the report on the basis of its questionable research methods, its failure to designate a cause, and 'because they felt researchers didn't spend enough time talking to people who live in Fort Chipewyan'.[47]

There have been a number of reports published since Dr O'Connor's 2006 findings, however, which corroborate not only his original medical conclusions, but his conviction 'that the governments of Alberta and Canada have been deliberately ignoring evidence of toxic contamination on downstream indigenous communities' as a result of tar sands mining,[48] such that even if we were to invoke the narrow legal definition of genocide these governments would have a case to answer. In 2007, Kevin Timoney, on behalf of the Nunee Health Board Society, released a study on water and sediment quality as it pertains to wildlife contaminants, the ecosystem and public health in Fort Chipewyan (Timoney 2007). Along with providing further hard scientific evidence supporting the claims of the residents of Fort Chipewyan, it heavily criticized previous reports undertaken by the Alberta government (ibid.: n87), emphasizing their dubious research methods and the government's vested interests in the tar sands industry. Timoney (ibid.: 71–2) also called to account the screening procedures of the Regional Aquatics Monitoring Program (RAMP), arguing that they cannot possibly be impartial when much of the information gathered is then classified as 'private data', and when RAMP has as its funding source a steering committee which is dominated by the oil industry and the Albertan government – both of which have nothing to gain and everything to lose should tar sands mining be definitively connected to serious public health risks. 'The result is the appearance of monitoring and management of environmental concerns in the public interest. The reality is a lack of timely publicly available information and the perpetuation of business as usual' (ibid.: 72).

Timoney concluded that 'based on the contaminant spill documentation, data, and observations of elders' it is reasonable to deduce that inadvertent and intentional pollution events associated with the explosive growth of the tar sands industry in north-eastern Alberta 'have and will continue to impact the aquatic health of the lower Athabasca River and adjacent Lake Athabasca' (ibid.: 56, 73) – posing grave risks to 'environmental and public health that demand immediate attention independent of provincial and industrial oversight' (ibid.: 73). The most authoritative water quality research to date was conducted by Kelly et al. and published in the *Proceedings of the National Academy of Sciences (PNAS)* in 2010, entitled 'Oil sands development contributes elements toxic at low concentrations to the Athabasca River and its tributaries' (Kelly et al. 2010). The study argues that tar sands mining is a greater source of air, land and water pollution in the Athabasca region than industry and government sources would have us believe. As one of the authors, David Schindler, summarizes: 'We have shown the assumption of industry and government, that all pollution of the oil sands comes from natural sources, is false ... Some of the chemicals we document are known carcinogens. The concentrations as a result of industry are high enough to harm fish. So there is good reason to be concerned.'[49]

The report found that water pollution levels were ten to fifty times higher than normal downstream of tar sands mining, and that a major oil spill's worth of bitumen is deposited on the land *each year*.[50] The report also criticized the government of Alberta and RAMP's previous findings and the methods used to gather them.[51] Kelly et al. concluded: 'contrary to claims made by industry and government in the popular press, the oil sands industry substantially increases loadings of toxic ['priority pollutants'] to the [Athabasca river] and its tributaries via air and water pathways' (Kelly et al. 2010: 5).

The report caused significant 'controversy' and resulted in the inevitable denialist questioning of 'methodology'. For example, a report by the Royal Society of Canada (RSC) on the 'Environmental and health impacts' of the tar sands[52] included an implicit criticism of Kelly et al.'s methodology. Even so, a recently convened government of Alberta panel, the Water Monitoring Data Review Committee,[53] nevertheless concluded that:

Taking into consideration all data and critiques, we generally agree with the conclusion of Kelly et al. that PACs (polycyclic aromatic compounds) and trace metals are *being introduced into the environment by oil sands operations* ... The Royal Society of Canada (2010) noted that Kelly et al. (2009) sampled at only one location in the river at each site (although at two depths). Kelly et al. have subsequently elaborated upon details of the sample collection protocols in written comments submitted to this Committee (E. Kelly, pers. comm. 2011). *There is nothing to suggest that the methods they used in sample collection were not scientifically rigorous.*

It should also be noted that the Royal Society team did not conduct their own original scientific research and in the usual Western 'scientific' fashion, as Chief Allan Adam of the Athabasca Chipewyan First Nation points out, they completely ignored indigenous peoples' experiences and traditional knowledge of the environment.[54]

Thus, the Kelly et al. findings could yet prove to be a key instrument in the struggle to bring about decisive action on tar sands mining. Indeed, taken together with the rest of the studies published in recent years, industry or government claims that the current level of rising carcinogens has been produced 'naturally' have been refuted.[55] Furthermore, the media attention given to these reports has increased pressure on the Alberta government such that they recently committed to undertake another investigation into the cancer rates in Fort Chipewyan.[56]

Bearing all the evidence in mind, especially the views of indigenous peoples from the affected communities, it could be argued that a kind of reckless 'biological warfare' is being conducted. It certainly would not be the first time in North American history that indigenous people were knowingly or even *intentionally* exposed to disease. The spread of disease has been employed as part of the Euro-American/ Euro-Canadian campaign to bring about the disappearance of Native North America at least since 1763, 'when Lord Jeffery Amherst ordered small-pox infected blankets to be distributed to the Ottawas as a means of "extirpat[ing] this execrable race"'.[57] As Andrea Smith (2005: 69) asserted, Native peoples 'will continue to be seen as expendable and inherently violable as long as they continue to stand in the way of the theft of Native lands'. Although strategy has varied over the centuries, adapting 'to the times and regions in which it played out', the North American 'logic of elimination' – namely to eliminate 'all indigenous populations that would not leave their lands and resources' and 'abolish their own cultures and languages' (Annett 2005: 44) – has never wavered. What's more, the situation is only set to worsen further, as the USA is soon hoping to 'extract up to 25 percent of their daily oil needs from tar sands-based operations in the region' (Stainsby 2007: 89); a plan that will involve the decimation of 'an area the size of Florida'[58] in north-eastern Alberta, and the construction and expansion of colossal pipelines that will extend across unceded indigenous territory in B.C. and the North West Territories, before heading south and through Indian Country in the USA (ibid.: 89) – consequently impacting indigenous communities not only in Canada, but *across the continent*.

While the USA has been receiving oil from northern Alberta tar sands operations via its pipeline infrastructure at varying levels for decades now, up until recently most of it by far was transported in the form of synthetic crude oil, a substance similar to conventional crude oil produced by putting the thick, raw bitumen through an 'upgrading' process. Historically, this process has taken place in refineries in Canada that have developed the capacity to handle exceptionally heavy crudes.[59] However, with Canadian processing operations running at full capacity, oil companies have started transporting more of the raw tar sands to US refineries that can either already take the heavier oil or which need upgrading.[60] This heavier tar-sands-derived crude, referred to as 'DilBit' (diluted bitumen), is different from conventional oil in important ways. It is 'a highly corrosive, acidic, and potentially unstable blend of thick raw bitumen and volatile natural gas liquid condensate',[61] characteristics which can lead to major weakening of pipelines, giving rise to significantly higher risks while transporting it.

A clear indication of the exceptionally caustic nature of DilBit is the fact that, despite its relatively recent construction,[62] between 2002 and 2010 Alberta's pipeline network had a rate of spills due to internal corrosion *sixteen times higher* than that in the USA.[63] This disparity is almost certainly the result of the considerably higher quantity of DilBit being funnelled through Alberta pipelines – for, as mentioned above, DilBit has not been common in the USA until recently.[64] Nonetheless, US pipelines are carrying increasing amounts of this corrosive raw form of tar sands oil without any proper review or change of pipeline/spill response safety standards which would take into account the different traits and properties of DilBit, as compared with conventional oil. On the contrary, in October 2009 the US Pipeline and Hazardous Materials Safety Administration – the agency charged with oversight of the nation's 2.1 million miles of pipeline – actually *loosened* safety regulations pertaining to pipe strength.[65] This in spite of the fact that, over the last ten years, DilBit exports to the United States have increased almost fivefold, to 550,000 barrels per day (bpd) in 2010, more than half of the approximately 900,000 bpd of tar sands oil currently flowing into the United States, and by 2019 Canadian tar sands producers plan to triple this amount.[66]

In addition to the caustic effect on internal pipeline infrastructure, this volatile and gummy substance also decreases the ability of engineers to detect leaks,[67] and makes any clean-up excruciatingly difficult – the consequences have *already* been catastrophic, with perhaps the worst example to date in the USA being the 800,000-gallon spill caused by a ruptured Enbridge pipeline carrying DilBit in south-western Michigan on 25 July 2010, which devastated local communities and the Kalamazoo river. The federal government called it the 'worst oil spill in Midwestern history'.[68] This spill was followed on 1 July 2011 by a spill of 42,000 gallons of oil into the Yellowstone river in Montana caused by a ruptured Exxon pipeline carrying DilBit.[69] These disasters have brought heightened media attention to the issue of tar sands oil mining generally and to the issue of its transport throughout the USA in unsafe pipelines specifically. In recent months, attention has turned to these issues as a result of opposition to and protests surrounding the extension of the 'Keystone XL pipeline'. A potentially enormous new line is slated to run from Hardisty, Alberta, through the south-west corner of Saskatchewan and across the US border, thence diagonally across Montana, South Dakota and Nebraska, to the Steele City to Cushing segment.[70] John Stansbury, a University of Nebraska water resources engineer who conducted an independent assessment, argues that a pipeline of this nature is likely to average some ninety-one major spills, and since the proposed pipeline will transect at least eleven major river crossings, such spills could contaminate the Ogallala Aquifer, a major Great Plains watershed, the Missouri and Mississippi rivers and the Yellowstone river with such deadly toxins as benzene[71] – and be yet another contributor to the 'slow industrial genocide' being inflicted on many indigenous peoples in these regions.

The perilous position of tar-sands-affected indigenous communities has been greatly facilitated by the governments of the USA and Canada failing to comply with many of their own laws and through the de facto extinguishment of treaty rights, prioritizing mining over local concerns.[72] The text of Treaty 8 suggests that the lands of First Nations would not be compromised by uncontrolled development which threatened First Nations culture and traditional ways of life, and yet the remote community of Fort Chipewyan relied on an 80 per cent subsistence diet until tar sands pollution, boreal forest and ecosystem destruction and loss of habitat made it impossible to sustain.[73] Thus, the tar sands now directly threaten the cultural survival of Fort Chipewyan and other First Nation peoples living within the so-called tar sands 'sacrifice zone'. Many people are simply too afraid to drink the water or harvest plants and animals, while others value their traditional knowledge so much that they are prepared to take the risks.[74] While some First Nations have legally forced the government of Canada to consult with indigenous communities about development projects they have no ability to veto such development of their land. So-called 'consultation' processes invariably mean simply telling a community a project is being proposed which may or may not have impacts on a First Nation and the recognition of its treaty rights. To date there is no legal framework within the Constitution of Canada that recognizes the international principle of Free, Prior and Informed Consent (FPIC) for the right of First Nations to say 'No' to a proposed development, a central tenet of the United Nations Declaration on the Rights of Indigenous Peoples (UNDRIP).

As George Poitras, a member of the Mikisew Cree First Nation in Fort Chipewyan, states:

> There's been a de facto extinguishment of our treaty rights because the government continues to take up land without any consideration or consultation with the First Nations [Petersen 2007] ... [The treaty] obligates the government to consult with us any time there is a potential or adverse impact on our

treaty rights – to hunt, fish, trap and so on. Historically they attempted to colonize us through policies and legislation that are paternal, colonial, imperial and they continue that attitude ... [the government is] simply not dealing with us as priority rights holders of these lands. (Ibid.)

Just as earlier genocidal policies of assimilation disguised themselves as philanthropic instruments of 'progress' and 'material advancement' for Native North Americans, resource extraction initiatives have professed an interest in 'helping' Native communities by way of offering them 'steady employment' and 'economic development'. This is exactly how the Alberta government first 'enticed First Nations council leadership to lease their treaty reserve lands to the tar sands industry' in the 1960s – allowing 'the first tier of tar sands operations ... to come into a region mostly inhabited by Dene, Cree and Métis'.[75] In reality, this mega-project has paid such a meagre fraction of prevailing market royalty rates that no such advancement has been discernible; rather it has brought only more death and ruin. Moreover, the loss of land and the ensuing physical and cultural erosion have led to a loss of hope and growing apathy, with many not speaking out 'because of the perceived inevitability of tar sands mining' (Stainsby 2007: 18). And so, 'the battle over the ongoing mining comes down to the *fundamental right to exist*' (Petersen 2007: 31, emphasis added). As George Poitras of the Mikisew Cree First Nation asserted: 'If we don't have land and we don't have anywhere to carry out our traditional lifestyles, we lose who we are as a people. So, if there's no land, then it's equivalent in our estimation to genocide of a people' (ibid.: 31).

This chapter has discussed the history of treaty-making and highlighted the differing views of the Indians and the settlers. The primary concern for the Indians was the continuation of their traditional way of life, to be able to hunt, fish and roam their territories as they always had done. For the settlers the primary concern was the 'extinguishment' of any underlying Indian rights to land and the opening up of the area to settler populations and industrial exploitation. That the treaties were 'agreed' and signed despite these contradictory objectives is testament to the duplicitous nature of the settler-led 'negotiations'. Empty promises were made by priests and the Commissioners themselves, e.g. Commissioner

Laird: the 'Indians who take treaty will be just as free to hunt and fish all over as they now are' (Daniel 1999: 76). Any rights seemingly conferred by the terms of the treaties were always subject to the Crown's assertion of underlying sovereignty. This is acutely evident in the following passage of Treaty 8:

> And Her Majesty the Queen HEREBY AGREES with the said Indians that they shall have right to pursue their usual vocations of hunting, trapping and fishing throughout the tract surrendered as heretofore described, **subject to** such regulations as may from time to time be made by the Government of the country, acting under the authority of Her Majesty, and saving and excepting such tracts as may be required or taken up from time to time for settlement, mining, lumbering, trading or other purposes.[76]

Thus, in the text of the treaty, rights to continue traditional practices were subordinate to settler property interests such as mining leases and the like. Rights to hunt, trap and fish could operate only around the fringes of such property interests. And with the inevitability of settler colonial expansion the treaties afforded the Indians very little protection indeed. Much as with the diseases both inadvertently and deliberately forced on their communities by settlers, they have been unable to resist development on their traditional lands and have had little or no say in mining projects that nonetheless have an enormous impact on their way of life, and cultural and physical health and well-being.

The tar sands mega-project is undoubtedly the worst offender in this regard. As we have seen, the environmental impact of the tar sands is enormous and the impact on the lives of the indigenous peoples is equally dramatic. As George Poitras writes: 'if Canada and Alberta today ignore and repeatedly, knowingly infringe on our Constitutionally protected Treaty Rights, will our future generations be able to meaningfully exercise their right to hunt, fish and trap? Will our people in 20 years from now be able to enjoy a traditional diet of fish, moose, ducks, geese, caribou?'[77] Tar sands development has entirely changed the Athabasca delta and watershed landscape with massive deforestation of the boreal forests, open-pit mining, depletion of water systems and watersheds, toxic contamination, destruction of habitat and biodiversity, and the severe forcible disruption of the indigenous Dene, Cree and Métis trap-line cultures.[78]

> The river used to be blue. Now it's brown. Nobody can fish or drink from it. The air is bad. This has all happened so fast. (Elsie Fabian, an elder in a Native Indian community along the Athabasca river, quoted in ibid.)

Many people in indigenous communities feel that they are in the final stages of a battle for survival that began in North America in the fifteenth century, and have called their past and present situation, brought about by settler and colonial governments, genocide. Their use of the term is not emotive or imprecise, but rather, as we have argued, is in keeping with Lemkin's concept and highlights the enormity of what the tar sands are doing to the Indians of Treaty 8 and beyond.

Thus, the Alberta government should halt tar sands expansion, clean up and address the root causes of tar-sands-associated pollution and environmental degradation, and ameliorate the effects of the health issues facing indigenous peoples as a result of tar sands operations. National and international financial and banking institutions should immediately withdraw funding from the tar sands expansion and operations.[79] If these steps are not taken, it behoves the international community to intervene and force the hands of both the Canadian and US governments and the financial and banking institutions to take these necessary steps.

Many indigenous peoples have been calling for this kind of action from the international community for some time now – feeling that they will not find remedy or justice from the very institutions that are committing these crimes. To be sure, they 'have been very interested in engaging international law, arguing that as descendants of indigenous nations, they deserve protection under international human rights laws' (Smith 2005: 182). The clearest recent example of this to date being the indigenous participation in and willpower behind the drafting and passing of the UN Declaration on the Rights of Indigenous Peoples, which arguably allows their sovereign rights to take precedence over US or other nation-states' domestic laws (ibid.), so long of course that the 'territorial integrity' (Article 46) of the colonial nation-state is not compromised.

## Conclusion

The chapter began with a discussion of genocide and indigenous peoples' right to exist as distinct peoples. It explored the settler colonial historical and legal context which dispossessed the indigenous peoples of the Treaty 8 region and ultimately facilitated tar sands production and its accompanying environmental and social harms. The case study highlighted the key themes of this book: historic and contemporary dispossession, a continuing colonial and genocidal relationship that continues into the present and which is driven by the resource thirst of global neoliberal capitalism. The Alberta tar sands are close to the worst end of the extreme energy spectrum, along with mountain-top removal, and are indicative of an increasingly desperate oil-soaked global economy that refuses to systematically turn to renewable energy. They are also the poster child of extreme energy, the epitome of scraping the bottom of the barrel, and are so energy intensive to extract that their continued production threatens the very survival of us all. The time for action to halt tar sands expansion is long overdue for the reasons discussed, but also because of the wider issue of anthropogenic climate change – which has been discussed in Chapter 2 and to which we will return in the last chapter. Indeed, if we take the latest climate science,[80] or even the warnings of the notoriously conservative International Energy Agency,[81] seriously then indigenous peoples and the rest of us are fast approaching the 'tipping point' of runaway climate change (quite possibly eventually resulting in the small matter of an 'extinction event'), such that investing further in tar sands production is tantamount to throwing bucketfuls of petrol on a fire.[82]

# 7 | LOOKING TO THE FUTURE: WHERE TO FROM HERE?

From the individual case study chapters the reader will be able to gauge my relative pessimism/optimism about a possible turnaround in the fortunes of those currently experiencing genocidal and ecocidal pressures. In this final section, however, I want to tentatively look to the future more broadly, the future not just for genocide and ecocide studies but also for humanity as a whole. So, I now ask the question: where to from here?

## For the field of genocide studies

> We do not err because truth is difficult to see. It is visible at a glance. We err because this is more comfortable. (Alexander Solzhenitsyn, cited in Jensen 2006: 367)

> In the light of what the science is telling us, the entirety of the 'developed' world's standard operating procedure encompassing economics, technologies, socio-cultural behaviour, not to say fundamental value systems, can no longer be sustained as viable or beneficial for ourselves, let alone for the planet's many millions of other species upon whom we also fundamentally depend. The knock-on effects for all academic disciplines, genocide studies included, are equally stark. Either we rethink some of our first principles, not to say standard modus operandi in the light of anthropogenic climate change, or we literally consign ourselves to the dustbin of history. (Levene and Conversi 2014: 282)

When introducing a groundbreaking special issue of the *International Journal of Human Rights* on Genocide and Climate Change, editor Jürgen Zimmerer pointed out that April 2014 saw the most recent report of the Intergovernmental Panel on Climate Change (IPCC) confirm, once more, the stark reality of anthropogenic climate change and its likely consequences; while at the same time the twentieth anniversary of the beginning of the Rwandan genocide focused global attention on this gruesome act of collective violence and many politicians and activists the world over stated (yet again) their commitment to genocide prevention, thus renewing the call 'Never again' so enthusiastically proclaimed after the Second World War II. Both events seem unconnected, yet:

> Whereas research into the human consequences of climate change at least deals with violence, conflict and resilience, and therefore, one could argue also with genocide, genocide studies is almost completely ignoring climate change as a cause for violence, thus neglecting probably the biggest trigger of genocide in the twenty-first century. This ignorance comes at a huge price for genocide prevention and human security more generally. (Zimmerer 2014: 267)

The special issue aimed at changing this and initiating an interdisciplinary dialogue between scholars working in the areas of climate change and genocide. In Zimmerer's opening contribution, 'Climate change, environmental violence and genocide', he argued that 'anthropogenic climate change is the most fundamental challenge for humankind in the twenty-first century and will drastically alter the living conditions of millions of people, mainly in the global south. Therefore environmental violence, including resource crises such as peak fossil fuel, should be of major concern to genocide studies.' Moreover, since violence is likely to be a major effect of climate change, conflict and peace research and security studies are engaged with climate change research and so what is 'strangely amiss, despite the fact that many see in climate change the scourge of the twentieth century, and one would assume also of the twenty-first century, is the integration of genocide studies in the climate change debate' (ibid.: 267).

Zimmerer contends that this state of affairs is due to genocide scholarship's lopsided emphasis on ideology on the one hand and on legal prosecution on the other hand, leading to a much too narrow understanding of the driving forces of genocide. In an article in the same special issue, Martin Crook and I took a similar position: with the impending threat of runaway climate change in the twenty-first century, the advent of the Anthropocene (Zalasiewicz 2008) – 'the climate change equivalent to Raphael Lemkin's big idea – in this case, with the responsible neologists, earth scientists, Paul Crutzen and Eugene F. Stoermer – [whereby] humanity writ-large now constitutes a geological actor on the planetary stage with the ability to change the most basic physical processes of the earth' (Levene and Conversi 2014: 282), and the attendant rapid extinction of species, destruction of habitats, ecological collapse and the self-evident dependency of the human race on our biosphere, ecocide (both 'natural' and 'man-made') will likely become a primary driver of genocide (see Crook and Short 2014). It is therefore incumbent upon genocide scholars to attempt a paradigm shift in the greatest traditions of science (Kuhn 2012) and enable a synthesis of a range of academic perspectives that have been so far underutilized in order to construct a theoretical apparatus which can illuminate the links between, and drivers of, ecocide and genocidal social death.

Genocide studies needs to rigorously explore insights from political ecology, environmental sociology and the burgeoning field of 'green criminology'. The balance of power between political interests, both within states and in the international arena, defines not only what is understood as crime but who, or even what, can be understood as a victim. Consequently, green criminologists argue that social and/or ecological harm is worthy of criminological research and analysis even if the state does not acknowledge the phenomenon as illegal, while some would argue that such analysis is needed *precisely* because of that fact (Shelley and Opsal 2014). Rob White outlines this basic premise: 'many conventional, and legal, forms of human production and interaction do far worse things to the natural environment than those activities which are deemed illegal' (White 2013a, 2013b).

From this ontological position critical criminologists have examined a plethora of criminal and harmful legal phenomena that produce environmental degradation[1] and have focused on the 'externalities' of production and the associated social and environmental costs, regulation or lack thereof and the social, economic and environmental dynamics of resource extraction and development,[2] environmental justice and the 'disproportionate harmful effects of industrial production on particular individuals and groups' (White 2013a, 2013b). Modern-day neoliberal capitalism is the vital structural context to many of the phenomena currently studied by green criminologists, because the 'problem is capitalism',[3] 'the enemy of nature' (Kovel 2007). It may be obvious to some, but growth-driven capitalism is antithetical to a physical reality of finite resources. As the natural world is finite, capitalism is inherently ecologically unsustainable and 'sustainable development' a dangerous oxymoron.

Political economy and Marxist ecology highlight the way class relations, and political power and influence, affect resource development choices and benefits, as well as whom and what is affected by corporate externalities. To fully encapsulate such dynamics, environmental sociologists and, more recently, green criminologists have invoked Schnaiberg's notion of the 'treadmill of production' (Shelley and Opsal 2014; Stretesky et al. 2013), which refers to a system whereby advancing technology increases production and rapidly intensifies environmental degradation. Technological advances are required by capitalism's need for raw materials and driven by the requirements of the process of extreme energy: as the easier to extract resources dwindle, new technological advances are required to get at the more difficult to extract and produce resources. Importantly, however, benefits and 'profits' from capital accumulation, along with the concomitant externalities of environmental degradation and social costs, are not justly shared or evenly distributed. Disadvantaged minorities, indigenous peoples and the working class often benefit the least but bear the most significant burdens of environmental degradation and pollution, while the employment situation for production staff can often get worse on account of decreasing investment and production levels, especially in Ponzi-scheme-financed industries like unconventional gas, where production peaks very soon, all while shareholders and owners of the means of production see increased profits.

The treadmill's perpetuation is dependent on a counterfactual ideological trick which invokes anti-ecological, limitless growth, reasoning that continued industrial expansion, and its required resource extraction, is essential for social progress, 'jobs' and the 'national interest'. This rhetorical feat is not solely the domain of corporate interests, of course, but crucially state ideology plays a vital role in maintaining the treadmill. Indeed, the corporate state is vested in economic development and assists in industrial expansionism by endorsing, promoting and legitimizing an economics that results in ecological disorganization as well as promoting dominant class relations and existing power structures (Stretesky et al. 2013).

The state also plays a conflicting role as the ultimate regulatory body responsible for protecting the public and limiting harmful practices, and thus Schnaiberg argued that the state could disrupt treadmill practices if it so desired. But as we have seen, in practice neoliberal ideology is so pervasive that existing regulation which seeks to protect populations is successfully depicted as unnecessary 'red tape', stopping corporations from 'getting on with business', while proposals for new regulations are often met with the suggestion that existing regulations are sufficient. Even where existing regulations are breached the state enforcement mechanisms are often impotent and of no deterrent value. For example, Stretesky et al.'s work on US Environmental Protection Agency fiscal penalties showed that corporations simply absorb such costs as the price of doing business on the treadmill and are not deterred from future harmful activities.

Green criminology has utlized the key insights of both the treadmill of production theory and political economy to better explain ecological destruction and its associated human and non-human impacts, consequences and 'harms'. Indeed, green criminology takes 'harm' as a central concept and involves 'a focus on all the different types of harms which people experience from the cradle to the grave' (Carrabine et al. 2008). Green criminology counts among its avenues of investigation the 'why, how and when' of the generation and control of such harms and related exploitation, abuse, loss and suffering. Gender inequalities, racism, speciesism and classism are all key categories for such an approach, but a vital aspect of green criminology is the way that it directs attention to causes of harms, crimes and conflicts, and related connections and consequences, usually overlooked or neglected in traditional criminology. By way of example, Carrabine et al. point to discussions about policy in the Middle East:

> these now recognize that conflict management is also a matter
> of resource management, where access to water is open to
> contestation. This is, of course, not a source of difficulty limited
> only to this region but given the absolute importance of water,
> has been, and will increasingly be, reproduced around the
> globe. As climate change makes new, devastating contributions
> to the incidence and scale of 'disasters', these occur alongside

continuing inequalities that mean the impacts of such disasters have unequal and differentially distributed results. (Ibid.)

Given the arguments presented in this book, especially those that mirror the concerns of Zimmerer above, the basic green criminological typology for investigation – i.e. four clusters of harms and crimes causing and/or resulting from the destruction and degradation of the Earth's resources: air pollution; deforestation; species decline and animal abuse; and water pollution and resource depletion – should be highly relevant to genocide studies today, and the sociology of genocide in particular. Indeed, alongside the insights of environmental sociology, green criminology can make a significant contribution to our understanding of the structural roots of the social and environmental harms that are pertinent to genocide studies. I hope this book, sitting alongside the important Zimmerer collection above, stimulates a significant ecological turn in genocide studies.

If such a turn were to take hold, could it influence the international legal order? It would certainly expand the scope of inquiry into a vital area of concern, but I seriously doubt that the Genocide Convention will be revisited any time soon to include either a more robust Lemkin-inspired cultural method, or an environmental method as envisaged in the 1980s and 1990s, as we saw in Chapter 2. I think that opportunity has passed, but I hope I am wrong, as a revised Genocide Convention that includes the cultural and ecological method could offer minority social groups considerably more legal protection than currently available.

However, a genuine process of decolonization would offer such peoples far more hope than international legal protections because, as we have seen, colonization, dispossession, exploitation, cultural assimilation and control are the greatest threats to the survival of such social groups as have been considered in the case studies of this book. But of course, the resource needs of colonial corporate states make continued colonial relations desirable, as the subordinate social groups within such relationships don't count politically and are one less competing voice to consider in the global 'race for what's left' (Klare 2014).

## For social groups, humanity and ecosystems

The nexus between ecocide and genocide as a lived experience, while far from a recent development for many indigenous peoples around the world, will likely become a far more frequent occurrence if we take the warnings of climate scientists seriously. Indeed, the survival of many non-indigenous minorities, and discrete cultural groups, and with it their 'future contributions to the world' that Lemkin spoke of, will be threatened by current levels of climate change as they are often the most vulnerable within vulnerable states (see Crook and Short 2014). In their necessarily provocative contribution to the Zimmerer collection above, Mark Levene and Daniele Conversi run with some familiar 'genocide' terminology, but 'radically recast it in order to delineate some of the power relationships which are making some peoples on the planet ostensibly more vulnerable to climate change than others, and, by implication, more threatened with violent extinction'. They argue that 'Holocaust research has given us the notion of 'perpetrators' and 'victims' (as well as 'bystanders') and use the terms to make a simple distinction between those most and least responsible for climate change. Their key point is worth quoting at length as it puts starkly that which needs to be said:

> The lion's share of carbon emissions can be directly or indirectly attributed to the lifestyles, working and consumer patterns of people in the First World, a category, incidentally, which would include nearly all, if not all, genocide scholars ... One might forcefully object that describing any population segment as perpetrators by dint of their carbon footprint is not appropriate, proportionate or kind. Perpetrators are people who kill and harm others, usually (though not always) knowingly. By contrast, the energy use of ordinary First World people is not so much consciously determined but rather predetermined by the function of the society they live in. If this leads indirectly to rising sea levels and methane emissions, glacial or Arctic melt, increased drought or flooding, deforestation, the death of the oceans, and so on, the evidence for intentionalist malice may still be absent. On the other hand, just as in cases of genocide where individuals and communities 'go along' with a regime's actions because they are unwilling to question its behaviour, or possibly fear the consequences, so here on the climate issue a general Western failure to change addictive behaviour associated with our normal quotidian consumerist activity does raise questions

about the degree of 'ordinary' complicity with what amounts
to systemic violence against people and planet. (Levene and
Conversi 2014: 283)

Levene and Conversi correctly identify 'ourselves' as climate
perpetrators and place us at one end of the culpability spectrum
and subsistence societies, whose modus operandi involves almost no
carbon emissions whatsoever, at the other. Crucially, they caution
that we shouldn't conflate 'poor' with 'subsistent'. Indeed, while
billions of 'poor' may be dependents of the global system, subsistence
cultures have traditionally created a high degree of socio-economic
autonomy, largely achieved through deploying their own labour or
that of domesticated animals, aligned with a usually conservation-
minded utilization of whatever renewable energy sources are available
to them for their basic sustenance (ibid.: 283).

While other creatures responded to harsh or varied conditions
with biological change over time, humans have generally relied
upon their ingenuity to survive by creating innovative ways to live
and communicate, and pass down knowledge to children – for the
human species, *culture is our primary adaptive mechanism* (Johnston
2000: 96). But with the culturally genocidal tendencies of global
capitalism and its path of accumulation we are losing our adaptive
edge in the midst of not only a climate crisis but, as Joel Kovel argues,
a worldwide 'ecological crisis' generated by, and extending deeply
into, 'an ecologically pathological society' and capitalist economy
(see Kovel 2007: xiii). Indeed, as Levene and Conversi point out,
'*homo anthropocenus* ... is entirely dependent as a consumer within
a globalised, inherently non-sustainable monoculture – one which
takes from the global commons but gives nothing back in return
and when it finally breaks down, as it must under the weight of this
negative equity, will have no obvious access to, or ability to work
with, nature for survival, let alone renewal' (Levene and Conversi
2014: 283).

The structural features of capitalism, in particular its tendency
to span the globe and impose a world market and world division of
labour, make it best understood as a form of *ecological imperialism*.
Capitalism is the first economic structure in human history that not
only has the potential to destroy ecosystems and local environments
but, through the process of the metabolic rift, imperil the very

biosphere itself and potentially induce forms of *pan-global ecological genocides and auto-genocides.*[4] Anthropogenic climate change is perhaps the most vivid and stark expression of the ruination of the biosphere, and the most devastating and ominous symptom of the metabolic rift. The process of extreme energy will exacerbate the ecological crisis, and if it is not halted will condemn whole human societies and ecosystems to the effects of runaway climate change as known *conventional fossil fuel reserves contain three times* the amount of $CO_2$ it would take to ensure this outcome. If we are to avoid such a scenario, and a potential extinction event for mankind, then, as leading climate scientist James Hansen puts it, 'we must rapidly phase out coal emissions, leave unconventional fossil fuels in the ground, and not go after the last drops of oil and gas. In other words, we must move as quickly as possible to the post-fossil fuel era of clean energies' (Hansen 2009: 289). Tyndall Centre climate scientist Kevin Anderson concurs: 'the only responsible action with regard to shale gas, or any "new" unconventional fossil fuel, is to keep it in the ground'.[5] The new technologies of extreme energy, such as fracking, are tantamount to sprinting in the wrong direction.

But of course, many of us know deep down, whether we choose to admit it or not, a number of simple truths: the global capitalist economy is incompatible with life. As numerous environmentalist authors, from Joel Kovel and Vandana Shiva to Derrick Jensen have noted, the global economy effectively creates infinite demand and no natural community can support infinite demand, especially when nothing beneficial is given back. A global economy is extractive, it gives nothing back, but follows the ecocidal pattern of a genocidal machine converting raw materials into power at the expense of living things and living systems. Traditional subsistence-based communities do not usually give up or sell the resources on which their communities depend, or allow their land bases to be damaged so that other resources – gold, oil, gas, etc. – can be extracted, until their communities have been effectively destroyed (Jensen 2006: 383).

# CONCLUSION

In writing this book I sought to make a contribution to a number of important areas of scholarship, but also to draw attention to the plight of the victims of the under-discussed genocides and ecocides analysed herein, while at the same time emphasizing the vulnerability of all humanity given the ecological crisis we now face.

From the outset, I placed this book in the recent school of genocide studies that has produced what I think can reasonably be termed a colonial/cultural turn, e.g. those works that highlighted the connection between colonization and genocides and the importance of culture to the concept of genocide. It also sought to explore the under-explored, and investigate some important cases of genocide which have received little or no scholarly attention in genocide studies: Palestine, Sri Lanka, Australia and Alberta, Canada. Unlike much of the genocide scholarship in the colonial/cultural school, it sought to highlight the *continuing* nature of the genocides in question through a broad sociological analysis which included recent empirical data in addition to vital historical contextualizing. The book will also add to the small number of studies that have shown how ecocide can be a method of genocide if, for example, such destruction results in conditions of life that fundamentally threaten a social group's cultural and/or physical existence (see Short 2010b).

It was crucial to place the discussions of genocide and ecocide in the empirical context of planetary boundaries, 'the Limits to Growth' and the '*process* of extreme energy', and suggest that this combination of factors will likely create a perfect storm for current and future human rights abuses, with ecocidal and genocidal consequences. In this area in particular, I utilized the key insights of a number of 'green criminologists'.

The case studies in this book have all invoked a Lemkin-inspired analysis, highlighting to differing extents, as the context determined, some of his key techniques of genocide alongside an additional method – ecocide, which can produce what Martin Crook and I have termed 'ecologically induced genocide'. The case studies began with an investigation into the history and current situation in Palestine. I suggested that by considering this case through the lens of settler colonialism the 'genocidal' massacres identified could be viewed within a wider context of a continuing 'Nakba'; and that the broader cultural, political, economic and environmental impacts of Israeli policies towards Palestinians are intrinsically related to this inherently genocidal and continuing process of colonization and dispossession. It was also suggested that the effects of these techniques of genocide against the entire Palestinian *genos*, beyond the scope of this book, should be analysed and that there is a distinct need for further research through a genocide and settler colonial lens, particularly with regard to the potential ecocidal impacts of Israeli policies towards Palestinians, which include deforestation, pollution and destruction of water resources and poor agricultural management.

The second case study focused on the conflict in Sri Lanka and its social, political, economic and environmental impacts on the Tamil minority. Even though aspects of the conflict have been described as genocidal, the chapter took a holistic approach that involved analysing the development of a comprehensive identity among the Tamil population, as a result of alienating and discriminatory policies since independence, and the subsequent stratification and subordination which led to the creation of a vulnerable minority population susceptible to the peculiar harm of genocide. The chapter also discussed important issues in post-war Sri Lanka, including ecological destruction following the government's neoliberal 'development' agenda and its effect on the people in the former war zone and former 'rebel-held' territories in the north and east. The case study outlined how a neoliberal 'development' agenda is now the favoured rationale for contemporary population dispersal and relocations of Tamil people from their lands and their livelihoods. Neoliberal 'democratization' has resulted in entrenched stratification with no possibility of meaningful 'reconciliation' as a racist paradigm has become dominant. Even so, the military's occupation of and dominion over the minority Tamil population, coupled with systematic land grabs, are but the latest elements of a genocidal process that is destroying the land-based political, economic, social, cultural and environmental foundations of the Tamil people.

The case studies then moved on to two non-violent conflicts, 'liberal democratic', indigenous/settler contexts in which colonialism dies hard. Beginning with the settler colonial context of Australia, the chapter outlined a *continuing* genocidal context in which many, but not all, indigenous peoples in Australia live, the seriousness of *present-day* culturally destructive state policies and the 'relationship of genocide' (Barta 2000). The chapter discussed important resource-based ecological dimensions of genocide: settler colonial land grabs which fuel the relentless 'mining' of Australia (Diamond 2006: 13) through the process of extreme energy via CSG production in particular, followed by the question of human adaptation possibilities, and the potential for survival in an even harsher Australian environment, which are jeopardized by the continuing culturally genocidal pressures on indigenous traditional knowledge systems and cultural diversity.

The final case study focused on the impacts on indigenous communities of the world's most destructive mining project – Alberta's tar sands. The chapter showed how many people in indigenous communities felt that they are in the final stages of a battle for survival that began in North America in the fifteenth century, and have called their past and present situation, brought about by settlers and colonial governments, genocide. As with the indigenous peoples of Australia, their use of the term genocide is not emotive or imprecise, but rather, as we have seen, is in keeping with Lemkin's concept and highlights the enormity of what the tar sands are doing to the Indians of Treaty 8 and beyond.

There are a plethora of reasons why the Alberta government should halt the expansion of tar sands extraction and immediately ameliorate the negative impacts on affected indigenous communities; production should be halted immediately, as the continued exploitation of this grotesquely inefficient resource could take us past our global carbon tipping point all on its own. This is one of the reasons why the tar sands are often held up, by supporters of an international law to ban ecocide, as reason alone for the need for such a law – as we saw in Chapter 2. While 'corporate social responsibility' is a fairly obvious oxymoron, there may indeed be hope that an international law against ecocide, if enacted, will prove a vital tool in the fight against such corporate externalities as those produced by the tar sands, and the myriad of other destructive and polluting corporate activities that are driving so much of our ecological crisis.

That said, we have systemic problems that run far deeper. No amount of negative 'Environmental Impact Assessments', or even of criminal prosecutions of corporations, is going to address the problem of planetary boundaries and limits to growth. While we can't spend our way to sustainability, in the dominant culture 'less' is a four-letter word.[1] For our politicians and their corporate sponsors 'growth' is still the ultimate good – our national and international political systems are catastrophically failing the ecological challenge. And so to the vital question, unfortunately beyond the investigative scope of this book: *what should we do about it?*

My research to date is better at telling us what won't work and, by implication, can point us in the right direction, but it offers little or no guidance on the best path to get us there. Even so, I can offer this: it may well be that our 'civilization' built on 'progress'[2] is inherently ecocidal and genocidal and hence irredeemable. We have created a system so divorced from the natural world that sustains us that even those millions who live in cities in developed countries are in fact 'nine meals from anarchy'.[3] Despite this inherent systemic vulnerability it is arguably naive to think that the dominant capitalist culture will undergo any sort of voluntary transformation to a sustainable way of living. 'Civilization' will continue to immiserate the vast majority of human life and ecosystems until we have witnessed incalculable extinction events inevitably leading to our own, unless we put a stop to it very soon. On this point I will leave the final word to a man, Derrick Jensen, who deserves our utmost respect for not immersing himself in comfortable denial and calling for, in no uncertain terms, a *deep green resistance*, an idea which I encourage the reader to investigate:[4]

> when dams were erected on the Columbia, salmon battered themselves against the concrete, trying to return home. We too must hurl ourselves against and through the literal and metaphorical concrete that keeps us imprisoned within an economic and political system that does not blanch at committing genocide and ecocide. (Jensen 2006: 383)

# NOTES

## Introduction

1 See Elder (2005: 470). And for a more detailed exploration of his life and works on the Genocide Convention see (2008).

2 Lemkin (1944: 79–95). For further discussion on this see Moses (2010).

3 For a good summary of Lemkin's tireless lobbying efforts see Power (2003), and for a detailed discussion of the political wrangles during the Convention's construction see Schabas (2000: 51–101).

4 'In the present Convention, genocide means any of the following acts committed with intent to destroy, in whole or in part, a national, ethnical, racial or religious group, as such: (a) Killing members of the group; (b) Causing serious bodily or mental harm to members of the group; (c) Deliberately inflicting on the group conditions of life calculated to bring about its physical destruction in whole or in part; (d) Imposing measures intended to prevent births within the group; (e) Forcibly transferring children of the group to another group' (United Nations, Convention on the Prevention and Punishment of the Crime of Genocide, 9 December 1948, UN Treaty Series, 78: 277).

5 United Nations Treaty Collection, 'Status of Treaty: Convention on the Prevention and Punishment of the Crime of Genocide', treaties.un.org/pages/ViewDetails.aspx?src=TREATY&mtdsg_no=IV-1&chapter=4&lang=en, accessed 10 June 2012).

6 Moshman (2001). For further discussion of Holocaust uniqueness in genocide studies see Churchill (1997: 63–75).

7 Scholars such as Dirk Moses, John Docker and Tanya Elder have explored Lemkin's archives at length and their analysis has been hugely influential to me. Regrettably, I have only had the chance to investigate Lemkin's letters and correspondence held in the UN archive in Geneva; and so I rely heavily on the work of others when articulating Lemkin's position based on his unpublished works, apart from those few occasions when I cite material from the UN archive in Geneva.

8 Frieze (2013: 247) and Lemkin (2012). This is perhaps the first book written on the history of genocide. See also Lemkin (2013).

9 Key writings from these researchers are: Moses (2010), Docker (2008: 81–101), Elder (2005: 470), Schaller and Zimmerer (2005), which appeared in book form as Schaller and Zimmerer (2009), Frieze (2013).

10 In addition to the works above, it is worth noting here that Lemkin's writing didn't occur in a vacuum and, various writers influenced his thinking: e.g. see David Denby's excellent article on the influence of Johann Herder (Denby 2005) and the influential J. A. Hobson's seminal work (Hobson 1975 [1902]). It is also worth highlighting that the idea of 'cultural diffusion' was particularly influential in the 1940s, sparked by A. L. Kroeber's important contribution to cultural anthropology: Kroeber 1940. As Michael McDonnell and A. Dirk Moses note, however, for Lemkin's essays on colonialism in

Spanish America he drew mainly upon the work of Spanish witness Bartolomé de las Casas, derived mainly from Brion (1929), which Lemkin notes was his chief source for Spanish colonial genocide, and MacNutt (1909); see McDonnell and Moses (2005: 504).

11 For a particularly illuminating example of how 'common everyday' and 'plain and ordinary' understandings of genocide are often at odds with not only Lemkin's work, but the understandings of those groups, such as many indigenous peoples, the concept was designed to protect, see Churchill (2002), particularly pp: 220–26.

12 Key examples from this perspective are: South (1998), South (2010), South and Brisman (2013), White (2013b) and White (2010).

13 See Short (2010b) and Huseman and Short (2012).

14 Much of the material on the history of ecocide in this book is taken from a version of a report we produced for the Ecocide Project. I am indebted to the researchers and Polly Higgins for their work on the project (Gauger et al. 2013).

15 The treaty area most affected by tar sands projects.

16 For a brief summary of the relevance of green criminology to these topics see Higgins et al. (2013).

## 1 Definitional conundrums: a sociological approach to genocide

1 See Short (2009: 102). Also note that some of the material and analysis in this chapter previously appeared in Short (2010).

2 For example, Gerald E. Markle has stated: 'The sad truth appears to be that the Holocaust has not been terribly significant to my discipline, and my discipline has not been terribly significant to the study of the Holocaust'

(Markle 1999); on this point see also Shaw (2010a) and Abowitz (2002: 27) (and yet this overlooks some highly influential sociological studies such as Bauman 1990), Dadrian (1975), Hamilton (1982) and Porter (1993).

3 On this point see Shaw (2007: 7), and for an example of such ideological 'wars' see the now classic book *Is the Holocaust Unique?* (Rosenbaum 1995).

4 For further discussion on this point see Curthoys and Docker (2008: 26) and Jones (2006: 20–21).

5 See Shaw (2010a: 148, 145).

6 We should not downplay the significance of the following important sociological studies: Chalk and Jonassohn (1990), Fein (1993), Kuper (1981). Add to these the more recent sociological contributions: Powell (2007), Shaw (2007), Van Kreiken (1999, 2004 and 2008).

7 For a discussion of the narrowing of the definition of genocide in the 1980s, see Curthoys and Docker (2008: 26).

8 In British common law 'foresight and recklessness are evidence from which intent may be inferred'; see J. Wien J. in *R* v. *Belfon* (1976) 3 All ER 46.

9 Some key writings from the main authors in the area: Barta (2000); Docker (2004); Moses (2000); Moses (2004); Moses (2008); and Moses and Stone (2006). See also these two excellent pieces: Schaller (2008); Zimmerer (2008).

10 Barta (2008c: 297).

11 For a summary of these see the UN web page, www.hrweb.org/legal/undocs.html.

12 For a discussion of a prime example of a rights institutionalization project that demonstrates the importance of Freeman's warning, see Short (2007).

13 See Power (2003), and for a detailed discussion of the political

wrangles during the Convention's construction see Schabas (2000: 51–101).

14  On the social construction of the genocide convention and the question of cultural genocide, see generally the pieces by Van Kreiken (1999) and (2004); and in particular (2008).

15  For the final text of the 2007 Declaration, see www.un.org/esa/socdev/unpfii/en/drip.html, and for a discussion of the global indigenous movement's impact on international law see Morgan (2004).

16  Lemkin (1944: 79–95). For further discussion on this, see Moses (2010).

17  Rome statute of the International Criminal Court, Article 7: Crimes against humanity. For a discussion of these crimes see Bassiouni (1999).

18  For more on the drafting process of the Genocide Convention, see Kuper (1981: 19–39).

19  'In the present Convention, genocide means any of the following acts committed with intent to destroy, in whole or in part, a national, ethnical, racial or religious group, as such: (a) Killing members of the group; (b) Causing serious bodily or mental harm to members of the group; (c) Deliberately inflicting on the group conditions of life calculated to bring about its physical destruction in whole or in part; (d) Imposing measures intended to prevent births within the group; (e) Forcibly transferring children of the group to another group' (United Nations, Convention on the Prevention and Punishment of the Crime of Genocide, 9 December 1948, UN Treaty Series, 78: 277).

20  Churchill (1997: 423). See e.g. Jones (2006: 22): 'I consider mass killing to be definitional to genocide. The inclusion of what some would call "ethnocide" (cultural genocide) is important, valid, and entirely in keeping with Lemkin's original conception.

It is also actionable under the UN Convention; but in charting my own course, I am wary of labelling "genocide" cases where mass killing has not occurred.'

21  For an interpretation of the difference between 'colonization' and 'colonialism' see Fieldhouse (1981: 4–5).

22  See e.g. Kuper (1981), Barta (1985), Docker (2008), Curthoys (2008) and Moses (2008).

23  United Nations, 'Draft United Nations declarations on the rights of indigenous peoples', 1994/45, www.unhchr.ch/huridocda/huridoca.nsf/%28Symbol%29/E.CN.4.SUB.2.RES.1994.45.En, accessed 16 June 2015.

24  United Nations, Convention on the Prevention and Punishment of the Crime of Genocide.

25  See www.cpsu.org.uk/index.php?id=75. For a detailed discussion on these issues see Samson and Short (2006).

26  In particular the right to 'free prior and informed consent' of those indigenous peoples affected by them – now an established international core principle most recently enshrined in Article 19 of the United Nations Declaration on the Rights of Indigenous Peoples – available at www.un.org/esa/socdev/unpfii/en/drip.html.

27  A damning report on waterway pollution, highlighting arsenic among other highly toxic substances, can be found in Timoney (2007).

28  For example, the Dene, Cree and Metis communities in Treaty 8 and Treaty 11 Territories.

29  See Docker (2004) on this point.

30  Secretariat Draft, 'First Draft of the Genocide Convention', Prepared by the UN Secretariat, May 1947, UN Doc. E/447.

31  In contemporary terms if cultural change were to occur while indigenous

peoples were exercising their right to Free, Prior and Informed Consent (FPIC) – which is a requirement, prerequisite and manifestation of the exercise of their fundamental right to self-determination as defined in international law – then such changes would not be genocidal. See United Nations Declaration on the Rights of Indigenous Peoples, 2007, especially Article 19, at www.un.org/esa/socdev/unpfii/en/drip.html.

32 The work of Talcott Parsons is arguably the prime example of this; see Parsons (1937) and more generally Parsons (1960).

33 See Wolfe (2006) on this point.

34 See the seminal report of UN Special Rapporteur Erica Daes, 'Indigenous Peoples and Their Relationship to Land, Final Working Paper', Commission on Human Rights, Sub-Commission on the Promotion and Protection of Human Rights, Fifty-third session, at www.unhchr.ch/Huridocda/Huridoca.nsf/0/78d418c307faa00bc1256a9900496f2b/$FILE/G0114179.pdf.

35 Ibid.

36 Which, while in a process of continual change, had a definite historical form. This point is made by Powell (2007: 538) with a Cree example.

## 2 The genocide–ecocide nexus

1 The Sub-Commission on Prevention of Discrimination and Protection of Minorities undertakes studies and makes recommendations to the Commission concerning the prevention of discrimination against racial, religious and linguistic minorities. Composed of twenty-six experts, the Sub-Commission meets each year for four weeks. It has working groups and established Special Rapporteurs to assist it with certain tasks; www.un.org/rights/dpi1774e.htm, accessed 16 July 2012.

2 In international forums the UN Sub-Commission on Prevention of Discrimination and Protection of Minorities used the term 'ecocide' to describe a potential crime involving environmental destruction, while in later years the International Law Commission preferred narrower formulations based around the notion of 'severe damage to the environment'.

3 Sub-Commission on Prevention of Discrimination and Protection of Minorities, *Study of the Question of the Prevention and Punishment of the Crime of Genocide*, Prepared by Mr Nicodème Ruhashyankiko, 4 July 1978, E/CN.4/Sub.2/416.

4 *New York Times*, 26 February 1970, cited in Weisberg (1970).

5 An independent organisation (1970–76) which built awareness among governments and society of damage to nature by human misuse of technology and chemical products.

6 The purpose of the Convention was to describe the destruction of the Indochinese peoples and environments by the United States government; and to call for a United Nations Convention on Ecocidal Warfare, which would receive evidence of the devastation of the human ecology of Indochina caused by the Indochina War, determine which belligerent caused that devastation, request reparations from the responsible belligerent or belligerents, and seek to define and proscribe 'Ecocide' as an international crime of war; www.aktivism.info/rapporter/ChallengingUN72.pdf, accessed 16 July 2012.

7 Austria, Holy See, Poland, Romania, Rwanda, Congo and Oman; see E/CN.4/Sub.2/416, pp. 11–117.

8 E/CN.4/Sub.2/SR.658, p. 53.

9 E/CIT.4/Sub.2/416, p. 185.

10  E/CN.4/Sub.2/1985/6.

11  E/CN.4/Sub.2/1985/6, para. 33.

12  Ibid.

13  Ibid., p. 124. Supportive governments: Austria, Holy See, Ecuador, Israel, Oman and Romania.

14  Report of the Sub-Commission on Prevention of Discrimination and Protection of Minorities on its 38th session, Geneva, 5–30 August 1985, E/CN.4/Sub.2/1985/57.

15  Draft Code of Offences Against the Peace and Security of Mankind until 1987; see General Assembly Resolution 42/151 of 7 December 1987.

16  treaties.un.org/pages/ ViewDetails.aspx?src=TREATY&mtdsg_ no=XVIII-10&chapter=18&lang=en, accessed 16 July 2012.

17  Statute of the International Law Commission, 1947. Adopted by General Assembly Resolution 174 (II) of 21 November 1947, amended by Resolutions 485 (V) of 12 December 1950, 984 (X) of 3 December 1955, 985 (X) of 3 December 1955 and 36/39 of 18 November 1981.

18  untreaty.un.org/ilc/ilcmembe. htm, accessed 16 July 2012.

19  untreaty.un.org/ilc/ilcsessions. htm; www.un.org/en/ga/sixth/66/66_ session.shtml, accessed 16 July 2012.

20  General Assembly Resolution 177 (II) of 21 November 1947.

21  *Yearbook of the ILC*, 1954, vol. II, pp. 151–2.

22  The Special Rapporteur refers to following international instruments: the Treaty on the Prohibition of the Emplacement of Nuclear Weapons and Other Weapons of Mass Destruction on the Sea-Bed and the Ocean Floor and in the Subsoil Thereof; the Treaty Banning Nuclear Weapon Tests in the Atmosphere in Outer Space and Under Water; the Treaty on Principles Governing the Activities of States in the Exploration and Use of Outer Space, including the Moon and other Celestial Bodies; and the Convention on the Prohibition of Military or any other Hostile Use of Environmental Modification Techniques; see A/ CN.4/377 and Corr. 1, paras 44 and 51, pp. 94–6.

23  A/CN.4/377 and Corr. 1, para. 46, p. 95.

24  This was the wording used in 1984; see A/CN.4/377 and Corr. 1, para. 79, p. 100.

25  *Yearbook of the ILC*, 1986, vol. I: Mr Stephen C. McCaffrey (USA), pp. 119–20, para. 10; Mr Andreas Jacovides (Cyprus), p. 121, para. 28; Mr Ahmed Mahiou (Algeria), p. 128, para. 11; Mr Doudou Thiam (Senegal; Special Rapporteur on the draft Code), p. 175, paras 17–18.

26  *Yearbook of the ILC*, 1986, vol. II, Pt 2, p. 46, para. 96.

27  One provision of Art. 22 on war crimes covers damage caused to the environment in times of war. 'Article 22. Exceptionally serious war crimes: 2. For the purposes of this Code, an exceptionally serious war crime is an exceptionally serious violation of principles and rules of international law applicable in armed conflict consisting of any of the following acts: [...] (d) employing methods or means of warfare which are intended or may be expected to cause widespread, long-term and severe damage to the natural environment; [...]'. See: *Yearbook of the ILC*, 1995, vol. II, Pt 2, p. 97.

28  *Yearbook of the ILC*, 1996, vol. II, Pt 1, p. 18, para. 27.

29  *Mens rea* is the necessary element of a crime – in this case intent to inflict environmental damage.

30  A/CN.4/448 and Add. 1, contained in *Yearbook of the ILC*, 1993, vol. II, Pt 1, p. 66, para. 50 (Australia), and p. 68, para. 30 (Austria).

31  A/CN.4/448 and Add. 1, contained

in *Yearbook of the ILC*, 1995, vol. I, 2386th m., p. 52; and 2387th m., pp. 52–3.

32  ILC(XLVIII)/DC/CRD.3 (included in *Yearbook of the ILC*, 1996, vol. II, Pt 1, para. 1).

33  The Working Group was established at the 2404th meeting. See vol. I and vol. II, Pt 2, of the *Yearbook of the ILC*, 1995.

34  *Yearbook of the ILC*, 1996, vol. I, 2428th meeting, p. 5, para. 5. Draft articles on State Responsibility (adopted in 1980). Article 19. International crimes and international delicts (adopted 1980). '3. Subject to paragraph 2, and on the basis of the rules of international law in force, an international crime may result, inter alia, from [...] d) a serious breach of an international obligation of essential importance for the safeguarding and preservation of the human environment, such as those prohibiting massive pollution of the atmosphere or of the seas.'

35  ILC(XLVIII)/DC/CRD.3 (included in *Yearbook of the ILC*, 1996, vol. II, Pt 1).

36  *Yearbook of the ILC*, 1996, vol. I, 2431th meeting, Tuesday, 21 May 1996.

37  Ibid. Including environmental damage in the context of war crimes: 12 votes in favour to 1, 4 abstentions; in the context of crimes against humanity: 9 votes to 9, 2 abstentions.

38  A/CN.4/466, 13th report on the draft code of crimes against the peace and security of mankind, by Mr Doudou Thiam, Special Rapporteur. Draft code of crimes against the peace and security of mankind (Part II) – including the draft statute for an international criminal court. Extract from the *Yearbook of the International Law Commission*, 1995, vol. II(1), p. 35 para. 8.

39  Ibid., para. 2.

40  Article 8. War crimes: 2. For the purpose of this Statute, 'war crimes' means:

(a) Grave breaches of the Geneva Conventions of 12 August 1949, namely, any of the following acts against persons or property protected under the provisions of the relevant Geneva Convention: [...]

(b) Other serious violations of the laws and customs applicable in international armed conflict, within the established framework of international law, namely, any of the following acts: [...] (iv) Intentionally launching an attack in the knowledge that such attack will cause [...] widespread, long-term and severe damage to the natural environment which would be clearly excessive in relation to the concrete and direct overall military advantage anticipated; [...]

41  Article 19. International crimes and International Delict. 3 [A]n international crime may result, inter alia, from:

(d) a serious breach of an international obligation of essential importance for the safeguarding and preservation of the human environment, such as those prohibiting massive pollution of the atmosphere or of the seas. See: *Yearbook of the ILC*, 1980, vol. II, Pt 2, p. 32, and *Yearbook of the ILC*, 1996, vol. II, Pt 2, p. 60.

42  International liability for injurious consequences arising out of acts not prohibited by international law.

43  *Yearbook of the ILC*, 1980, vol. II, Pt 2, p. 32: 'a serious breach of an international obligation of essential importance for the safeguarding and preservation of the human environment, such as those prohibiting massive pollution of the atmosphere or of the seas'.

44  Penal Code Viet Nam 1990 Art. 278. 'Ecocide, destroying the natural environment', whether committed in time of peace or war, constitutes a crime against humanity.

45  Criminal Code Russian Federation 1996 Art. 358.

46  Criminal Code of the Republic of Armenia 2003 Art. 394.

47  Criminal Code Belarus 1999 Art. 131.

48  Penal Code Republic of Moldova 2002 Art. 136.

49  Criminal Code of Ukraine 2001 Art. 441.

50  Criminal Code of Georgia 1999 Art. 409.

51  Penal Code Kazakhstan 1997 Art. 161.

52  Criminal Code Kyrgyzstan 1997 Art. 374.

53  Criminal Code Tajikistan 1998 Art. 400.

54  As oil and natural gas production peaks and declines, coal becomes increasingly pivotal in maintaining global energy consumption rates; however, this renewed focus on coal, seen in the 'record rate' of coal gasification and coal-to-liquid plant construction of the last decade, will only further exacerbate strained coal resources. Indeed, world coal production continues to increase annually, with an overall increase of over 67 per cent between 1990 and 2013. Even with more conservative estimates of coal production growth and the most opportunistic estimates of global coal reserves – relying on the World Coal Association's production growth rate of 0.4 per cent between 2012 and 2013 remaining constant and the German Federal Institute for Geosciences and Natural Resources' estimate of 1,052 billion tonnes of reserves – the world will 'run out' of coal in just over a century. As that figure assumes no 'updates' to reserve figures (despite nearly every state with 'significant coal resources' reporting a 'substantial downward revision' in reserve estimates made since 1986) or increase in production rate (despite the sharp decreases in available oil and natural gas during the upcoming decades), it is reasonable to conclude that the limits to coal-dependent growth will also soon be reached. Heinberg (2007).

55  Natural gas liquids (NGLs) are 'hydrocarbons with longer molecular chains', such as propane and butane, within natural gas that are captured and used for heating and industrial purposes. Heinberg (2014: 25).

56  Conventional natural gas production follows a similar peak and decline bell-curve and is expected to reach its plateau before the mid-twenty-first century. See Mobbs (2013a); Maggio and Cacciola (2012).

57  I have in mind here both the Gulf War of 1990/91 and the Iraq War of 2003–2011, though the UN Security Council sanctions against Iraq in the interim also indicate the willingness of Western states to take international action to gain control of oil exports when native governments are considered unreliable.

58  See *US National Security Strategy, A National Security Strategy for a New Century*, The White House, Washington, DC, 1998.

59  Exxon's revenue is greater than the GDP of Thailand, for instance. Trivett (2011).

60  See the excellent work of investigative journalist Greg Palast on this point – Palast (2002).

61  United States Congress, Energy Policy Act, Pub.L. 109–58 (2005).

62  BBC, 'Lords: Fracking should be "urgent priority" for UK', BBC News: Business, 8 May 2014, www.bbc.co.uk/news/business-27312796.

63  Damian Carrington, 'UK defeats European bid for fracking regulations', *Guardian*, 14 January 2014, www.theguardian.com/environment/2014/

jan/14/uk-defeats-european-bid-fracking-regulations.

64  The Economist, 'Energy firms and climate change: unburnable fuel', *The Economist*, 4 May 2013, www.economist.com/news/business/21577097-either-governments-are-not-serious-about-climate-change-or-fossil-fuel-firms-are.

65  For more on corporate–state connections, see Chomsky (2013); Palast (2002).

66  For example, the American Enterprise Institute, which receives funding from ExxonMobil and other companies in the energy sector, 'offered a $10,000 incentive to scientists and economists to write papers challenging the IPCC findings' after the Intergovernmental Panel on Climate Change released its fourth assessment report in 2007. Jones and Levy (2009).

67  IPCC, 'Summary for Policymakers', in IPCC (2013).

68  IPCC, 'Summary for Policymakers', in IPCC (2013).

69  Hinkley (2002); Bakan (2005). For further reading on the economic model and psychology under which corporations operate, see Elson (2002) and Connolly (2012). Notably, even privately held companies, such as Koch Industries, have a monetary interest in maintaining global fossil fuel use, as long as non-renwable energy sources continue to generate profit.

70  US Energy Information Administration, 'Renewable & alternative fuels', www.eia.gov/renewable/.

71  For example, in 2009 approximately $43–46 billion was provided to renewable and biofuel technologies, projects and companies by the governments of the world, compared with the $577 billion spent on fossil fuel subsidies in 2008. Bloomberg: New Energy Finance, 'Subsidies for renewables, biofuels dwarfed by supports for fossil fuels', about.bnef.com/press-releases/subsidies-for-renewables-biofuels-dwarfed-by-supports-for-fossil-fuels/.

72  This concept is perhaps best illustrated by the insistence from both industry and governments that hydraulic fracturing will allow natural gas to replace the use of coal and thus reduce the emission of greenhouse gases, when in actuality the abundance of hydraulic fracturing in the United State has simply lowered the price of US coal and driven up exports. Damian Carrington, 'Fracking boom will not tackle global warming, analysis warns', *Guardian*, 15 October 2014, www.theguardian.com/environment/2014/oct/15/gas-boom-from-unrestrained-fracking-linked-to-emissions-rise; Grose (2013).

73  Ibid.

74  UNEP, 'Athabasca oil sands, require massive investments and energy and produce massive amounts of oil and $CO_2$ – Alberta (Canada)', United Nations Environment Programme 54, Global Environment Alert Service (2011): 1–5; UNEP, 'Oil palm plantations: threats and opportunities for tropical ecosystems', United Nations Environment Programme 73, Global Environment Alert Service (2011): 1–10.

75  Euran Mearns, 'The global energy crises and its role in the pending collapse of the global economy', Paper presented at the Royal Society of Chemists, Aberdeen, Scotland, 29 October 2008.

76  At the time of writing oil prices were in decline but the finite nature of the resource guarantees that prices will again rise.

77  David J. Murphy, 'EROI, insidious feedbacks, and the end of economic growth', Paper presented at the Sixth Annual Conference of the Association

for the Study of Peak Oil (ASPO), Washington, DC, 7–9 October 2010.

78  On this point see also Heinberg (2014).

79  Notwithstanding the current, inevitably temporary, geopolitically induced price reduction, prices will undoubtedly rise over time as supply declines; see Mobbs (2015).

80  IPCC, 'Summary for Policymakers', in IPCC (2007).

81  Laboratory for Aviation and the Environment, 'Air pollution causes 200,000 early deaths each year in the US', Massachusetts Institute of Technology, lae.mit.edu/?p=2821.

82  Alok Jha, 'Boiled alive,' *Guardian*, 26 July 2006, www.theguardian.com/environment/2006/jul/26/science.g2.

83  IPCC, 'Projections of Future Changes in Climate', in IPCC (2007).

84  World Health Organization (WHO) Regional Office for Europe, *Euroheat: Improving Public Health Responses to Extreme Weather Heat-Waves. Summary for Policy-Makers*, World Health Organization, Copenhagen, 2009.

85  IPCC, 'Projections of Future Changes in Climate', in IPCC (2007).

86  See Barry and Woods (2010); Nafeez Ahmed, 'Are you opposed to fracking? Then you might just be a terrorist', *Guardian*, 21 January 2014, www.theguardian.com/environment/earth-insight/2014/jan/21/fracking-activism-protest-terrorist-oil-corporate-spies; Human Rights Council, 'Report of the Special Rapporteur on the Human Right to Safe Drinking Water and Sanitation: Mission to the United States of America', A/HRC/18/33/Add.4, 2011: 10–11.

87  See Huseman and Short (2012) for a full definition of this extraction process.

88  See Crook and Short (2014). Marx's analysis of the accumulation crisis brought on by materials-supplies disturbances operates on two levels: first, it focuses on the conditions of crisis caused by fluctuations in the value of the materials in question brought on by shortages; and secondly, it relates to the indirect fluctuations in 'prices' brought on by the resultant competition, speculation and the credit system. See Marx, *Theories of Surplus Value*, vol. 2, Progress Publishers, Moscow, 1968, p. 515. For further elaboration of the contradiction between 'nature's time' and 'labour's time' see Marx and Engels (1967: 118).

89  For more on this see Short et al. (2015).

90  Reports of considerable negative impacts go well beyond the anecdotal realm; see, for example, environmental and health studies such as Brown (2014); McDermott-Levy et al. (2013); Moore et al. (2014); Osborn et al. (2011); and Vengosh et al. (2014). And social scientific enquiries such as Perry (2012); Anderson and Theodori (2009); Apple (2014); Beach (2013); Gramling and Freudenburg (1992); Fleming and Measham (2014).

91  Environment and Human Rights Advisory, *A Human Rights Assessment of Hydraulic Fracturing for Natural Gas*, EHRA, Oregon, 2011, www.earthworksaction.org/files/publications/EHRA_Human-rights-fracking-FINAL.pdf.

92  See Short et al. (2015); Elliot and Short (2014); Grear (2014); Grear et al. (2014).

93  UNEP, 'Gas fracking: can we safely squeeze the rocks?', United Nations Environment Programme, Global Environment Alert Service, 2012.

94  Ibid., pp. 6–7.

95  Ibid., pp. 7–9 12.

96  Howarth et al. (2011); Howarth et al. (2012); Howarth (2014).

97  Osborn et al. (2011). See also Isaac Santos and Damien Maher,

*Fugitive Emissions from Coal Seam Gas*, Centre for Coastal Biogeochemistry Research Submission to Department of Climate Change and Energy Efficiency, 2012, www.scu.edu.au/coastal-biogeochemistry/index.php/70/.

98  Environment and Human Rights Advisory, 'A Human Rights Assessment'.

99  E.g. *Gasland*, Directed by Josh Fox, HBO Productions, New York, 2012; *Drill Baby Drill*, Directed by Lech Kowalski, Kowalski Productions, France, 2013.

100  Anderson and Theodori (2009); Schafft et al. (2013); Schafft et al. (2014).

101  See www.endecocide. org/examples/ and see the *Guardian* newspaper's ten worst ecocides at www.theguardian. com/environment/gallery/2010/ may/04/top-10-ecocides?#/ ?picture=361634449&index=0.

102  For a personal background see pollyhiggins.com/.

103  See eradicatingecocide.com/.

104  E.g. Survival International, Forest Peoples' Alliance, Raven Trust, Cultural Survival and many more.

105  Eradicating Ecocide, 'Closing the door to dangerous industrial activity: a concept paper for governments to implement emergency measures', eradicatingecocide. com/connect/documents/.

106  www.endecocide.org/strategy/.

107  See James Perkins, 'Biggest weekly oil rig decline since 1987', *The Shale Energy Insider*, 2 February 2015, www.shaleenergyinsider. com/2015/02/02/biggest-weekly-oil-rig-decline-since-1987/, and for a UK perspective Anthony Hilton, 'Fracking just doesn't pay so why bother?', *Evening Standard*, 3 February 2015, www. standard.co.uk/business/markets/ anthony-hilton-fracking-just-doesnt-pay-so-why-bother-10020898.html.

108  Damian Carrington, 'Owen Paterson held urgent meeting for fracking boss, documents show', *Guardian*, 21 March 2014, www. theguardian.com/environment/2014/ mar/21/owen-paterson-urgent-meeting-fracking-cuadrilla-lord-browne; 'Emails reveal UK helped shale gas industry manage fracking opposition', *Guardian*, 17 January 2014, www.theguardian. com/environment/2014/jan/17/emails-uk-shale-gas-fracking-opposition; 'George Osborne urges ministers to fast-track fracking measures in leaked letter', *Guardian*, 26 January 2015, www. theguardian.com/environment/2015/ jan/26/george-osborne-ministers-fast-track-fracking.

109  David Cameron, 'We cannot afford to miss out on shale gas', *Telegraph*, 11 August 2013, www.telegraph.co.uk/news/ politics/10236664/We-cannot-afford-to-miss-out-on-shale-gas.html.

110  Paul Mobbs, 'Fracking policy and the pollution of British democracy', *The Ecologist*, 20 January 2015, www. theecologist.org/News/news_ analysis/2721027/frackingnbsppolicy_ and_the_pollution_of_british_democracy. html.

## 3 Palestine

1  Haifa Rashed is a Research Associate at the Human Rights Consortium and a graduate of the MA programme in Understanding and Securing Human Rights at the University of London. She has researched the Palestine question for many years. We have published numerous articles together, the first of which was Haifa Rashed and Damien Short, 'Can a Lemkin inspired genocide perspective aid our understanding of the Palestinian situation?', *International Journal of Human Rights*, 16(8), 2012, pp. 1142–69. Some of the data and analysis in this chapter can be found in that paper.

2 See Rashed et al. (2014); Martin Shaw, 'Palestine and genocide: an international historical perspective revisited', *Holy Land Studies*, 12(1), 2013, pp. 1–7; Rashed and Short (2012); Docker (2012); Shaw (2010b); and Martin Shaw and Omer Bartov, 'The question of genocide in Palestine, 1948: an exchange between Martin Shaw and Omer Bartov', *Journal of Genocide Research*, 12(3/4), 2010, pp. 243–59.

3 This recognition of the fragmentation of Palestinian identity has produced studies such as Matar (2011).

4 For more on this see Rashed and Short (2012).

5 On this see Ram 2007: 56) and Rodinson (1973).

6 For an interesting analysis of the Zionist settler colonial project and its two outcomes (successful in Israel proper, unsuccessful in the West Bank and Gaza) see Veracini (2013). See also Rodinson (1973); Ram (2007); Kimmerling (2003); Gregory (2004); Veracini (2006); Ilan Pappé, 'Zionism as colonialism: a comparative view of diluted colonialism in Asia and Africa', *South Atlantic Quarterly*, 107(4), Fall 2008; Piterberg (2008); Collins (2011); Masalha (2012); and David Lloyd, 'Settler colonialism and the state of exception: the example of Palestine/Israel', *Settler Colonial Studies*, 2(1), 2012, pp. 59–80.

7 Elkins and Pederson (2005: 1). For a comparison between settler colonialism, founding violence and reconciliation in Israel and Australia see Veracini (2006) and for a comparison between settler colonialism in Israel and North America see Finklestein (1995).

8 Ilan Pappé, 'When Israeli denial of Palestinian existence becomes genocidal', *The Electronic Intifada* (online), 20 April 2013, electronicintifada.net/content/when-israeli-denial-palestinian-existence-becomes-genocidal/12388.

9 See, e.g., Palestinian Media Watch 'Hamas's "genocide ideology"' (online), palwatch.org/main.aspx?fi=584.

10 Genocide Watch, 'Countries at risk report', 2014 (online), genocidewatch.net/wp-content/uploads/2012/06/2014-Countries-at-Risk-Report5.htm.

11 Indeed, Israeli minister Naftali Bennett even accused Hamas of 'self-genocide' during Operation Protective Edge in 2014 – Sky News, 'Israel minister accuses Hamas of "self-genocide"', 20 July 2014 (online), news.sky.com/story/1304322/israel-minister-accuses-hamas-of-self-genocide.

12 See Rashed et al. (2014) for more on this.

13 See, e.g., Morris (2004); Pappé (2006); Shlaim (2000).

14 For more on this see Masalha (2011).

15 For recent studies on rape as a potential feature of genocide, see Daniela De Vito, Aisha Gill and Damien Short, 'Rape characterised as genocide', *SUR International Journal on Human Rights*, 6(10), 2009, pp. 29–52, and Levene (2005).

16 See Pappé (2006); Benvenisti (2000); Kovel (2007b); White (2009).

17 Martin Shaw and David Hirsh, 'Antisemitism and the boycott: an exchange between Martin Shaw and David Hirsh', *Democratiya*, 105, 2008, dissentmagazine.org/democratiya/article_pdfs/d14ShawHirsh-1.pdf.

18 See, e.g., Ali (2013). See also Mahmoud Darwish, 'Not to begin at the end', *Al-Ahram* weekly, 533, 10–16 May 2001), online, weekly.ahram.org.eg/2001/533/op1.htm: 'We are not looking back to dig up the evidence of a past crime, for the Nakba is an extended present that promises to continue in the future'; Joseph Massad,

'Resisting the Nakba', *Al-Ahram* weekly, 897, 15–21 May 2008, online, weekly. ahram.org.eg/2008/897/op8.htm: 'I submit, therefore, that this year is not the 60th anniversary of the Nakba at all, but rather one more year of enduring its brutality; that the history of the Nakba has never been a history of the past but decidedly a history of the present'; and Masalha (2012: 254): 'While the Holocaust is an event in the past, the Nakba did not end in 1948. For Palestinians, mourning sixty-three years of al-Nakba is not just about remembering the "ethnic cleansing" of 1948, it is also about marking the ongoing dispossession and dislocation.'

19  See Robert Ross, '"Price tag" attacks and the ethnic cleansing of Palestine', *Mondoweiss*, 2 July 2013, mondoweiss.net/2013/07/attacks-cleansing-palestine.html; UN News Centre, 'UN rights office voices concern over forced evictions of Palestinians in West Bank', UN News Centre, 27 August 2013, www.un.org/apps/news/story. asp?NewsID=45707&Cr=palestin&Cr1#. UpUefZSgbOX.

20  See, e.g., Marcy Newman, 'Ethnic cleansing in East Jerusalem', *The Electronic Intifada*, 10 March 2009, online, electronicintifada. net/content/ethnic-cleansing-east-jerusalem/8123; Marian Houk, 'Ethnic cleansing continues: Israeli lawyers tell UN Palestinian Jerusalemites targeted', *Jerusalem Quarterly*, 48(91), 2011, www.jerusalemquarterly.org/ ViewArticle.aspx?id=397; Gideon Levy, 'Ethnic cleansing of Palestinians, or, democratic Israel at work', *Haaretz*, 12 May 2011, www.haaretz.com/print-edition/opinion/ethnic-cleansing-of-palestinians-or-democratic-israel-at-work-1.361196; Associated Press, 'Palestinians' Abbas accuses Israel of "ethnic cleansing"', CBS, 27 September 2012, www.cbsnews.

com/news/palestinians-abbas-accuses-israel-of-ethnic-cleansing/; Jonathan Cook, 'Israel's ethnic cleansing zones', *Counterpunch*, 10 July 2013, www. counterpunch.org/2013/07/10/israels-ethnic-cleansing-zones/; Institute for Middle East Understanding, 'Ethnic cleansing by bureaucracy: Israel's policy of destroying Palestinian homes', *Mondoweiss*, 3 October 2013, mondoweiss.net/2013/10/bureaucracy-destroying-palestinian.html; Ben Lynfield, '"Israel's ethnic cleansing in Jerusalem is a blow to peace efforts" say Palestinian leaders', *Independent*, 26 August 2013, www.independent.co.uk/ news/world/middle-east/israels-ethnic-cleansing-in-jerusalem-is-a-direct-blow-to-peace-efforts-say-palestinian-leaders-8784982.html; War On Want, 'Help us stop ethnic cleansing in Palestine', War on Want, 2013, online, www.waronwant. org/help-us-stop-ethnic-cleansing-in-palestine; and Teju Cole, 'Slow violence, cold violence', *Guardian*, 18 April 2015, www.theguardian.com/books/2015/ apr/17/bad-law-east-jerusalem-ethnic-cleansing-palestines-teju-cole.

21  UN Human Rights Council, 'Report of the Special Rapporteur on the situation of human rights in the Palestinian territories occupied since 1967, Richard Falk', A/HRC/25/67, March 2014, paras 36–37, 11–12.

22  Footnote 41, 'Submission to Special Rapporteur by the Civic Coalition for Palestinian Rights in Jerusalem', November 2013; UN Human Rights Council, 'Report of the Special Rapporteur on the situation of human rights in the Palestinian territories occupied since 1967, Richard Falk', A/ HRC/25/67, March 2014, paras 36–37, 11–12.

23  UN Human Rights Council, 'Report of the Special Rapporteur on the situation of human rights in the Palestinian territories occupied since

1967, Richard Falk', A/HRC/25/67, March 2014, para. 34, 11.

24  See, e.g., Cook, 'Israel's ethnic cleansing zone', Institute for Middle East Understanding, 2013; 'Ethnic cleansing by bureaucracy: Israel's policy of destroying Palestinian homes', *Mondoweiss*, 3 October 2013, mondoweiss.net/2013/10/bureaucracy-destroying-palestinian.html; Jillian Kestler-DAmours, 'Israel, no place for Bedouin', Al Jazeera, 29 June 2011, www.aljazeera.com/indepth/opinion/2011/06/20116238174269364. html; Palestine Solidarity Campaign, 'Ethnic cleansing', Palestine Solidarity Campaign, online, www.palestinecampaign. org/campaign/ethnic-cleansing/.

25  David Bernstein, 'Forcible removal of Arabs gaining support in Israel', *The Times* (London), 24 August 1988, cited in Masalha (2000: ch. 2, n117).

26  For detailed statistics on Palestinian fatalities inflicted by Israeli forces, see B'Tselem, 'Statistics', 2014, online, www.btselem.org/statistics.

27  During the Israeli invasion of Lebanon a massacre took place in the Palestinian refugee camps of Sabra and Shatila by Christian Phalangists who were allowed admission to the camps by Israeli forces who were controlling access to the camps. For more, see Cohn-Sherbok and El-Alami (2001). For a detailed report see International Commission, 'Israel in Lebanon: Report of the International Commission to Enquire into Reported Violations of International Law by Israel during Its Invasion of the Lebanon', *Journal of Palestine Studies*, 12(3), Spring 1983.

28  The UN General Assembly declared the massacre to be 'a genocide'; United Nations, GA Res. 37/123 D, 1982. See Schabas (2000: 234) on the legal import of this resolution.

29  For detailed reports on the events in Jenin, see United Nations, General Assembly 10th emergency session, Agenda item 5, A/ES-10/186 (30 July 2002), 'Illegal Israeli actions in Occupied East Jerusalem and the rest of the Occupied Palestinian Territory', and Amnesty International, 'Israel and the Occupied Territories: shielded from scrutiny: IDF violations in Jenin and Nablus', 2002, www.amnesty. org/en/library/asset/MDE15/143/2002/ en/c4ef6642-d7bc-11dd-b4cd-01eb52042454/mde151432002en.pdf.

30  For more on this see Rashed and Short (2012: 1144).

31  Nehad Khader, 'Interview with Dr Basil Baker: quick death under fire, slow death under siege', *Journal of Palestine Studies*, 44(1) (Special issue: Operation Protective Edge), Autumn 2014, p. 132.

32  UNRWA, *Gaza Emergency*, 2014, online (figure correct as of 11 September 2014), www.unrwa.org/gaza-emergency.

33  UNOCHA, 'Protection of Civilians Reporting Period: 20–26 January 2015', online, www.ochaopt.org/documents/ ocha_opt_protection_of_civilians_ weekly_report_2014_01_30_english.pdf.

34  See, e.g., Abukar Arman, 'On Gaza, genocide, and impunity', Al Jazeera, 27 July 2014, online, www.aljazeera.com/indepth/ opinion/2014/07/gaza-genocide-impunity-201472616564887960 8.html.

35  See, e.g. Charles Davis, 'Israel's war on Palestine: it's bad, but is it "genocide"?', *Vice*, www.vice.com/read/ israels-war-on-gaza-is-it-genocide-813, and Soraya Sepahpour-Ulrich, 'Israel and the "G" word: Gaza genocide and Arab fratricide', *Global Research*, 1 August 2014, www.globalresearch. ca/the-g-word-gaza-genocide-and-arab-fratricide/5394391.

36  Haaretz, 'Penelope Cruz, Javier Bardem, Pedro Almodovar denounce Israel's "genocide" in Gaza', *Haaretz*,

29 July 2014, online, www.haaretz.com/life/arts-leisure/1.607866.

37  Two activist campaigns of note are 'Israel Genocide?', which is appealing for the UN Special Adviser on the Prevention of Genocide to investigate whether Israel is committing genocide against Palestinians – see Israel Genocide?, 2015, online, israelgenocide.com. A 'Jews Against Genocide' activist group was also established during the military operation – for more on this see Miko Peled, '"Jews Against Genocide" hold memorials for killed Palestinian children in front of Israeli govt buildings around the world', *Mondoweiss*, 18 July 2014, online, mondoweiss.net/2014/07/memorials-palestinian-buildings.

38  See, e.g., Marjorie Cohn, 'US leaders aid and abet Israeli war crimes, genocide & crimes against humanity', *Jurist*, Forum, 8 August 2014, online, jurist.org/forum/2014/08/marjorie-cohn-israel-crimes.php, and Luke Peterson, 'Is Israel committing a genocide against the Palestinians of Gaza?', *Juan Cole*, Informed Comment, 2 August 2014, online, www.juancole.com/2014/08/committing-genocide-palestinians.html. For a comprehensive list of articles relating to Israel and 'genocide', see Israel Genocide?, 2015, online, israelgenocide.com/articles/.

39  Ilan Pappé, 'Israel's incremental genocide in the Gaza ghetto', *The Electronic Intifada*, 13 July 2014, electronicintifada.net/content/israels-incremental-genocide-gaza-ghetto/13562.

40  AFP The Express Tribune, 'Nawaz urges world to stop Israel's "genocide" in Gaza', 16 July 2014, online, tribune.com.pk/story/736313/nawaz-urges-world-to-stop-israels-genocide-in-gaza/.

41  Russia Today, '"Stop the genocide"! S. American leaders condemn Israeli operation in Gaza', 2014, online,

rt.com/news/174144-south-america-gaza-genocide/.

42  Khaled Abu Toameh, 'Abbas accuses Israel of "genocide" in its Gaza operation', *Jerusalem Post*, 7 September 2014, online, www.jpost.com/Diplomacy-and-Politics/Abbas-accuses-Israel-of-genicide-in-its-Gaza-operation-362125, and Peter Beaumont and Julian Borger, 'Mahmoud Abbas calls on UN to back deadline for Israeli withdrawal', *Guardian*, 26 September 2014, online, www.theguardian.com/world/2014/sep/26/mahmoud-abbas-un-israeli-withdrawal-occupied-territories.

43  AFP, 'Erdogan accuses Israel of seeking "systematic genocide in Gaza"', *The Times of Israel*, 17 July 2014, online, www.timesofisrael.com/erdogan-says-israel-atempting-systematic-genocide-in-gaza/.

44  See, e.g., Richard Silverstein, 'Israeli professor calls for Palestinian genocide', 14 October 2014, online, www.richardsilverstein.com/2014/10/14/israeli-professor-calls-for-palestinian-genocide/.

45  Gideon Resnick, 'Israeli politician declares war on "the Palestinian people"', *Daily Beast*, 7 July 2014, online, www.thedailybeast.com/articles/2014/07/07/israeli-politician-declares-war-on-the-palestinian-people.html.

46  Translation provided by Ali Abunimah, 'Israeli lawmaker's call for genocide of Palestinian gets thousands of Facebook likes', *The Electronic Intifada*, 7 July 2014, online, electronicintifada.net/blogs/ali-abunimah/israeli-lawmakers-call-genocide-palestinians-gets-thousands-facebook-likes.

47  Annie Robbins, 'Israel should pay 1.4 million Palestinians to leave Gaza, Moshe Feiglin says', *Mondoweiss*, 26 December 2014, online, mondoweiss.net/2014/12/million-palestinians-feiglin.

48  United Nations, 'Statement by the Special Advisers of the Secretary-General on the Prevention of Genocide, Mr Adama Dieng, and on the Responsibility to Protect, Ms Jennifer Welsh, on the situation in Israel and in the Palestinian Occupied Territory of Gaza Strip', 24 July 2014, unispal.un.org/UNISPAL.nsf/47D4E277B48D9D3685256DDC00612265/99CB7C1CE4CEEC6F85257D1F006FD34E#sthash.wdKzhU7Q.dpuf.

49  Russell Tribunal on Palestine, 'Extraordinary Session on Gaza: Summary of Findings, Brussels 25 September 2014', 37, 2014, online, www.russelltribunalonpalestine.com/en/wp-content/uploads/2014/09/TRP-Concl.-Gaza-EN.pdf. This is not the first time such an accusation has been levelled against the Israeli government – in December 2013, the then UN Special Rapporteur on the situation of human rights in Palestinian territories occupied since 1967, Richard Falk, accused Israel of acting with genocidal intent against the Palestinian people, saying 'when you target an ethnic group and inflict ... punishment upon them, you are in effect nurturing a criminal intention that is genocidal'. *Russia Today*, 15 December 2013, online, www.youtube.com/watch?v=4GwApvroWkE&feature=youtu.be&t=3m30s.

50  UN General Assembly, A/HRC/16/G/1, 10 January 2011, 'Letter dated 9 December 2010 from the Permanent Representative of Israel addressed to the President of the Human Rights Council', Human Rights Council Sixteenth session, Agenda item 7, unispal.un.org/UNISPAL.NSF/0/3ADF03D82EDC046C8525781800679B9F, and Israel Ministry of Foreign Affairs, 'Operation Protective Edge – Q&A', mfa.gov.il/MFA/ForeignPolicy/Issues/Pages/Operation-Protective-Edge-QA.aspx.

51  Stephanie Nebehay, '"No safe place for civilians" in Gaza, UN says', Reuters, 22 July 2014, online, www.reuters.com/article/2014/07/22/us-palestinians-israel-un-aid-idUSKBN0FR14820140722.

52  Breaking the Silence, 'This is how we fought in Gaza: soldiers' testimonies and photographs from Operation "Protective Edge"', 106, 2014, www.breakingthesilence.org.il/pdf/ProtectiveEdge.pdf.

53  UN General Assembly, Convention on the Prevention and Punishment of the Crime of Genocide, 9 December 1948, United Nations, Treaty Series, vol. 78, p. 277, www.refworld.org/docid/3ae6b3ac0.html.

54  Raphael Lemkin, 'Genocide as a crime under international law', *American Journal of International Law*, 41(1), 1947, p. 147.

55  2013 report by the United Nations Conference on Trade and Development on the Palestinian economy in East Jerusalem cited by UN Human Rights Council, 'Report of the Special Rapporteur on the situation of human rights in the Palestinian territories occupied since 1967, Richard Falk', A/HRC/25/67, March 2014, para. 35, 11.

56  See, e.g., Sara Roy, 'The Gaza Strip: a case of economic de-development', *Journal of Palestine Studies*, 17(1), Autumn 1987, pp. 56–88.

57  Ibid., p. 83.

58  United Nations Conference on Trade and Development, Sixty-second session, 'Report on UNCTAD assistance to the Palestinian people: developments in the economy of the Occupied Palestinian Territory', 6 July 2015, para. 60, refers to Office of the United Nations Special Coordinator for the Middle East Peace Process, 'Gaza in 2020: a liveable place?', August 2012.

59  United Nations Conference on Trade and Development, Sixty-second session, 'Report on UNCTAD assistance to the Palestinian people: developments in the economy of the Occupied Palestinian Territory', 6 July 2015, Executive Summary.

60  Nehad Khader, 'Interview with Dr Basil Baker: quick death under fire, slow death under siege', *Journal of Palestine Studies*, 44(1) (Special issue: Operation Protective Edge), Autumn 2014, p. 131.

61  Wafa, 'Experts say 2014 worst for Gaza in decades', Wafa Palestinian News & Info Agency, 29 December 2014, online, english.wafa.ps/index. php?action=detail&id=27424.

62  International Committee of the Red Cross, 'Gaza, 1.5 million people', 2009, p. 6.

63  Office of the United Nations Special coordinator for the Middle East Peace Process (UNScO), 'Gaza in 2020: a livable place?', August 2012, p. 2, www. unrwa.org/userfiles/file/publications/ gaza/Gaza%20in%202020.pdf.

64  Center On Housing Rights and Evictions, 'Israel's violations of the International Covenant on Civil and Political Rights with regard to house demolitions, forced evictions and safe water and sanitation in the Occupied Palestinian Territory and Israel', 2010, p. 32, www2.ohchr.org/english/bodies/ hrc/docs/ngos/COHRE_AlHaq_Israel99. pdf.

65  Office of the United Nations Special coordinator for the Middle East Peace Process (UNScO), 'Gaza in 2020: a livable place?', August 2012, p. 2, www. unrwa.org/userfiles/file/publications/ gaza/Gaza%20in%202020.pdf.

66  UNOCHA, 'Joint statement: 30 international aid agencies: "We must not fail in Gaza"', 26 February 2015, online, www.ochaopt.org/documents/30_aid_ agencies_joint_statement_26_feb_2014_ eng.pdf.

67  Oxfam International, 'Vital building in conflict damaged Gaza to take more than a century at current rate', 26 February 2015, online, www.oxfam.org/en/pressroom/ pressreleases/2015-02-26/vital-building- conflict-damaged-gaza-take-more- century-current.

68  Reuters, 'WikiLeaks: Israel aimed to keep Gaza economy on brink of collapse', *Haaretz*, 5 January 2011, www. haaretz.com/news/diplomacy-defense/ wikileaks-israel-aimed-to-keep-gaza- economy-on-brink-of-collapse-1.335354.

69  United Nations General Assembly Human Rights Council, 12th session, Agenda item 7, A/HRC/12/48, 25 September 2009, para. 27, 'Human Rights in Palestine and other Occupied Arab Territories: Report of the United Nations Fact-Finding Mission on the Gaza Conflict' (also referred to as the 'Goldstone Report').

70  Harriet Sherwood, 'Israel accused over "cruel" Gaza blockade', *Guardian*, 30 November 2010, www.guardian. co.uk/world/2010/nov/30/israel- accused-over-gaza-blockade.

71  Amira Hass, '2,279 calories per person: how Israel made sure Gaza didn't starve', *Haaretz*, 17 October 2012, online, www.haaretz.com/news/ diplomacy-defense/2-279-calories-per- person-how-israel-made-sure-gaza-didn- t-starve.premium-1.470419.

72  Food security is defined by the UN as 'when all people, at all times, have physical, social and economic access to sufficient, safe and nutritious food that meets their dietary needs and food preferences for an active and healthy life' – World Health Organization, 'Food security", online, www.who. int/trade/glossary/story028/en/.

73  UNWRA, 'Food insecurity in Palestine remains high', 2014, online, www. unrwa.org/newsroom/press-releases/ food-insecurity-palestine-remains-high.

74 Ibid.

75 Hilmi S. Salem, 'Impacts of climate change on biodiversity and food security in Palestine', Paper for the International Conference on 'Climate Change, Biodiversity and Food Security in the South Asian Region', in Neelima Jerath, Ram Booj and Gurharminder Singh (eds), 'Climate change, biodiversity and food security in the South Asian region, 2010', Sponsored by the United Nations Educational, Scientific and Cultural Organization (UNESCO) and the Punjab State Council for Science and Technology (PSCST), Chandigarh, India, 3/4 November 2008, p. 232.

76 Ibid.

77 Chris Gunness, 'The world has broken its promises about rebuilding Gaza – and the children will suffer', *Guardian*, 21 February 2015, online, www. theguardian.com/commentisfree/2015/feb/21/chris-gunness-gaza-aid-broken-promises-children-suffer.

78 UNDP, 'Climate Change Adaption Strategy and Programme of Action for the Palestinian Authority', 2011, www.ps.undp.org/content/dam/papp/docs/Publications/UNDP-papp-research-climatechange.pdf, p. 68.

79 Weizmann to David Lloyd George, 29 December 1919, CZA Z4/16024, cited by Jehuda Reinharz, 'Chaim Weizmann as political strategist: the initial years, 1918–1920', in Frances Malino and Phyllis Cohen Albert (eds), *Essays in Modern Jewish history: A tribute to Ben Halpern*, East Brunswick and London, Associated University Presses, 1982, p. 276.

80 *Boston Sunday Globe*, 18 October 1998 cited by Jad Isaac, 'Israeli Palestinian water relationships: paternalistic neo-colonialism', Applied Research Institute Jerusalem, 2009, p. 10, www.arij.org/index.php/publications/papers/103-2009-papers/372-israeli-palestinian-water-relationships-paternalistic-neocolonialism.

81 UN News Centre, 'Right to water and sanitation is legally binding, affirms key UN body', 1 October 2010, www.un.org/apps/news/story.asp?NewsID=36308.

82 BTSELEM, 'Water crisis', www.btselem.org/water.

83 Office for the Coordination of Humanitarian Affairs, 'The humanitarian impact on Palestinians of Israeli settlements and other infrastructure in the West Bank', 2007, p. 114, www.ochaopt.org/documents/TheHumanitarianImpactOfIsraeliInfrastructureTheWestBank_full.pdf.

84 Applied Research Institute Jerusalem, 'The water rights and the water wrongs in Palestine', 2008, p. 3, online, www.arij.org/files/admin/2008/The%20Water%20Rights%20and%20the%20Water%20Wrongs%20in%20Palestine.pdf.

85 Qatar News Agency, 'Israel violates Palestinian people's right to water and sanitation', Waterworld, 2011, www.waterworld.com/index/display/news_display/1469693117.html.

86 Jad Isaac and Jane Hilal, 'Palestinian landscape and the Israeli–Palestinian conflict', *International Journal of Environmental Studies*, 68(4), 2011, pp. 426–7. For a study on the effects of industrial waste from an industrial Israeli settlement on residents of a Palestinian village, see Khloud Hammad and Mazin Qumsiyeh, 'Genotoxic effects of Israeli industrial pollutants on residents of Bruqeen village (Salfit district, Palestine)', *International Journal of Environmental Studies*, 70(4), 2013, pp. 655–62.

87 Office of the United Nations Special coordinator for the Middle East Peace Process (UNScO), *Gaza in 2020: A Livable Place?*, August 2012, www.unrwa.

org/userfiles/file/publications/gaza/
Gaza%20in%202020.pdf, p. 3.

88  Emergency Water Sanitation
and Hygiene in the occupied Palestinian
territory (EWASH), 'Gaza water disaster',
Factsheet, 2014, online, www.ewash.
org/files/library/Gaza%20water%20disa
ster%20info%20graphic.pdf.

89  Palestine Solidarity Campaign,
'Israel, Palestine and the environment',
2012, online, www.palestinecampaign.
org/wp-content/uploads/2012/12/
environment-factsheet.pdf.

90  See, e.g., Mohammed Omer,
'Closure turns Gaza's streets into
sewers', *The Electronic Intifada*, 28
January 2008, electronicintifada.
net/content/closure-turns-gazas-
streets-sewers/7325, and Alex Shams,
'Sewage floods Gaza streets as lack
of fuel plunges strip into darkness',
*Ma'an News*, 15 November 2013, online,
www.maannews.net/eng/ViewDetails.
aspx?ID=647697.

91  COHRE (Centre On Housing
Rights and Evictions), 'Israel's violations
of the International Covenant on Civil
and Political Rights with regard to house
demolitions, forced evictions and safe
water and sanitation in the Occupied
Palestinian Territory and Israel', 2010,
p. 34.

92  Emergency Water Sanitation and
Hygiene in the occupied Palestinian
territory (EWASH), 'Gaza water disaster'.

93  COHRE (Centre On Housing
Rights and Evictions), 'Israel's violations
of the International Covenant on Civil
and Political Rights', p. 33.

94  Amnesty International, 'Thirsting
for justice: Palestinian access to water
restricted', 27 October 2009, online,
www.amnesty.org/en/library/asset/
MDE15/028/2009/en/634f6762-
d603-4efb-98ba-42a02acd3f46/
mde150282009en.pdf.

95  Patrick Wolfe, 'Settler colonialism
and the elimination of the native',

*Journal of Genocide Research*, 8(4),
December 2006, p. 388, and Da'Na
(2013).

96  See Mazin Qumsiyeh, 'The
coming environmental Nakba' in
*The Third Palestinian Environmental
Awareness and Education Conference*,
EEC, Bethlehem, 2013, pp. 57–9.

97  Jad Isaac and Nader Hrimat,
'Assessing the impact of Israel's
segregation wall on the Palestinian
agricultural biodiversity', Applied
Research Institute Jerusalem, paper
presented at the International
Conference on Promoting Community-
driven Conservation and Sustainable
Use of Dryland Agrobiodiversity,
Sponsored by the International Center
for Agricultural Research in the Dry
Areas (ICARDA), Aleppo, Syria, 18–21
April 2005, p. 3.

98  Salem, 'Impacts of climate
change', p. 233.

99  UNDP, 'Climate Change Adaption
Strategy and Programme of Action for
the Palestinian Authority', p. 68.

100  Ibid., p. 68.

101  See, e.g., UNEP, 'Desk study
on the environment in the Occupied
Palestinian Territories', Nairobi, Kenya,
2003, p. 126; Isaac and Hilal, 'Palestinian
landscape and the Israeli–Palestinian
conflict', pp. 413–29; Jon Pattee, 'Ecocide:
war lays waste to Palestine', Albawaba.
com, online, www.albawaba.com/news/
ecocide-war-lays-waste-palestine.

102  Palestine Solidarity Campaign
'Israel, Palestine and the environment'.

103  Ari Briggs, 'Is government and
Supreme Court inaction poisoning our
children?', *Jerusalem Post*, 15 July 2012,
online, www.jpost.com/Opinion/Op-
Ed-Contributors/Is-government-and-
Supreme-Court-inaction-poisoning-our-
children.

104  Ibid.

105  World Wildlife Fund,
'Deforestation and climate change',

2014, online, www.wwf.org.uk/what_we_do/forests/deforestation_and_climate_change/.

106  Arab Group for the Protection of Nature, 2014, online, apnature.org/en/node/719.

107  Fadi Dweik, 'Changes of the Palestinian agricultural land use under drought', Applied Research Institute Jerusalem, 2012, online, www.arij.org/files/admin/2012/Changes%20of%20the%20Palestinian%20agricultural%20Land%20use%20under%20Drought.pdf.

108  Arab Group for the Protection of Nature, 2014.

109  Ethan Ganor, 'Holy Land or living hell? Ecocide in Palestine', Indybay, 21 September 2005, online, www.indybay.org/newsitems/2005/09/21/17689901.php.

110  Max Ajl, 'The ecocide of Palestine', 26 July 2009, online, www.maxajl.com/the-ecocide-of-palestine/.

111  Rosina Hassoun, 'Water between Arabs and Israelis: researching twice promised resources', in John M. Donahue and Barbara Johnston (eds), *Water, Culture, and Power: Local Struggles in a Global Context*, Island Press, Washington, DC, 1998.

112  Salem, 'Impacts of climate change', p. 230.

113  For a detailed study of the decline of vertebrate biodiversity in the Bethlehem area, see Mazin B. Qumsiyeh, Sibylle S. Zavala and Zuhair S. Amr, 'Decline in vertebrate biodiversity in Bethlehem, Palestine', *Jordan Journal of Biological Sciences*, 7(2), June 2014, pp. 101–7.

114  UNEP, 'Desk study on the environment in the Occupied Palestinian Territories', p. 95.

115  See also Dweik, 'Changes of the Palestinian agricultural land use under drought'.

116  UNEP, 'Desk study on the environment in the Occupied Palestinian Territories', p. 95.

117  See, e.g., Salem, 'Impacts of climate change', p. 230.

118  UNEP, 'Desk study on the environment in the Occupied Palestinian Territories', p. 95.

119  Ibid., p. 95.

120  Palestine Solidarity Campaign, 'Israel, Palestine and the environment'.

121  Alon Tal, *Pollution in a Promised Land: An Environmental History of Israel*, University of California Press, Berkeley, and London, 2002, pp. 6–13, cited in Palestine Solidarity Campaign, 'Israel, Palestine and the environment'.

122  Arab Association for Human Rights, 'Israel's poisonous aerial spraying of Negev crops is illegal, endangers health of Bedouin villagers', *The Electronic Intifada*, 6 July 2004, electronicintifada.net/content/israels-poisonous-aerial-spraying-negev-crops-illegal-endangers-health-bedouin-villagers/385.

123  Balfour Declaration, 1917, cited by BBC, 'Balfour Declaration', 29 November 2001, online, news.bbc.co.uk/1/hi/in_depth/middle_east/israel_and_the_palestinians/key_documents/1682961.stm.

124  Some exceptions include Jiryis (1976), Zureik (1979), Grossman (1993), Masalha (2005), Cook (2006) and Pappé (2011).

125  Joseph Massad, 'Resisting the Nakba', *Al-Ahram weekly*, 897, 15–21 May 2008, online, weekly.ahram.org.eg/2008/897/op8.htm. See Sa'di and Abu-Lughod (2007) for more on the Nakba as an ongoing experience.

126  Minority Rights International, 'Israel overview', Last updated March 2011, online, www.minorityrights.org/5002/israel/israel-overview.html.

127  For an analysis of Israeli governmental policies towards its Palestinian minority during the military government period of 1948–66, see As'ad Ghanem, 'Palestinians in Israel

under the Israeli "ethnocratic" regime', in Ilan Pappé (ed.), *The Israel/Palestine Question: A Reader*, 2nd edn, Routledge, London and New York, 2007, pp. 207–31.

128  In 2014 there were approximately 1,694,000 Israeli Palestinians out of total 8,180,000 Israeli citizens (Israel Central Bureau of Statistics, online, www.cbs.gov. il/reader/newhodaot/hodaa_template. html?hodaa=201411111 (in Hebrew)).

129  International Crisis Group, 'Identity crisis: Israel and its Arab citizens', 4 March 2004, online, www. crisisgroup.org/en/regions/middle-east-north-africa/israel-palestine/025-identity-crisis-israel-and-its-arab-citizens.aspx.

130  Ibid.

131  Associated Press, 'Israel's Arab minority not celebrating Independence Day', Ynet, 5 July 2008, online, www. ynetnews.com/articles/0,7340,L-3540821,00.html.

132  Alon and Benn, 'Netanyahu: Israel's Arabs are the real demographic threat' *Haaretz*, 2003, online, www. haaretz.com/print-edition/news/ netanyahu-israel-s-arabs-are-the-real-demographic-threat-1.109045.

133  BBC, 'UN blasts Israeli marriage law', 15 August 2003, online, news.bbc. co.uk/1/hi/world/middle_east/3152651.stm.

134  It is worth noting the argument that the term 'Bedouin' is denationalizing and divisive to the Palestinian collective. See Ahmad Amara, 'The Negev land question: between denial and recognition', *Journal of Palestine Studies*, 42(4), Summer 2013.

135  Human Rights Watch, 'Off the map: land and housing rights violations in Israel's unrecognized Bedouin villages', March 2008, www.hrw.org/ sites/default/files/reports/iopt0308_1.pdf.

136  Amara, 'The Negev land question', p. 27.

137  Nasser Rego, 'Israel, 1948 and memoricide: the 1948 Al-'Araqib/Negev massacre and its legacy', *Holy Land Studies*, 11(2), 2012, pp. 205–15.

138  Shirly Siedler, 'Minister: Israel looking at ways to lower Bedouin birthrate', *Haaretz*, 29 September 2014, online, www.haaretz.com/news/ national/.premium-1.618119.

139  B. Michael, 'This too, is genocide', *Haaretz*, 8 October 2014, online, www.haaretz.com/opinion/. premium-1.619773.

140  Ismael Abu-Saad, 'Present absentees: the Arab school curriculum in Israel as a tool for de-educating indigenous Palestinians', *Holy Land Studies*, 7(1), 2008, p. 39.

141  Ian Black, '1948 no catastrophe says Israel, as term nakba banned from Arab children's textbooks', *Guardian*, 22 July 2009, online, www.theguardian. com/world/2009/jul/22/israel-remove-nakba-from-textbooks.

142  Abu-Saad, 'Present absentees'.

143  Adalah, 'Discriminatory Laws: Update', April 2011, adalah. org/upfiles/2011/Discriminatory_Laws_ update_April_2011.pdf.

144  Rania Dabaneh and Dalia Hatuqa, 'Israel's road signs policy "erases memory of place"', Al Jazeera, 4 February 2015, online, www.aljazeera. com/news/2015/02/israel-road-signs-policy-erases-memory-place-150202105553841.html.

145  Liora R. Halperin, 'The irony of erasing Arabic: making Hebrew Israel's only language ignores history', *The Jewish Daily Forward*, 10 October 2014, online, forward.com/articles/206861/ the-irony-of-erasing-arabic/.

146  Ibid.

147  See, e.g., BBC, 'Row over "standard" Hebrew signs', 13 July 2009, online, news.bbc.co.uk/1/hi/8148089.stm.

148  Maoz Azaryahu, 'Hebrew, Arabic, English: the politics of

multilingual street signs in Israeli cities', *Social & Cultural Geography*, 13(5), 2012, p. 476.

149  Jonathan Cook, 'Israel conducts population transfer training exercises', *The Electronic Intifada*, online, electronicintifada.net/v2/article11570. shtml.

150  UNHRC 25th session, Agenda item 7, Report of the Special Rapporteur on the situation of human rights in the Palestinian territories occupied since 1967, Richard Falk, 13 January 2014, para. 51, p. 14.

151  Ibid.

152  See Boyle (2003); Boyle, 'The United States promotes Israeli genocide against the Palestinians', Z Space, 11 January 2009, online, www. zcommunications.org/the-united-states-promotes-israeli-genocide-against-the-palestinians-by-francis-boyle.html; and Boyle, 'The Palestinian genocide by Israel', 30 August 2013, www. countercurrents.org/boyle300813.htm.

153  Boyle (2003: 159).

154  See, e.g., israelgenocide.com for a citizen's campaign petitioning the UN Office of the Special Adviser on the Prevention of Genocide to 'Investigate the Possibility that Israel is Committing the Crime of Genocide Against the Palestinian People', as well as 'Jews Against Genocide', a group of activists particularly active during Operation 'Protective Edge' in 2014: www. facebook.com/Jews-Against-Genocide-694634937278932/timeline/.

155  Russell Tribunal on Palestine, Findings of the Final Session, Brussels, 16/17 March 2013. www. russelltribunalonpalestine.com/en/full-findings-of-the-final-session-en.

156  Claudia Card, 'Genocide and social death', *Hypatia*, 18(1), Winter 2003.

157  Mohammed Abed, 'Clarifying the concept of genocide', *Metaphilosophy*, 37(3/4), p. 326.

158  Including, non-exhaustively, 'politicide' (e.g. Kimmerling 2003), 'indigenocide' (e.g. Raymond Evans, '"Crime without a name": colonialism and the case for indigenocide', in Moses (2008: 133–47), 'ethnocide' and 'memoricide' (e.g. Masalha 2012). For more on these terms, see Patrick Wolfe, 'Structure and event', in Moses (2008: 120).

159  Kuala Lumpur Foundation to Criminalise War, 'Israel found guilty of genocide', 2013, online, criminalisewar. org/2013/israel-found-guilty-of-genocide/.

160  Ibid.

161  See Rashed and Short (2012) for more on this.

162  Massad 2006: 171). Presumably, therefore, any just and peaceful resolution to the 'Palestinian Question' would necessarily incorporate a process of decolonization, although it is beyond the remit of this chapter to elaborate on this.

## 4  Sri Lanka

1  Vinay Prakash specializes in researching human rights, nationalism, security and defence in South Asia, Africa and the Balkans. He is currently associated with the Human Rights Consortium as a research associate and was formerly a researcher at SEESAC-UNDP in Belgrade, Serbia, where he worked on illicit proliferation of small arms and light weapons, and gender mainstreaming in the security sector. Vinay holds a Master's degree in International Peace and Security from King's College London, and a Bachelor's degree in Economics (Honours) from Christ University, Bangalore, India.

2  ABC News, 'Up to 100,000 killed in Sri Lanka's Civil War: UN', 20 May 2009, goo.gl/uUcQcl. A study conducted by Harvard Medical School

and the University of Washington says at least 215,000 people have been killed in Sri Lanka's civil war, with the likely estimate being around 338,000. The numbers, first published in the *British Medical Journal*, are quoted at goo. gl/Vo58D4.

3 J. Lunn, C. Taylor and I. Townsend, 'War and peace in Sri Lanka', Research Paper 09/51, House of Commons Library, 2009.

4 The UNSC panel states that 40,000 civilians may have been killed during the last stages of the civil war, other reports suggest more; Francis Harrison claims 100,000 Tamil civilians have been missing since the war and may have been killed; 'One hundred thousand Tamils missing after Sri Lanka war', 17 December 2012, goo. gl/7Djo9M.

5 BBC, 'Why Sri Lankan Tamils won't remember war dead this year', 27 November 2010, goo.gl/7HDfkb.

6 Report of the Office of the United Nations High Commissioner for Human Rights on Promoting Reconciliation, *Accountability and Human Rights in Sri Lanka.*

7 Kshatriyas is a Sanskrit term for one of four broad social groups (*varnas*) that comprise the military and ruling elite. They are economically and politically active and second to the Brahmins in the social hierarchy.

8 Obeyeskere (2006), cited in DeVotta (2007: 7).

9 Gananath Obeyesekere, 'Religious symbolism and political change in Ceylon', *Modern Ceylon Studies*, 1970, p. 45; DeVotta (2007).

10 The tiger was the state symbol of the Tamil Cholas, whose reign and influence extended beyond southern India and Sri Lanka to include South-East Asia. The political upheaval in Sri Lanka saw the LTTE utilize the myth of the Cholan tiger in the fight for

independence against the Sri Lankan state.

11 The Portuguese brought Catholicism in the sixteenth century, the Dutch and later the British brought with them different branches of Christianity. See De Silva (1981).

12 Although the popular belief is that the Tamils benefited the most from English education, it is clear that this was primarily the Jaffna Tamils and not the eastern or Indian Tamils. Similarly, the same can be said about the Sinhalese in western Sri Lankan, particularly in and around Colombo, who were more anglicized and formed the elite.

13 This is reflected in Whitaker (1990).

14 For more see Obeyesekere (1984); Kapferer (1988); Gunawardana (1990).

15 The Kandy kings were Hindus who embraced Buddhism and DeVotta states that this proved effective in ruling the kingdom as the Buddhist clergy (sanga) cared only for the kings to provide 'subventions and protection to Buddhism more than their ethnicity' (DeVotta 2007: 13).

16 DeVotta (2007: 314). This is further enunciated in the Mahavamsa.

17 Tennent (1860: 400). Tennent's use of Malabar clearly refers to the Tamils. However, the term today refers to the people from the northern part of Kerala, India. While Tennent's use of the word could be an unintentional error, it must be noted that many scholars considered that medieval Lanka was a cosmopolitan melting pot with the presence of communities from as far as the Deccan and South-East Asia. See Gunawardana (1990).

18 Arunachalam in Rogers (1990: 97).

19 Shaivism is a branch of Hinduism that reveres Shiva as the principal supreme deity as opposed to Vaishnavism, where reverence is given

to Vishnu. Although reverence is given to a principal deity, many practitioners of this faith do acknowledge and worship other deities within the Hindu pantheon but to a lesser extent.

20 Department of Census and Statistics, 2012, www.statistics.gov.lk/.

21 The Indian and the Sri Lankan Tamils are classified as two different ethnic groups in Sri Lanka; ibid.

22 For first-hand information on the politics in colonial Sri Lanka, see *British Documents on the End of the Empire Part 1: The Second World War and the Soulbury Commission 1939–1945*, ed. K. M. Silva, Stationery Office, London, 1997, and *British Documents on the End of Empire Part II: Towards Independence 1945–1948*, ed. K. M. De Silva, Stationery Office, London, 1997.

23 The 'repatriation' of Indian Tamils took place in three phases, with the Nehru-Kotelwala Pact, 1954, the Sirima-Shastri Pact, 1964, and the Sirima-Gandhi Pact, 1972. The percentage of the Indian Tamil population in Sri Lanka today stands at 4.8 per cent, down from 11 per cent in 1948; the 'Grant of Citizenship to Persons of Indian Origin Act (2003)' regularized the remaining stateless Indian Tamils on the island.

24 The SLFP sought to win the votes of the majority by exploiting the language issue; however, many Sinhalese political parties first opposed this move but were forced to endorse the Sinhala-only view when realization dawned that failure to do so would lead to permanent loss of the Sinhalese electorate.

25 The Official Language Act failed to recognize Tamil. The law saw protests from Tamils and moderate Sinhalese. See Arasarathnam (1964).

26 De Silva stated: 'The qualifying mark for admission to the medical faculties was 250 (out of 400) for Tamil students, whereas it was only 229 for the Sinhalese. Worse still, this same pattern of a lower qualifying mark applied even when Sinhalese and Tamil students sat for the examination in English. In short, students sitting for examinations in the same language, but belonging to two ethnic groups, had different qualifying marks.' In Wilson (1988).

27 The enrolment percentage of Tamil medium students into engineering courses fell from 40.8 per cent in 1970/71 to 24.4 per cent in 1973/74. Implementation of district quotas saw it fall further to 13.2 per cent in 1975. Tamil enrolment into medical courses fell from 36.9 per cent in 1973 to 25.9 per cent in 1974 and just 20 per cent in 1975. See C. R. de Silva, 'The impact of nationalism on education: the school takeover (1961) and the university admission crisis, 1970–75', 1978. The Tamils were considered a 'privileged race' (Coomaraswamy) under the British, hence the Tamil districts in the north and east faced the brunt of the quota system along with people in Colombo, which was the bastion of anglicized Sinhalese elites.

28 Prior to the Vaddhukoddai resolution, all the Tamil political parties demanded devolution of powers in the north and east and always pursued non-violent means.

29 Report by the Fact Finding Mission to Trincomalee (Eastern Province) Sri Lanka, 16/17 April 2006, goo.gl/K4niG4.

30 International Crisis Group, 'Sri Lanka's North I: The denial of minority rights', *Asia Report*, 219, 16 March 2012, p. 17.

31 Sri Lanka's land mass is divided into three zones; eastern and northern Lanka constitute the island's Dry Zone, while the Central Highlands and south-western part of the island form the Wet Zone. Added to this there is a third

intermediate zone circling the highlands which serves as a buffer between the Wet and the Dry Zones. See Patrick Peebles, 'Colonisation and ethnic conflict in the Dry Zone of Sri Lanka', *Journal of Asian Studies*, 49(1), 1990; Muggah (2008).

32  G. H. Peiris, 'Agrarian transformations in British Sri Lanka', *Sri Lanka Journal of Agrarian Studies*, 2, 1981, p. 5. Also cited in Peebles, 'Colonisation and ethnic conflict', p. 37.

33  H. M. Gunaratne, *For a Sovereign State*, Sarvodaya Publications, Colombo, 1988, p. 201.

34  Federal Party, *Ilankai Tamil Arasu Kadchi Silver Anniversary Volume*, Jaffna, 1974, in Peebles (1990: 38).

35  N. Sanderatne, 'Agricultural development: controversial issues', in S. Kelegama (ed.), *Economic Policy in Sri Lanka, Issues and Debates*, Vijitha Yapa Publications, Colombo, 2004.

36  Vaddukoddai Resolution, 14 May 1976.

37  Radhika Coomaraswamy, *The 1972 Republican Constitution in the Postcolonial Constitutional Evolution of Sri Lanka*, p. 137.

38  The Gal-Oya Riots of 1956 are considered the first of many anti-Tamil pogroms, and began when Sinhalese mobs attacked peaceful protesters in Gal-Oya, Eastern Province. *Sunday Times*, 16 October 2005, sundaytimes. lk/051016/plus/4.html.

39  Amerasinghe, in Peebles (1990: 37).

40  The People's Tribunal on State-aided Sinhala Colonisation, p. 13, ptsrilanka.org/en/evidence/sri-lanka/ colonisation/10-state-aided-sinhala-colonisation.

41  Ministry of Mahaweli Development, *Mahaweli: Project and Programme*, Ministry of Land and Land Development and Ministry of Mahaweli Development, 1984, p. 93.

42  J. R. Jayawardene, 'Remembering Black July', *Daily Telegraph*, 11 July 1983, blackjuly.info/quotestext.html. Statement to the press just a few weeks prior to the anti-Tamil pogroms.

43  Eleanor Pavey, 'The massacres in Sri Lanka during Black July riots of 1983', *Online Encyclopedia of Mass Violence*, Science Po, 2008, p. 5.

44  Tambiah (1986); Pavey, 'The massacres in Sri Lanka'.

45  *The Review*, International Commission of Jurists, December 1983.

46  Ana Pararajasingham, 'State terror: Black July revisited', 2006, blackjuly.wordpress.com/2006/07/03/ state-terror-black-july-of-1983-revisited/ or www.sangam.org/ANALYSIS/ AnaJuly83.htm.

47  E. O Ballance, *The Cyanide War: Tamil Insurrection in Sri Lanka 1973–1988*, Brassey's, 1989; Amnesty International, *Rapport annuel pour l'année civile 1983*, 1984; Pavey, 'The massacres in Sri Lanka'.

48  *Daily Express*, 19 July 1983; Pararajasingham, 'State terror'.

49  P. Seighart, 'Sri Lanka mounting tragedy of errors', International Committee of Jurists, March 1984, p. 76, icj.wpengine.netdna-cdn.com/wp-content/uploads/1984/03/Sri-Lanka-mounting-tragedy-of-errors-fact-finding-mission-report-1984-eng.pdf.

50  *New York Times*, 7 August 1983.

51  Seighart, 'Sri Lanka mounting tragedy', p. 76.

52  Ibid.

53  'Sri Lanka: racism and the authoritarian state', *Race & Class, a Journal for Black & Third World Liberation*, XXVI(1), Summer 1984, p. 4.

54  Pararajasingham, 'State terror'.

55  Ibid.

56  Gamini Dissanayake, addressing Tamil estate workers on 5 September 1983, just a month after anti-Tamil pogroms; in DeVotta (2007: 30).

57 N. Murray, 'The state against Tamils', *Race & Class*, XXVI(1), 1984, p.100.

58 Ibid., p.100.

59 BBC, 'Sri Lanka's historic Jaffna Library "vandalised"', 10 November 2010.

60 Pavey, 'The massacres in Sri Lanka', 11.

61 The Hindu, 'Tiger vs Tiger in eastern Sri Lanka', 15 March 2004, www.thehindu.com/2004/03/15/stories/2004031504231400.htm.

62 Permanent People's Tribunal, 'People's Tribunal Sri Lanka', 7–10 December 2013.

63 Report of the Secretary-General's Panel of Experts on Accountability in Sri Lanka, 31 March 2011, p. 41, para. 137.

64 Report of the Office of the United Nations High Commissioner for Human Rights on Promoting Reconciliation, Accountability and Human Rights in Sri Lanka, p. 6, para. 24.

65 Ibid., p. 11, para. 53.

66 Report of the Commission of Inquiry on Lessons Learnt and Reconciliation, 4.171, November 2011, p. 92.

67 *Telegraph*, 'More than 280,000 Sri Lankan refugees could be held in camps for up to two years', November 2011.

68 Report of the Office of the United Nations High Commissioner for Human Rights on Promoting Reconciliation, Accountability and Human Rights in Sri Lanka, p. 7.

69 N. Malathy, 'A fleeting moment in my country: the last years of the LTTE de-facto state', *Clarity Press Atlanta*, 2012, p. 106.

70 'Sri Lanka: women's insecurity in the north and east', *Crisis Group Asia Report*, 217, December 2011, p. 23.

71 Human Rights Watch, 'We will teach you a lesson; sexual violence against Tamils by the Sri Lankan security forces', 2013, p. 43.

72 Human Rights Watch (2013), 'We Will Teach You a Lesson; Sexual Violence against Tamils by the Sri Lankan Security Forces', p.19

73 Ibid., p. 20.

74 Sri Lanka Supporting Regional Governance program (SuRG), 'Post-war support for widowed mothers: a gender impact assessment', prepared for the US Agency for International Development (USAID), May 2011, p. 6.

75 Report of the Office of the United Nations High Commissioner for Human Rights on Promoting Reconciliation, Accountability and Human Rights in Sri Lanka, p. 5, para. 18.

76 Read more in Human Rights Watch, 'We will teach you a lesson'.

77 Muggah (2008); Land Acquisition Act 1950 at goo.gl/g43vf7.

78 'As fighting flares in civil war, key Buddhist shuns nonviolence', *Washington Post*, 26 March 2008, goo.gl/Uxx8D6.

79 Champika Ranawaka, interview with Juliana Rufus of Al Jazeera, 29 August 2007.

80 The Tamils and the Muslims of the east share cultural ties, including the matrilineal clan structure, marriage patterns, and other cultural and religious practices; joint paddy cultivations and other forms of economic cooperation were commonplace between the Eastern Tamils and Muslims. This also helped reinforce distinctions with the higher-caste Tamils of the north; International Crisis Group, 'Sri Lanka's Eastern Province: land, development, conflict', *Asia Report*, 159, 15 October 2008, p. 21.

81 Ibid., p. 9.

82 Ibid., p. 23.

83 Easwaran Ratnam, 'Curfew in Ampara as Muslims clash with STF', *Daily Mirror*, 21 September 2006; International Crisis Group interview, representative of the Peace Secretariat for Muslims, Colombo, May 2008.

84 International Crisis Group, 'Sri Lanka's Eastern Province', p. 21.

85 Basic population information on Trincomalee district, 2007, based on special enumeration report, Department of Census and Statistics. See also Appendix C, International Crisis Group, 'Sri Lanka's Eastern Province'.

86 Christina Williams, 'Land grabs jeopardize peace in Sri Lanka', Terra Nullius: Land Rights, Human Rights and Law, 2014, goo.gl/CfMCZH.

87 IRIN Humanitarian News and Analysis, 'Sri-Lanka's northern housing funding gap', 25 February 2014.

88 'Notes on the military presence in Sri Lanka's Northern Province', *Economic and Political Weekly of India*, July 2012.

89 IHS Jane Defence Academy, 'Sri Lanka outline 12% defence budget increase', 28 September 2014, goo.gl/st89P1.

90 International Crisis Group interview, fisherman, Selvanagar and Mullaitivu, August/September 2011, *Asia Report*, 219, 16 March 2012.

91 Ellis Eric, Brother Grip e-link, sri-lanka.theglobalmail.org/brothers-grip.

92 Inter Press Service 'Women battle on after Lanka war', 30 October 2013.

93 Tamil National Alliance (TNA), Situation report, 21 October 2011.

94 International Crisis Group interview, September 2011, *Asia Report*, 219, 16 March 2012.

95 International Crisis Group interviews, farmers, Weli Oya, September 2011.

96 Ibid.

97 International Crisis Group interviews, villagers, Maritimepattu, Mullaitivu, August 2011.

98 International Crisis Group interview, farmer in Weli Oya, August/September 2011.

99 TNA Situation Report: North and East, 21 October 2011, p. 4.

100 'Rajapaksa's "War Heroes' Day" to counter Sirisena's "Remembrance Day"', *New Indian Express*, 17 May 2015.

101 'Tamils say barred from commemorating war dead, Sri Lanka denies', Reuters, 19 May 2014, goo.gl/pAKeFl.

102 Ibid.

103 'Army occupation angers Sri Lankan Tamils four years after war ends. Methods of intimidation include "text message, a phone call and a delivery of two cow skulls", an animal sacred to Tamil Hindus', Reuters, 15 November 2013, full text available at goo.gl/coPK7A.

104 'Tamil National Alliance wins northern provincial elections in Sri Lanka', *Times of India*, 22 September 2013, goo.gl/9A9fr1.

105 '3 roads close to A9 highway in Kanyakaranakulam have been renamed', two after fallen soldiers and one after a Buddhist monk, International Crisis Group report, 16 March 2012, p. 17, cited by TNA situation report.

106 International Crisis Group report, 16 March 2012, p. 17.

107 Ibid., p. 18.

108 Al Jazeera interview with Dr Saravanamuttu, www.youtube.com/watch?v=XE_T42f3gfY.

109 Ibid.

110 Medananda Thera in De Votta (2007: n2).

111 'Sri Lanka president wins constitutional power boost', Reuters, 8 September 2010, goo.gl/QFr2WA.

112 Janaki Lenin, 'On track to "go beyond the critical point": Sri Lanka still losing forests at rapid clip', 2014, goo.gl/MY1JKN.

113 Ibid.

114 Conservation International, *Western Ghats and Sri Lanka*, www.biodiversityhotspots.org/xp/hotspots/ghats/Pages/default.aspx.

115 Ibid.

116  Lenin, 'On track to "go beyond ... "'

117  Ibid.

118  For the best description of all that such an agenda entails see Harvey (2005).

119  S. Fernando, 'People and the environment should be first', Movement for National Land and Agricultural Reform (MONLAR), 2012, goo.gl/RBygsy.

120  Government of Sri Lanka, 'Connecting to growth: Sri Lanka's Poverty Reduction Strategy, in regaining Sri Lanka: vision and strategy for accelerated development', 2002, p. 83.

121  M. Hardy, 'Poverty in Sri Lanka', *Sunday Leader*, 4th April 2010, goo. gl/90jDFk.

## 5  Australia

1  A variation of some of the arguments and data analysis presented in this chapter was previously published as Short (2010b).

2  Indeed, Dirk Moses (2004: 16) writes: 'the term genocide is used to refer to two phenomena in Australian history: frontier violence, mainly in the nineteenth century, and the various policies of removing Aboriginal children of mixed decent from their families, mainly in the twentieth century'. For detailed discussion on the question of cultural genocide in Australia see Van Kreiken (1999, 2004 and in particular 2008)

3  Tony Barta (2000: 249) ends his paper suggesting that 'relations of genocide are alive', while Patrick Wolfe (2006) argues, correctly in my view, that settler colonialism is structure not an event.

4  Such as Kevin Buzzacot and Darren Blomfeld from the Tent Embassy, Michael Anderson and John Ah Kitt, to name a few.

5  As of 17 February 2015 there are at least 250 indigenous groups in Australia that have proved to the satisfaction of the Native Title Tribunal that they have a continuing attachment to their land and live by 'traditional laws and customs'; see www.nntt.gov.au/searchRegApps/ NativeTitleClaims/Pages/default.aspx.

6  Although such indigenous peoples are not the focus of the arguments presented here, this is not to suggest that they are not therefore to be considered indigenous. As Yin Paradies (2006: 363) writes, 'although the poor and the rich Indigene, the cultural reviver and the quintessential cosmopolitan, the fair, dark, good, bad and disinterested may have little in common, they are nonetheless all equally but variously Indigenous'.

7  Broadly speaking, this concept incorporates the political rights to autonomy and self-government and can be achieved without impacting upon the territorial integrity of the settler state itself. Furthermore, as Pritchard notes, 'the right to self-determination embraces a comprehensive scale of realisation-possibilities, including: the creation of a State, secession, self-government and self-administration'. See Pritchard (1992). In the Australian context the realization of this right will stretch across the range of possibilities Pritchard lists, varying according to the nature of the indigenous group to which it is directed. For at least those 250 groups which have, to date, proved a continuing connection to their ancestral lands, and which still primarily live in accordance with distinct 'traditional' laws and customs, referred to earlier, it could involve the negotiation of a decolonizing international legal instrument (with the indigenous peoples being regarded as nations equal in status but not in form to the settler state) independent of the institutions of all parties and the establishment of an impartial implementation mechanism. This

approach was advocated by the National Aboriginal and Islander Legal Service Secretariat (NAILSS) to the UN in the 1990s – see Pritchard (ibid.) on this, and for a more theoretical outline of such 'treaty federalism' see the excellent chapter by Tully (2000). For those indigenous peoples whose indigeneity is primarily based on 'placelessness', as Paul Havemann (2005) has termed it, or on a lack of culture, and who have been dispossessed from their ancestral lands, it could simply involve having a meaningful role in the design and implementation of those government policies directed at them; loosely covered by Pritchard's notion of 'self-administration'.

8 Moran (1999). For a detailed critique of the Australian reconciliation process, see Short (2008).

9 CERD. Decision 1(53); Cerd/C/53/Misc.17/Rev.2, 11 August 1998.

10 M. Brough, Explanatory Memorandum Aboriginal Land Rights (Northern Territory) Act 1976 Amendment Bill 2006, Commonwealth Parliament of Australia, House of Representatives, 2006.

11 Ibid.

12 Altman (2007: 6) cites one community a whole year later. Consequently, under the new Northern Territory policy 'Stronger Futures', there is even more of a steer towards opening up indigenous land to economic development, with extractive industries no doubt at the top of the waiting list.

13 Sydney Morning Herald, 13 September 2007, www.theaustralian.news.com.au/story/0,25197,22409420-2702,00.html.

14 'Indigenous intervention "genocide"', AAP, 7 August 2007, www.news.com.au/story/0,23599,22202385-29277,00.html.

15 Ampe Akelyernemane Meke Mekarle, *Little Children Are Sacred*, Northern Territory Government, Board of Enquiry into the Protection of Aboriginal Children from Sexual Abuse, www.inquirysaac.nt.gov.au/pdf/bipacsa_final_report.pdf.

16 See UN Special Rapporteur James Anaya's comments, www2.ohchr.org/english/issues/indigenous/rapporteur/docs/ReportVisitAustralia.doc.

17 Langton (2007) and Noel Pearson, 'Noel Pearson discusses the issues faced by Indigenous communities', ABC Lateline Interview, 26 June 2007, www.abc.net.au/lateline/content/2007/s1962844.htm.

18 Copy on file with author.

19 Press release, Prescribed Area Peoples' Alliance, 7 November 2008, on file with author.

20 *Open Letter: Enough Is Enough*, Prescribed Area Peoples' Alliance, 3 February 2009.

21 Ibid.

22 P. O'Mara, 'Health impacts of the Northern Territory Intervention', *Medical Journal of Australia*, 192(10), 17 May 2010. Executive summary available at www.mja.com.au/public/issues/192_10_170510/oma10307_fm.pdf.

23 Ibid.

24 Ibid., my emphasis.

25 Ibid., my emphasis. The government has since engaged in 'consultations' with some indigenous peoples but on the understanding that the Intervention will continue – only the fine detail is up for discussion. These 'consultations' have since been exposed as grossly inadequate in a major response from the group known as 'concerned Australians' in conjunction with the relevant Aboriginal communities in the Northern Territory, and authors Michele Harris, Larissa Behrendt and Nicole Watson: *Will They Be Heard?*, intranet.law.unimelb.edu.au/staff/events/files/Willtheybeheard%20Report.pdf.

26  See www.gneppartnership.org/.

27  See comments by resources minister Martin Ferguson, who recently stated 'there's going to be uranium mining on an increasing basis in Western Australia, South Australia and the Northern Territory, we'll see uranium mining in Queensland in due course'; www.abc.net.au/news/stories/2009/07/21/2631570.htm.

28  For a basic introduction to and pictures of the surface impacts of these mines, see www.world-nuclear.org/info/Country-Profiles/Countries-A-F/Appendices/Australia-s-Uranium-Mines/, and for but one example of wider environmental impacts see Lindsay Murdoch, 'Polluted water leaking into Kakadu from uranium mine', *The Age*, 13 March 2009, www.theage.com.au/national/polluted-water-leaking-into-kakadu-from-uranium-mine-20090312-8whw.html.

29  The words 'as such' (interestingly absent from the draft Lemkin penned) in the UN Genocide Convention require that groups be intentionally targeted because of who they are and not for any other reason such as economic gain or self-defence. Given that perpetrators may well have multiple reasons for genocidal action it is not surprising that Helen Fein for one has advocated a more sociologically realistic approach – 'sustained purposeful action': see Fein (1993: 24). Under such a formula intent can also be inferred from action, which is entirely consistent with a long-established principle in British common law – in British common law 'foresight and recklessness are evidence from which intent may be inferred'; see Wien J. in *R* v. *Belfon* (1976) 3 All ER 46.

30  Stronger Futures in the Northern Territory Act 2012, 'An Act to build stronger futures for Aboriginal people in the Northern Territory, and for related purposes', No. 100, 2012, comloaw.gov.au/details/C2012A00100.

31  Mick Gooda and Helen Szoke, 'Opening statement to Senate Community Affairs Legislation Committee inquiry into the NTER (Stronger Futures) Bills', Australian Human Rights Commission, 2012, www.humanrights.gov.au/opening-statement-senate-community-affairs-legislation-committee-inquiry-nter-stronger-futures-bills.

32  See stoptheintervention.org/facts/stronger-futures-legislation/yolngu-statement-and-supporters#cA.

33  See the list of supporters at stoptheintervention.org/facts/stronger-futures-legislation/yolngu-statement-and-supporters#cA.

34  See stoptheintervention.org/facts/press-releases/leading-australians-angered-by-government-plans-that-will-continue-discrimination-in-the-nt.

35  indigenousjobsandtraining review.dpmc.gov.au/forrest-review.

36  www.fmgl.com.au/.

37  For more on this see Short (2008: ch. 3).

38  'Land rights under attack', *Land Rights News: Northern Edition*, 4, October 2014, p. 1, www.nlc.org.au/files/various/LRNOct2014v2.pdf.

39  The full NT government's submission can be found at www.aph.gov.au/Parliamentary_Business/Committees/Joint/Northern_Australia/Inquiry_into_the_Development_of_Northern_Australia/Submissions.

40  'Land rights under attack', p. 1.

41  Ian Viner, 'The plan to undermine the Land Rights Act', *Land Rights News: Northern Edition*, October 2014.

42  S. Kerins, 'The future of Homelands/Outstations', Centre for Aboriginal Economic Policy Research, Topical Issue no. 1/2010, Australian National University, www.anu.edu.au/caepr/.

43  John Altman, 'No movement on the outstations', *Sydney Morning Herald*, 26 May 2009.

44  Ibid.

45  See M. Moran, 'The viability of "hub" settlements', Academy of the Social Sciences, Dialogue 29, 1/2010, p. 38.

46  Ibid.

47  See 'Agreements, Treaties and Negotiated Settlements Project' at www.atns.net.au/agreement. asp?EntityID=5399.

48  www.australiasnorthernterritory. com.au/Living/nt-cities-towns/Pages/ remote-towns.aspx.

49  Kerins, 'The future of Homelands/Outstations'.

50  Altman, 'No movement on the outstations'. See also Kerins, 'The future of Homelands/Outstations', on this point.

51  Gumatj statement, Working Group on Aboriginal Rights Circular, 26 October 2008, on file with author.

52  S. Everingham, 'Killing us softly: Dodson slams outstations plan', *ABC News*, 2 June 2009, www.abc.net.au/ news/stories/2009/06/02/2587462. htm, my emphasis.

53  L. Trevaskis, 'Homelands need support over growth towns', *ABC Rural*, 6 December 2011, www.abc.net. au/site-archive/rural/nt/content/201112/ s3385010.htm.

54  A. Taylor, 'First insights: population change for Territory Growth Towns, 2001 to 2011', Northern Institute/Faculty of Law, Education, Business and the Arts, 2011, www.cdu. edu.au/sites/default/files/research-brief-2012-07.pdf.

55  D. Trigger, J. Keenan, K. de Rijke and W. Rifkin, (2014) 'Aboriginal engagement and agreement-making with a rapidly developing resource industry: coal seam gas development in Australia', *The Extractive Industries and Society*, 1, 2014, pp 176–88.

56  L. Keogh, 'Frack or frack-off? Coal seam gas', *Queensland Historical Atlas: Histories, Cultures, Landscapes*, 2014, www.qhatlas.com. au/frack-or-frack-off-coal-seam-gas.

57  Ibid.

58  Department of Natural Resources and Mines, 2014.

59  Trigger et al., 'Aboriginal engagement and agreement-making'.

60  For a general overview of CSG-related problems, see Mariann Lloyd-Smith, 'Is Australia's present Britain's future?', Extreme Energy Initiative, School of Advanced Study, University of London, 20 May 2013, extremeenergy. org/2013/05/31/licence-to-drill-is-australias-present-britains-future-podcast/.

61  Trigger et al., 'Aboriginal engagement and agreement-making'.

62  Ibid., p. 182.

63  National Native Title Tribunal, Githabul People's Native Title Determination, 2007, www.nntt. gov.au/news-and-communications/ publications/documents/multimedia and determination brochures.pdf.

64  H. Lovejoy, 'International court challenge over CSG mining', *EchoNet Daily*, 2 January 2013, www.echo. net.au/2013/01/international-court-challenge-over-csg-mining/.

65  E. Farrow-Smith, 'Aboriginal people reject Native Title over coal seam gas', *ABC News*, 2012, www. abc.net.au/news/2012-12-15/ githubulcsg/4429486.

66  Ibid.

67  Lovejoy, 'International court challenge over CSG mining'.

68  A. Macdonald-Smith, 'Aboriginal council takes on greens, farmers over gas', *Financial Review*, 14 October 2013, www.afr.com/p/australia2-0/ aboriginal_council_takes_on_greens_ OPdixfkeUqHKxoKTnLL14J.

69  Ibid.

70  B. Code, SBS, 13 February 2012, www.sbs.com.au/news/article/2013/02/13/nsw-aboriginal-land-council-battles-csg-fair-share.

71  Trigger et al., 'Aboriginal engagement and agreement-making', p.182.

72  'Native Title claimants fight CSG', *Moree Champion*, 23 May 2013, www.moreechampion.com.au/story/1521589/native-title-claimants-fight-csg/.

73  Ibid.

74  See www.lockthegate.org.au/missions_principles_aims.

75  See aidanricketts.com/media-release-author-provides-activist-training-for-csg-free-group/.

76  'Native Title claimants fight CSG'.

77  S. Smail, 'Aboriginal group takes Newman Government to United Nations over fracking in the Lake Eyre Basin', *ABC News*, 4 December 2014, www.abc.net.au/news/2014-12-04/aboriginal-group-takes-newman-government-to-un-over-fracking/5939046?WT.mc_id=newsmail.

78  Ibid.

79  Polly Higgins, 'Two views: deep disconnect or deep care', *Eradicating Ecocide*, 18 March 2014, ecocidealert.com/?tag=csg.

80  D. Maher, I. R. Santos and D. R. Tait, 'Mapping methane and carbon dioxide concentrations and $\delta 13C$ values in the atmosphere of two Australian coal seam gas fields', *Journal of Water, Air and Soil Pollution*, 225, 18 November 2014.

81  D. Chris, 'SCU researchers trace methane emissions to CSG mines', *EchoNet Daily*, 19 November 2014, www.echo.net.au/2014/11/scu-researchers-trace-methane-emissions-csg-mines/.

82  G. Readfearn, 'Australia named worst-performing industrial country on climate change', *Guardian*, 8 December 2014, www.theguardian.com/environment/2014/dec/08/australia-named-worst-performing-industrial-country-on-climate-change.

83  Ibid.

84  Ibid.

85  Ibid.

86  CSIRO and Bureau of Meteorology, www.climatechangeinaustralia.gov.au/en/about/.

87  My emphasis. The full draft is reproduced at www.preventgenocide.org/law/convention/drafts/.

88  For more on this point see Short (2003).

89  The Rudd government recently pledged to reinstate the application of the Racial Discrimination Act 1975 to the Intervention's enabling legislation. The resulting legislation (Social Security and Other Legislation Amendment (Welfare Reform and Reinstatement of the Racial Discrimination Act) Act, 2010) effects only a partial reinstatement and relies on many otherwise discriminatory measures being deemed 'special measures' for the benefit of Aboriginal people. However, the structural nature of Intervention measures such as compulsory land acquisition has been assessed by UN human rights bodies as inherently discriminatory and plainly inconsistent with the notion of 'special measures' – see Vivian and Schokman (2009) (while written before the Act's passage their analysis still stands), and the full reports: United Nations Human Rights Committee, Consideration of Reports Submitted by States Parties Under Article 40 of the Covenant, CCPR/C/AUS/CO/5, May 2009, and United Nations Special Rapporteur on the situation of human rights and fundamental freedoms of indigenous people, Observations on the Northern Territory Emergency Response, Advance Version, February 2010, at www2.ohchr.org/english/issues/indigenous/rapporteur/docs/ReportVisitAustralia.pdf. See also

Amnesty International, 'Submission to Senate Standing Committee on Community Affairs: Reinstating the RDA in the NTER legislation', February 2010, stoptheintervention.org/uploads/files_to_download/AI-RDA-NTER-legislation-11-2-10.pdf.

90 Moses (2010:13), and see Moses (2008: 15). Concerning the crime of genocide in international law, and its relationship to the emerging human rights order, in a letter to the UN secretary general on 6 May 1947 Lemkin wrote: 'Somehow the French Revolution which proclaimed the rights of man forgot about the most essential of our rights, namely the right to exist. It is inconceivable to have an orderly International life without effective International guarantees of the right of existence of entire human groups and their cultures.' Letter to H. E. M. Trygve Lie, Secretary General United Nations, 6 May 1947, UNOG Archives Registry Collection, Palais des Nations, Geneva, Box Folder reference SOA 318-1-01-4.

91 Raphael Lemkin, letter to Mrs Eleanor Roosevelt, 18 May 1946, p. 2, UNOG Archives Registry Collection, Palais des Nations, Geneva. Box Folder reference SOA 318-1-01-4.

92 Personal correspondence, November 2009.

93 RCIADIC, 'National Report', Royal Commission on Aboriginal Deaths in Custody, 1991, www.austlii.edu.au/au/other/IndigLRes/rciadic. But we should note once again that in contemporary Australia not all indigenous peoples' indigeneity is defined in such uniquely separate terms from the wider Australian community.

## 6 Tar sands and the indigenous peoples of northern Alberta

1 Jen Huseman is a Research Associate at the Human Rights Consortium, School of Advanced Study, University of London, and a graduate of the School's MA in Understanding and Securing Human Rights. She has researched indigenous issues in North America for all her adult life and is an active advocate for indigenous rights. We have worked together for many years. An alternate version of the arguments and data analysis presented in this chapter was published as Huseman and Short (2012).

2 From Liv Inger Somby's article, published on the Galdu (Resource Centre for the Rights of Indigenous Peoples) website, 3 November 2009, www.galdu.org/web/index.php?odas=3757&giella1=eng.

3 But of course not all people who define themselves as indigenous have a strong physical or spiritual connection to land generally or to a specific geographical setting. As Yin C. Paradies writes: 'although the poor and the rich Indigene, the cultural reviver and the quintessential cosmopolitan, the fair, dark, good, bad and dis-interested may have little in common, they are nonetheless all equally but variously Indigenous' (2006: 363).

4 Abed (2006: 327). As Abed (ibid.: 328) has so poignantly argued, 'social death is the harm that makes genocide an ethically unique form' of destruction.

5 Two examples of this perspective are Chalk and Jonassohn (1990: 25) and Jones (2006). Jones wrote: 'I consider mass killing to be definitional to genocide ... in charting my own course, I am wary of labelling as "genocide" cases where mass killing has not occurred' (ibid.: 22).

6 The 'Cold War' era began circa 1945, 'pitting the U.S. and its "Free World" allies against the "Communist Bloc" ...' (Churchill 1997: 289).

7 Indian land was also used extensively for nuclear weapons testing during this period.

8  In this way, the concept of a 'national sacrifice area' was first established in official North American governmental policy, whereby certain areas of the USA/Canada could be demarcated for overdevelopment and exploitation in the name of so-called 'national priorities', 'irrespective of the resulting permanent environmental damages' (Higgins-Freese Tomhave 2002). As Churchill (1997: 185) attested, having the last of their territory zoned 'so as to forbid human habitation' would obviously 'precipitate [the] ultimate dispersal' of the impacted Native group, thus 'causing its disappearance as a "human group" per se'. We must therefore conclude that this policy is genocidal, 'no more ... no less'. In addition, one can see how 'colonizers attempt to deny ... reality by forcing those people who have already been rendered dirty, impure, and hence expendable to face the most immediate consequences of environmental destruction' (Smith 2005:57).

9  'Although Canada is often seen as a junior partner in many imperial ventures, it has taken the lead in the subjugation of the people of Afghanistan and Haiti. Perhaps more significant, if less well known, is Canada's role in subordinating the planet to the needs of the oil and gas industry' (Stainsby 2007: 89).

10  Ibid.: 89.

11  'The recoverable oil reserves in Alberta's tar sands are so bountiful that they vie with oil reserves in Saudi Arabia and Venezuela for top status' (Petersen 2007: 12).

12  St Catherine's Milling and Lumber Co.v. The Queen (1888), 14 App. Cas. 46 (J.C.P.C.), summary available at www.bloorstreet.com/200block/rstcth.htm.

13  Treaty negotiations, and the ultimate extinguishment of Indian title, were facilitated by the imposition on the natives of colonizer forms of social and political organization. In the years following 1867, the new Dominion of Canada sought to 'enfranchise' Indians through a succession of Indian Acts which 'registered' Indians, gave them band numbers, defined them as 'wards of the state', created Indian 'reserves' under Crown title and arranged native-controlled local government (Samson 2003: 42).

14  Record Group 10, Public Archives of Canada, Ottawa, 3708: 19502-1.

15  Canada, Treaty 8, pp. 6–7.

16  McKenna, 26 July 1899, Record Group 10, Public Archives of Canada, Ottawa, 6732: 420–2.

17  See Daniel (1999: 83, and the interviews with elders, pp.144–60).

18  Canada, Treaty 8.

19  The United Nations Environment Programme, for example, has identified the tar sands 'as one of the world's top 100 hotspots of environmental degradation' (International Boreal Conservation Campaign (IBBC), 'Canada's tar sands: America's #1 source of oil has dangerous global consequences', 2008, www.borealbirds.org/resources/factsheet-ibcc-tarsands.pdf).

20  WWF, Scraping the Bottom of the Barrel?, 2008, p. 27, assets.panda.org/downloads/unconventional_oil_final_lowres.pdf.

21  G. Monbiot, 'The urgent threat to world peace is ... Canada', 2009, www.monbiot.com/2009/12/01/the-urgent-threat-to-world-peace-is-%E2%80%A6-canada/.

22  Ibid.: 3. 'The Syncrude tailings pond is now the largest dam on earth, to be rivaled only by China's Three Gorges Dam' (ibid.: 3).

23  For a conservative estimate, see the citation of a US Department of Energy study in Natural Resources

Defence Council, 'Setting the record straight: lifecycle emissions of tar sands', p. 2, www.docs.nrdc.org/energy/files/ene_10110501a.pdf, and for the upper range see Romm (2008) and www.greenpeace.org/france/PageFiles/266537/dirtyoil.pdf.

24  See www.netl.doe.gov/energy-analyses/pubs/Life%20Cycle%20GHG%20Analysis%20of%20Diesel%20Fuel%2oby%20Crude%20Oil%20Source%202.pdf.

25  www.columbia.edu/~jeh1/mailings/2011/20110603_SilenceIsDeadly.pdf.

26  M. Humphries, *North American Oil Sands: History of Development, Prospects for the Future*, Congressional Research Service, 2008, www.fas.org/sgp/crs/misc/RL34258.pdf, accessed September 2011.

27  E. Black, 'America with no plan for oil interruption: ironically, as price per barrel drops, American oil supply from Canada imperiled', *The Cutting Edge News*, 2008, online, www.thecuttingedgenews.com/index.php?article=896, accessed September 2011.

28  Smith (2005: 179). This is sometimes referred to as 'internal colonialism'.

29  W. C. Bradford, 'Beyond reparations: an American Indian theory of justice', Paper #170, Indiana University, 2004, p. 7, hosted by the Berkeley Electronic Press (bepress), law.bepress.com/expresso/eps/170, accessed February 2009.

30  Smith (2005: 122), and on the 'forcible' point see Short (2010).

31  The first forty years of its operation have already seen an incredible 'influx of workers, machinery and infrastructure' into the area, which has had severely detrimental impacts on local Native communities 'socially, politically, and culturally' (LaDuke 1999: 84). This has included rises in alcohol and drug abuse, 'violence, prostitution, elder and spousal abuse', and abandoned children 'fathered by workers who are long gone' (Stainsby 2007: 35). Sociologists have referred to these particular 'ramifications of … development as the "boom town syndrome". It is not considered to be a healthy environment for the host population and is exacerbated when the local host community is a different colour, race, and culture from the newcomers' (LaDuke 1999: 84).

32  See Timoney (2007: 52), citing Judge Michael Horrocks' judgement in the case. It reads: 'because of an earlier fire that had damaged a flare area, contaminated material escaped from a flare pond into the wastewater system. A major fire then took place on 21 January 1982 in the wastewater pond; one witness described the flames as being three hundred feet high.'

33  Timoney (2007: 53). Furthermore, 'a 2008 study by Environmental Defense showed that the tailings ponds were leaking 11 million litres of liquid into the surrounding environment everyday' (I. Willms, 'Photo essay: Fort Chipewyan lives in the shadow of Alberta's oil sands', *This Magazine*, 2011, online, this.org/magazine/2011/11/01/fort-chipewyan-photo-essay/, accessed November 2011.

34  IBBC, *Canada's Tar Sands*, p. 3: 'Tar sands companies are currently licensed to use over 90 billion gallons of water from the Athabasca River per year – enough water to satisfy the needs of a city of two million people'. Furthermore, 'most if not all of this water is taken out of the natural cycle and never replaced' (K. Thomas, 'A new wave of exploitation: Canada, Alberta defy UN, sell off rights to disputed Lubicon land', *The Dominion*, 48, 2007, p. 38).

35  IBBC, *Canada's Tar Sands*, p. 1.

36  ibid., p. 1.

37 'These are the communities of Mikisew Cree First Nation and the Athabasca Chipewyan First Nation at Fort Chipewyan, Fort McMurray First Nation, Fort McKay First Nation, and to the south, the Chipewyan Prairie First Nation. They are all members of the Athabasca Tribal Council' (Indigenous Environmental Network, *Tar Sands: Indigenous Peoples and the Giga Project*, Information Sheet no. 1, c. 2008, online, dirtyoilsands.org/files/IEN_CITSC_Tar_Sands_Info_Sheet.pdf, accessed November 2009).

38 'The observations of the elders are remarkably consistent. They say that the river water tastes differently now – oily, sour, or salty. When the river water is boiled, it leaves a brown scum in the pot. Fish (and muskrat) flesh is softer now, and watery. Ducks, muskrats, and fishes taste differently now. There is now a slimy, sticky, or gummy material ... in their fishing nets in winter; this started in perhaps the mid-1990s' (Timoney 2007: 46).

39 CBC News, 'Oilsands poisoning fish, say scientists, fisherman', 2010, online, www.cbc.ca/news/canada/edmonton/story/2010/09/16/edmonton-oilsands-deformed-fish.html, accessed September 2011.

40 M. Rolbin-Ghanie, 'What in Tar Nation? Life amongst the tar sands', *The Dominion*, 48, Autumn 2007, p. 21.

41 In response to O'Connor's findings, Alberta Health and Wellness released their own report in 2006 which 'declined to conclude the cancer rate in Fort Chipewyan was elevated' (Timoney 2007: 6). Timoney suggests that this was perhaps due to the fact that the government 'used questionable statistical methods and assumptions and underestimated levels of arsenic in water and sediment and the fish consumption rate of many Fort Chipewyan residents' (ibid: 4).

42 Tar Sands Watch, 'Will Dr. John O'Connor ever be cleared?', 2009, online, www.tarsandswatch.org/will-dr-john-o-connor-ever-be-cleared, accessed March 2010.

43 CBC News, 'Fort Chip cancer rates higher than expected: report', 2009, online, www.cbc.ca/news/health/story/2009/02/06/edm-fort-chip-cancer.html, accessed 2011.

44 Alberta Cancer Board, Division of Population Health and Information Surveillance, 'Cancer incidents in Fort Chipewyan, Alberta, 1995–2006', February 2009, www.ualberta.ca/~avnish/rls-2009-02-06-fort-chipewyan-study.pdf, accessed September 2011. The report concluded that levels of the rare cancer cholangiocarcinoma were not higher than expected, however (ibid.).

45 However, 'according to Natural Resources Defence Council Senior Scientist Dr. Gina Solomon ... almost all of the cancer types that were elevated have been linked scientifically to chemicals in oil or tar' (D. Droitsch and T. Simieritsch, on behalf of the Pembina Institute, 'Canadian aboriginal concerns with oil sands: a compilation of key issues, resolutions and legal activities', Pembina Institute, September 2010, online, www.pembina.org/pub/2083, accessed September 2011).

46 Alberta Health Services, 'Fort Chipewyan cancer study findings released', 2009, online, www.albertahealthservices.ca/500.asp, accessed September 2011.

47 CBC News, 'Fort Chip cancer rates higher than expected'.

48 Indigenous Environmental Network, Information Sheet no. 1, p. 2.

49 S. Bell, 'Oilsands pollution worse than expected', *Slave River Journal*, 2009, online, srj.ca/oilsands-pollution-worse-than-expected-p4362.htm, accessed September 2011.

50  Ibid.

51  As mentioned above, so did Timoney's 2007 report.

52  Royal Society of Canada, 'Expert panel report: environmental and health impacts of Canada's oil sands industry', www.rsc.ca/.../RSC%20report%20complete%20secured%209Mb.pdf.

53  Water Monitoring Data Review Committee, 'Evaluation of four reports on contamination of the Athabasca river system by oil sands operations', environment.alberta.ca/documents/WMDRC_-_Final_Report_March_7_2011.pdf.

54  Sierra Club Prairie, 'Royal Society report on tar sands ignores traditional knowledge of indigenous peoples, community members and allies, raise concerns', www.sierraclub.ca/en/node/3554.

55  Respecting Aboriginal Values and Environmental Needs, 'Making "cents" of the tar sands', 2011, online, raventrust.com/blog/2011-09/making-cents-of-the-tar-sands.html, accessed September 2011.

56  CBC News Canada, 'Cancer rates downstream from oilsands to be probed', 2011, online, www.cbc.ca/news/canada/edmonton/story/2011/08/19/edm-cancer-oilsands-fort-chipewyan-study.html, accessed September 2011.

57  Churchill (2004: 34). Another case in point, and contrary to popular belief, is that the expression 'Final Solution', in a genocidal sense, was not, in fact, coined by the Nazis, but by Canadian Indian Affairs Superintendent Duncan Campbell Scott in a letter from April 1910 written 'in response to a concern raised by a west coast Indian Affairs official about the high level of death in the coastal residential schools'. Scott wrote: 'It is readily acknowledged that Indian children lose their natural resistance to disease by habituating so closely in these schools, and that as a consequence they die at a much higher rate than in their villages. But this alone does not justify a change in the policy of this Department, which is geared towards a final solution to our Indian Problem' (Annett 2005: 15). That these deaths were the result of intentional infliction of disease was further corroborated by contemporary top Canadian Indian Affairs medical officer Doctor Peter Bryce, who stated in an official report in 1907: 'I believe the conditions are being deliberately created in our residential schools to spread infectious diseases ... The mortality rate in the schools often exceeds fifty percent. This is a national crime' (ibid.: 20).

58  IBBC, 'Canada's tar sands', p. 1. This will give Alberta the fastest rate of deforestation in the world outside the Amazon.

59  National Resource Defense Council et al., 'Tar sands pipelines safety risks', 2011, online, February 2011, www.nrdc.org/energy/files/tarsandssafetyrisks.pdf, accessed August 2011.

60  Ibid., p. 5.

61  Ibid., p. 4.

62  Ibid., p. 9. 'Over half of the pipelines currently operating in Alberta have been built in the last twenty years as the tar sands region developed' (ibid.: 8).

63  Ibid., p. 9.

64  Ibid., p. 8.

65  STL Today, 'Worries over defective steel force TransCanada to check oil pipeline', 2010, online, www.stltoday.com/news/local/metro/article_c0b2c3a6-ef66-532b-9266-2dd501b8df75.html, accessed September 2011.

66  NRDC et al., 'Tar sands pipelines safety risks', p. 5.

67  '... as DilBit flows through a pipeline, pressure changes within the pipeline can cause the natural gas liquid

condensate component to move from liquid to gas phase. This forms a gas bubble that can impede the flow of oil. Because this phenomenon – known as column separation – presents many of the same signs as a leak to pipeline operators, real leaks may go unnoticed. Because the proper response to column separation is to pump more oil through the pipeline, misdiagnoses can be devastating' (ibid.: 6–7).

68 Onearth Magazine, NDRC, 'Michigan spill increases concern over tar sands pipelines', 2010, online, www.onearth.org/article/michigan-oil-spill-tar-sands-concerns, accessed September 2011.

69 Onearth Magazine, NDRC, 'Montana's Yellowstone river oil spill: the shape of things to come?', 2011, online, www.onearth.org/article/yellowstone-river-oil-spill, accessed September 2011.

70 See 'Stop tar sands: scars upon sacred land IV: a slow industrial genocide', www.dailykos.com/story/2011/08/19/1007991/-Stop-Tar-Sands:-Scars-Upon-Sacred-and-IV:-A-Slow-Industrial-Genocide.

71 See this report on a recent benzene leak: switchboard.nrdc.org/blogs/aswift/suncor_spill_reveals_gaps_in_s.html.

72 For an in-depth discussion of this, see Stainsby (2007).

73 Indigenous Environmental Network, Tar Sands, p. 6.

74 Ibid., p. 6.

75 Ibid., p. 3.

76 See Treaty 8, available at www.ainc-inac.gc.ca/eng/1100100028813.

77 G. Poitras, 'Why am I attending?', Blog, 24 September 2011, edmortimer.wordpress.com/2011/09/24/cree-george-poitras-ottawa-tarsands-action-monday-/.

78 C. Thomas-Muller, 'Tar sands: environmental justice, treaty rights and Indigenous Peoples', 2008, canadiandimension.com/articles/1760.

79 See, for example, this damning exposé of the Royal Bank of Scotland's funding of the tar sands industry: peopleandplanet.org/dl/cashinginontarsands.pdf.

80 For example, see Anderson and Bows (2011).

81 See the IEA's latest report at www.worldenergyoutlook.org/.

82 See D. Carrington, 'The burning issue of energy cannot wait for economic good times', 2011, www.guardian.co.uk/environment/damian-carrington-blog/2011/nov/09/iea-energy-outlook-carbon-climate-change?INTCMP=SRCH.

**7 Looking to the future: where to from here?**

1 M. Atlas, 'Rush to judgment: an empirical analysis of environmental equity in U.S. environmental protection agency enforcement actions', Law and Society Review, 35, 2001, pp. 633–82; P. Stretesky and M. J. Hogan, 'Environmental justice: an analysis of superfund sites in Florida', Social Problems, 45, 1998, pp. 268–87; Stretesky et al. (2013).

2 M. A. Long, P. B. Stretesky, M. J. Lynch and E. Fenwick, 'Crime in the coal industry: implications for green criminology and treadmill of production', Organization & Environment, 25(3), 2012, pp. 328–46; M. Lynch, 'The greening of criminology: a perspective for the 1990s', The Critical Criminologist, 2(3), 1990, pp. 3–4, 11–12; M. Lynch, M. Long, K. Barrett and P. Stretesky, 'Why green criminology and political economy matter in the analysis of global ecological harms', British Journal of Criminology, 53, 2013, pp. 997–1016.

3 Lynch et al., 'Why green criminology and political economy matter'.

4  The term 'auto-genocide' is used because some genocides would arguably be the consequence of conscious and unconscious self-destructive actions, within the capitalist system, by members of the victim social figurations themselves. The plural 'genocides' is also used here because, despite global capitalism's culturally genocidal tendencies, there are still many thousands of distinct social figurations - *'geni'* – around the world today.

5  See Yale Environment, *360 Forum: Just How Safe Is 'Fracking' of Natural Gas?*, Opinion, 20 June 2011.

**Conclusion**

1  P. Mobbs, 'Less is a four letter word', Presentation to the Extreme Energy Initiative, University of London, 2015, www.fraw.org.uk/mei/temp/sas_

2015.html http://www.fraw.org.uk/mei/temp/sas_2015.html.

2  For a wonderfully insightful critique of the idea of 'progress', see C. Samson, *A World You Do Not Know: Settler societies, indigenous peoples and the attack on cultural diversity*, School of Advanced Study, University of London Press, London.

3  A. Simms, 'Nine meals from anarchy', *Guardian*, 7 January 2010, www.theguardian.com/commentisfree/2010/jan/11/nine-meals-anarchy-sustainable-system; E. Platt, 'Britain need not be nine meals from anarchy', *New Statesman*, 27 June 2011, www.newstatesman.com/society/2011/06/food-growing-urban-london-city.

4  See deepgreenresistance.org and his brutally frank and honest discussions over three volumes on the *Problem of Civilisation*.

# BIBLIOGRAPHY

Abed, M. (2006) 'Clarifying the concept of genocide', *Metaphilosophy*, 37(3/4): 308–30.

Abowitz, D. A. (2002) 'Bringing the sociological into the discussion: teaching the sociology of genocide and the Holocaust', *Teaching Sociology*, 30.

Ali, Z. (2013) 'A narration without an end: Palestine and the continuing Nakba', MA thesis, Birzeit University.

Altman, J. (2007) 'The "National Emergency" and land rights reform: separating fact from fiction: an assessment of the proposed amendments to the Aboriginal Land Rights (Northern Territory) Act 1976', Briefing paper for Oxfam Australia, Centre for Aboriginal Economic Policy Research, Australian National University, 7 August.

Amara, A. (2013) 'The Negev land question: between denial and recognition', *Journal of Palestine Studies*, 42(4): 27.

Anaya, J. (2004) *Indigenous Peoples in International Law*, Oxford: Oxford University Press.

Anderson, B. J. and G. L. Theodori (2009) 'Local leaders' perceptions of energy development in the Barnett Shale', *Southern Rural Sociology*, 24(1): 113–29.

Anderson, K. and A. Bows (2011) 'Beyond "dangerous" climate change: emission scenarios for a new world', *Philosophical Transactions of the Royal Society A*, 369(1934): 20–44, rsta. royalsocietypublishing.org/ content/369/1934/20.full.

Annett, K. D. (2005) *Hidden from History: The Canadian Holocaust – the Untold Story of the Genocide of Aboriginal Peoples by Church and State in Canada*, 2nd edn, sponsored by the Truth Commission into Genocide in Canada.

Apple, B. E. (2014) 'Mapping fracking: an analysis of law, power, and regional distribution in the United States', *Harvard Environmental Law Review*, 38: 217–44.

Arasarathnam, S. (1964) *Ceylon*, New York: Prentice-Hall.

Attwood, B. and A. Markus (1999) *The Struggle for Aboriginal Rights*, NSW: Allen and Unwin.

Azaryahu, M. (2012) 'English: the politics of multilingual street signs in Israeli cities', *Social & Cultural Geography*, 13(5): 461–79.

Badiou, A. (2006) *Polemics*, London and New York: Verso.

Bakan, J. (2005) *The Corporation: The Pathological Pursuit of Profit and Power*, London: Constable and Robinson.

Barnett, J. (2001) 'Environmental security and U.S. foreign policy', in P. G. Harris (ed.), *The Environment, International Relations, and U.S. Foreign Policy*, Washington, DC: Georgetown University Press.

Barry, J. and K. Woods (2010) 'The environment', in M. Goodhart (ed.), *Human Rights: Politics and Practice*, Oxford: Oxford University Press.

Barta, T. (1985) 'After the Holocaust: consciousness of genocide in Australia', *Australian Journal of Politics and History*, 31(1): 154–61.

— (2000) 'Relations of genocide: land and lives in the colonization of Australia', in I. Walliman and N. M. Dobrowski (eds), *Genocide and the Modern Age: Etiology and Case Studies of Mass Death*, pp. 237–52.

— (2008a) 'With intent to deny: on colonial intentions and genocide denial', *Journal of Genocide Research*, 10(1): 111–33.

— (2008b) '"They appear actually to vanish from the face of the Earth." Aborigines and the European project in Australia Felix', *Journal of Genocide Research*, 10(4): 519–39.

— (2008c) 'Decent disposal: Australian historians and the recovery of genocide', in D. Stone (ed.), *The Historiography of Genocide*, Basingstoke: Palgrave Macmillan, pp. 296–322.

Bassiouni, C. (1999) *Crimes against Humanity in International Criminal Law*, 2nd revised edn Kluwer Law International.

Bauman, Z. (1990) *Modernity and the Holocaust*, Ithaca, NY: Cornell University Press.

Beach, D. (2013) 'How the fracking boom impacts rural Ohio', *EcoWatch: Transforming Green*, 16 September, ecowatch.com/2013/09/16/fracking-boom-impacting-rural-ohio/.

Becker, H. (1997) *Outsiders*, New York: Free Press.

Bedell, F. (2014) 'Economic injustice as an understanding of the existence of two Americas – wealth and poverty', *Open Journal of Political Science*, 4(3): 101–8.

Behrendt, L. (2001) 'Genocide: the distance between law and life', *Aboriginal History*, 25: 132–47.

Benvenisti, M. (2000) *Sacred Landscapes: The Buried History of the Holy Land since 1948*, Berkeley: University of California Press.

Bird Rose, D. (1991) *Hidden Histories:*

*Black Stories from Victoria River Downs, Humbert River and Wave Hill Stations*, Canberra: Aboriginal Studies Press.

Björk, T. (1996) 'The emergence of popular participation in world politics: United Nations Conference on Human Environment 1972', Department of Political Science, University of Stockholm, www.folkrorelser.org/johannesburg/stockholm72.pdf, accessed 16 June 2012.

Boyle, F. (2003) *Palestine, Palestinians and International Law*, Atlanta, GA: Clarity Press Inc.

Brantlinger, P. (2004) '"Black armband" versus "white blindfold" history in Australia: a review essay', online, www.ideals.illinois.edu/bitstream/handle/2142/3506/brantlinger.pdf?sequence=2.

Brasch, W. (2012) *Fracking Pennsylvania: Flirting with Disaster*, California: Greeley and Stone.

Brion, M. (1929) *Bartolomé de las Casas: 'Father of the Indians'*, New York: E. P. Dutton.

Brody, H. (2002) *Maps and Dreams*, London: Faber & Faber.

Brook, D. (1998) 'Environmental genocide: Native Americans and toxic waste', *American Journal of Economics and Sociology*, 57(1): 105–13.

Brown, V. J. (2014) 'Radionuclides in fracking wastewater: managing a toxic blend', *Environmental Health Perspectives*, 122(2): A50–A55.

Butcher, T. (2013) 'A "synchronised attack": on Raphael Lemkin's holistic conception of genocide', *Journal of Genocide Research*, 15(3): 253–71.

Card, C. (2003) 'Genocide and social death', *Hypatia*, 18(1).

Carrabine, E., P. Cox, M. Lee, K. Plummer and N. South (2008) *Criminology: A sociological introduction*, 2nd edn, Oxford: Routledge.

Césaire, A. (1955) *Discourse on Colonialism*, www.bandung2.co.uk/Books/Files/Politics/Discourse on Colonialism.pdf, accessed 14 August 2011.

Chalk, F. and K. Jonassohn (1990) *The History and Sociology of Genocide: Analyses and Case Studies*, New Haven, CT: Yale University Press.

Charles A. (2009) 'Business strategies and climate change', in H. Selin and S. D. VanDeveer (eds), *Changing Climates in North American Politics*, Cambridge, MA: MIT Press.

Chomsky, N. (1999) *Profit over People: Neoliberalism and the Global Order*, New York: Seven Stories Press.

— (2013) 'Can civilization survive capitalism?', *AlterNet*, 5 March.

Chomsky, N. and I. Pappé (2010) *Gaza in Crisis: Reflections on Israel's War against the Palestinians*, London: Hamish Hamilton.

Churchill, W. (1997) *A Little Matter of Genocide: Holocaust and Denial in the Americas, 1492 to the Present*, San Francisco, CA: City Lights Books.

— (2002) *Struggle for the Land: Native American Resistance to Genocide, Ecocide and Colonisation*, San Francisco, CA: City Light Books.

— (2004) *Kill the Indian, Save the Man: The Genocidal Impact of American Indian Residential Schools*, San Francisco, CA: City Light Books.

— (2005) *Since Predator Came: Notes from the Struggle for American Indian Liberation*, 2nd edn, Oakland, CA, and Edinburgh: AK Press.

Codrington, H. W. (1927) *A Short History of Sri Lanka*, London: Macmillian and Co.

Collins, J. (2011) *Global Palestine*, London: C. Hurst & Co.

Connolly, N. (2012) 'Corporate social responsibility: a duplicitous distraction?', *International Journal of Human Rights*, 16(8): 1228–49.

Cook, J. (2006) *Blood and Religion: The unmasking of the Jewish and Democratic State*, London: Pluto Press.

Cook, W. A. (ed.) (2010) *The Plight of the Palestinians: A long history of destruction*, New York: Palgrave Macmillan.

Cooper, J. (2008) *Raphael Lemkin and the Struggle for the Genocide Convention*, Basingstoke: Palgrave Macmillan.

Crook, M. and D. Short (2014) 'Marx, Lemkin and the genocide ecocide nexus', *International Journal of Human Rights*, 18(3): 298–319.

Curthoys, A. (2008) 'Genocide in Tasmania', in D. Moses (ed.), *Empire, Colony, Genocide: Conquest, Occupation and Subaltern Resistance in World History*, New York and Oxford: Berghahn Books.

Curthoys, A. and J. Docker (2008) 'Defining genocide', in D. Stone (ed.), *The Historiography of Genocide*, Basingstoke: Macmillan.

Dadrian, V. (1975) 'A typology of genocide', *International Review of Modern Sociology*, 5: 201–12.

Da'Na, S. (2013) 'Israel's settler-colonial water regime: the second contradiction of Zionism', *Holy Land Studies*, 12(1): 43–70.

Daniel, R. (1999) 'The spirit and terms of Treaty 8', in R. Price, *The Spirit of the Alberta Treaties*, 3rd edn, Alberta: University of Alberta Press, pp. 47–100.

Davis, R. and M. Zannis (1973) *The Genocide Machine in Canada: The Pacification of the North*, Montreal: Black Rose Books.

De Rijke, K. (2013a) 'Hydraulically fractured: unconventional gas and anthropology', *Anthropology Today*, 29(2): 13–17.

— (2013b) 'Coal seam gas and social impact assessment: an anthropological contribution to current debates and practices', *Journal of Economic and Social Policy*, 15(3): 3.

— (2013c) 'The agri-gas fields of Australia: black soil, food, and unconventional gas', *Culture, Agriculture, Food and Environment*, 35(1): 41–53.

De Silva, K. M. (1981) *History of Sri Lanka*, London: C. Hurst and Co.

Deckard, S. (2010) 'Devouring reef: (post) colonial anxiety and ecocritique in Sri Lankan literature', in B. Roos and A. Hunt (eds), *Postcolonial Green: Environmental Politics and World Narratives*, Virginia: University of Virginia Press.

Denby, D. (2005) 'Herder: culture, anthropology and the Enlightenment', *History of the Human Sciences*, 18(1): 55–76.

DeVotta, N. (2007) *Sinhalese Buddhist Nationalist Ideology: Implications for Policy and Conflict in Sri Lanka*, Washington, DC: East West Centre.

Diamond, J. (2006) *Collapse: How Societies Choose to Survive or Fail*, London: Penguin.

Dimbleby, J. (1979) *The Palestinians*, London: Quartet Books.

Docker, J. (2004) 'Raphael Lemkin's history of genocide and colonialism', Contribution for the United States Holocaust Museum, Center for Advanced Holocaust Studies, Washington, DC, 26 February, www.ushmm.org/genocide/analysis/details/2004-02-26/docker.pdf.

— (2008) 'Are settler-colonies inherently genocidal?', in D. Moses (ed.), *Empire, Colony, Genocide: Conquest, Occupation and Subaltern Resistance in World History*, New York and Oxford: Berghahn Books.

— (2012) 'Instrumentalising the Holocaust: Israel, settler-colonialism, genocide (creating a conversation between Raphaël Lemkin and Ilan Pappé)', *Holy Land Studies*, 11(1).

Elder, T. (2005) 'What you see before your eyes: documenting Raphael Lemkin's life by exploring his archival papers, 1900–1959', *Journal of Genocide Research*, 7(4): 469–99.

Elkins, C. and S. Pederson (eds) (2005) *Settler Colonialism in the Twentieth Century: Projects, Practices, Legacies*, Oxford: Routledge.

Elliot, J. and D. Short (2014) 'Fracking is driving UK civil and political rights violations', *The Ecologist*.

Elson, D. (2002) 'Human rights and corporate profits: the UN Global Compact – part of the solution or part of the problem?', in L. Bernia and S. Bisnath (eds), *Global Tensions: Challenges and Opportunities in the Global Economy*, London: Routledge.

Engels, F. (1958) *The Condition of the Working Class in England*, Stanford, CA: Stanford University Press.

Falk, R. A. (1973) 'Environmental warfare and ecocide – facts, appraisal, and proposals', in M. Thee, *Bulletin of Peace Proposals*, vol. 1, Oslo, Bergen and Tromsö: Universitersforlaget, pp. 80–96.

Fein, H. (1993) *Genocide: A Sociological Perspective*, London: Sage.

Fieldhouse, D. K. (1981) *Colonialism 1870–1945: An Introduction*, New York: St Martin's Press.

Finklestein, N. (1995) 'History's verdict: The Cherokee case', *Journal of Palestine Studies*, 24(4): 32–45.

Fisher, A. D. (1973) 'The Cree of Canada: some ecological and evolutionary considerations', in B. Cox (ed.), *Cultural Ecology: Readings on the Canadian Indians and Eskimos*, Toronto: McClelland and Stewart, pp. 126–39.

Fleming, D. A. and T. G. Measham (2014) 'Local economic impacts of an unconventional energy boom: the coal seam gas industry in Australia', *Australian Journal of Agricultural and Resource Economics*, doi: 10.1111/1467-8489.12043.

Freeman, M. (2002) *Human Rights: An Interdisciplinary Approach*, Oxford: Polity.

Fried, J. H. E. (1972) 'War by ecocide', in M. Thee (ed.), *Bulletin of Peace Proposals*, vol. 1, Olso, Bergen and Tromsö: Universitetsforlaget.

Frieze, D. L. (2013) 'New approaches to Raphael Lemkin', *Journal of Genocide Research*, 15(3): 247–52, dx.doi.org/10.1080/14623528.2013.821219.

Fumoleau, R. (2004) *As Long as This Land Shall Last: A History of Treaty 8 and Treaty 11, 1870–1939*, University of Calgary Press.

Gauger, A., M. P. Rabatel-Fernel, L. Kulbicki, D. Short and P. Higgins (2012) 'Ecocide is the missing 5th crime against peace', The Ecocide Project, School of Advanced Study, University of London, sas-space. sas.ac.uk/4830/1/Ecocide_research_report_19_July_13.pdf.

Gramling, R. and W. Freudenburg (1992) 'Opportunity-threat, development, and adaptation: toward a comprehensive framework for social impact assessment', *Rural Sociology*, 57(2): 216–34.

Grear, A. (2014) 'Fracking – human rights must not be ignored!', *The Ecologist*, 30 October.

Grear, A., T. Kerns, E. Grant, K. Morrow and D. Short (2014) 'A human rights assessment of hydraulic fracturing and other unconventional gas development in the United Kingdom', *Extreme Energy Initiative Report*, commissioned by the Bianca Jagger Human Rights Foundation, www.sas.ac.uk/sites/default/files/files/UK%20HRIA%20w%20appdx-hi%20res.pdf.

Gregory, D. (2004) *The Colonial Present*, Oxford: Blackwell.

Grose, T. K. (2013) 'As U.S. cleans its energy mix, it ships coal problems abroad', *National Geographic: News*, 15 March, news.nationalgeographic.com/news/energy/2013/03/130315-us-coal-exports/.

Grossman, D. (1993) *Sleeping on a Wire: Conversations with Palestinians in Israel*, London: Cape.

Gunawardana, R. A. L. H. (1990) 'The people of the Lion: the Sinhala identity and ideology in history and historiography', in J. Spencer (ed.), *Sri Lanka: History and the Roots of Conflict*.

Hamilton, R. F. (1982) *Who Voted for Hitler?*, Princeton, NJ: Princeton University Press.

Hansen, J. (2009) *Storms of My Grandchildren: The truth about the coming climate catastrophe and our last chance to save humanity*, London: Bloomsbury.

Harris, S. (1979) *'It's Coming yet ...' Aboriginal Treaty within Australia between Australians*, Canberra: Aboriginal Treaty Committee.

Harvey, D. (2005) *A Brief History of Neoliberalism*, Oxford: Oxford University Press.

Havemann, P. (2005) 'Denial, modernity and exclusion: indigenous placelessness in Australia', *Macquarie Law Journal*, 5.

Heinberg, R. (2007) 'Peak coal: sooner than you think', On Line Opinion, 21 May, www.onlineopinion.com.au/view.asp?article=5869.

— (2014) *Snake Oil: How Fracking's False Promises of Plenty Imperils Our Future*, West Sussex: Clairview Books.

Higgins, P., D. Short and N. South (2013) 'Protecting the planet: a proposal for a law of ecocide', *Crime, Law and Social Change*, 59(3): 251–66.

Higgins-Freese, J. and J. Tomhave (2002) 'Race, sacrifice, and native lands', Earth Light Library: Essays, Articles and Reviews, *Earth Light Magazine*, 46, Summer, www.earthlight. org/2002/essay46_sacrifice.html, accessed March 2010.

Hinkley, R. C. (2002) 'How corporate law inhibits social responsibility', *Humanist*, 62(2): 26.

Hobson, J. A. (1975) *Imperialism: A Study*, New York: Gordon Press.

Hönisch, B. et al. (2012) 'The geological record of ocean acidification science', *Science*, 335(6072): 1058–63.

Horowitz, I. L. (1982) *Taking Lives: Genocide and State Power*, New Brunswick, NJ: Transaction.

Howard, J. (1988) 'Treaty is a recipe for separatism', in K. Barker (ed.), *A Treaty with the Aborigines?*, Melbourne: Institute of Public Affairs.

Howarth, R., R. Santoro and A. Ingraffea (2011) 'Methane and the greenhouse-gas footprint of natural gas from shale formations', *Climatic Change*, 106(4): 679–90.

Howarth, R. et al. (2012) 'Methane emissions from natural gas systems', Background paper for the National Climate Assessment, www.eeb. cornell.edu/howarth/publications/ Howarth_et_al_2012_National_ Climate_Assessment.pdf.

Howarth, R. A. (2014) 'A bridge to nowhere: methane emissions and the greenhouse gas footprint of natural gas', *Energy Science and Engineering*, 2(2): 47–60.

Hulme, K. and D. Short (2014) 'Ecocide and the "polluter pays" principle: the case of fracking', *Environmental Scientist*, April, pp. 7–10.

Humphreys, S. (2008) *Climate Change and Human Rights: A Rough Guide*, Geneva: International Council on Human Rights Policy.

Huseman, J. and D. Short (2012) '"A slow industrial genocide": tar sands and the indigenous peoples of northern Alberta', *International Journal of Human Rights*, 16(1): 216–37.

International Energy Agency (2013), *Key World Energy Statistics*, Paris: International Energy Agency.

IPCC (2007) *Climate Change 2007: The Physical Science Basis. Contribution of Working Group I to the Fourth Assessment Report of the Intergovernmental Panel on Climate Change*, ed. S. Solomon et al., Cambridge: Cambridge University Press.

— (2013) *Climate Change 2013: The Physical Science Basis. Contribution of Working Group I to the Fifth Assessment Report of the Intergovernmental Panel on Climate Change*, ed. T. F. Stocker et al., Cambridge: Cambridge University Press.

— (2014) *Climate Change 2014: Impacts, Adaptation, and Vulnerability. Part A: Global and Sectoral Aspects. Contribution of Working Group II to the Fifth Assessment Report of the Intergovernmental Panel on Climate Change*, Cambridge: Cambridge University Press.

Isaac, J. and N. Hrimat (2005) 'Assessing the impact of Israel's segregation wall on the Palestinian agricultural biodiversity', Applied Research Institute Jerusalem, paper presented at the International Conference on Promoting Community-driven Conservation and Sustainable Use of Dryland Agrobiodiversity, sponsored by the International Center for Agricultural Research in the Dry Areas (ICARDA), Aleppo, Syria, 18–21 April.

Jensen, D. (2006) *Endgame*, vol. 1: *The Problem of Civilisation*, New York: Seven Stories Press.

Jiryis, S. (1976) *The Arabs in Israel*, New York and London: Monthly Review Press.

Johnston, B. R. (2000) 'Human environmental rights', in A. Pollis and B. Schwab, *Human Rights: New Perspectives, New Realities*, London: Lynne Rienner, pp. 95–113.

Jones, A. (ed.) (2004) *Genocide, War Crimes and the West: History and Complicity*, London: Zed Books.

— (2006) *Genocide: A Comprehensive Introduction*, Routledge/Taylor & Francis.

Kalmus, J. (2013) 'Israel studies professor: 1948 really was ethnic cleansing, not genocide', *Jewish Chronicle*, online, www.thejc.com/news/uk-news/103408/israel-studies-professor-1948-really-was-ethnic-cleansing-not-genocide.

Kapferer, B. (1988) *Legends of People, Myths of State: Violence, Intolerance, and Political Culture in Sri Lanka and Australia*, Smithsonian Institute.

Karmi, G. (2007) *Married to Another Man: Israel's Dilemma in Palestine*, London: Pluto Press.

Kelly, E. N., D. W. Schindler, P. V. Hodson, J. W. Short, R. Radmanovich and C. C. Nielsen (2010) 'Oil sands development contributes elements toxic at low concentrations to the Athabasca River and its tributaries', *Proceedings of the National Academy of Sciences (PNAS)*, 2 July, www.pnas.org/content/early/2010/08/24/1008754107.full.pdf, accessed September 2011.

Kimmerling, B. (2003) *Politicide: Ariel Sharon's war against the Palestinians*, London and New York: Verso.

Klare, M. T. (2010) 'The relentless pursuit of extreme energy: a new oil rush endangers the Gulf of Mexico and the planet', *Huffington Post*, 19 May, www.huffingtonpost.com/michael-t-klare/the-relentless-pursuit-of_b_581921.html.

— (2011) 'The era of extreme energy: life after the age of oil', *Huffington Post*, 25 May, www.huffingtonpost.com/michael-t-klare/the-era-of-xtreme-energy_b_295304.html.

— (2014) *The Race for What's Left: The Global Scramble for the World's Last Resources*, New York: Picador.

Kovel, J. (2007a) *The Enemy of Nature: The End of Capitalism or the End of the World?*, 2nd edn, London: Zed Books.

— (2007b) *Overcoming Zionism: Creating a Single Democratic State in Israel/Palestine*, London: Pluto Press.

Kroeber, A. L. (1940) 'Stimulus diffusion', *American Anthropologist*, 42: 1–20.

Kuhn, T. S. (2012) *The Structure of Scientific Revolutions*, Chicago, IL: Chicago University Press.

Kuper, L. (1981) *Genocide: Its Political Use in the Twentieth Century*, New Haven, CT: Yale University Press.

LaDuke, W. (1999) *All Our Relations: Native Struggles for Land and Life*, Cambridge, MA: South End Press.

Langton, M. (2007) 'Trapped in the Aboriginal reality show', *Griffith Review*, 19: *Re-imagining Australia,* Griffith University, www.griffithreview.com/images/stories/edition_articles/ed19_pdfs/langton_ed19.pdf.

Lemkin, R. (1944) *Axis Rule in Occupied Europe: Analysis, Proposals for Redress*, Washington, DC: Carnegie Endowment for International Peace.

— (1945) 'Genocide: a modern crime', *Free World*, 4: 39–43, www.preventgenocide.org/lemkin/freeworld1945.htm.

— (2012) *Lemkin on Genocide*, ed. S. L. Jacobs, Plymouth: Lexington Books.

— (2013) *Totally Unofficial: The autobiography of Raphael Lemkin*, ed. D.-L. Frieze, New Haven, CT: Yale University Press.

Levene, M. (2004) 'Climate change and violence: a multidisciplinary and interdisciplinary initiative', Crisis Forum, www.crisis-forum.org.uk/projects/climate_change_and_violence.php.

— (2005) *Genocide in the Age of the Nation State*, vol. I: *The Meaning of Genocide,* vol. II: *The Rise of the West and the Coming of Genocide*, London: I. B. Tauris.

Levene, M. and D. Conversi (2014) 'Subsistence societies, globalization, climate change and genocide: discourses of vulnerability and resilience', *International Journal of Human Rights*, 18(3): 281–97.

Lieberman, B. (2010) '"Ethnic cleansing" and genocide', in D. Bloxham and A. D. Moses (eds), *The Oxford Handbook of Genocide Studies*, Oxford: Oxford University Press, pp. 42–60.

Lloyd-Davies, E. (2013) 'Defining extreme energy: a process not a category', Working Paper Series, Extreme Energy Initiative, 25 July, extremeenergy.org/2013/07/25/defining-extreme-energy-a-process-not-a-category/.

Lunn, J., C. Taylor and I. Townsend (2009) 'War and peace in Sri Lanka', Research Paper 09/51, London: House of Commons Library.

Lynch, M. J., R. G. Burns and P. B. Stretesky (2010) 'Global warming and state-corporate crime: the politicalization of global warming under the Bush administration', *Crime, Law and Social Change*, 54(3/4): 213–39.

MacNutt, F. A. (1909) *Bartholomew de las Casas: His Life, His Apostolate, and His Writings*, New York: Putnam.

Maggio, G. and G. Cacciola (2012) 'When will oil, natural gas, and coal peak?', *Fuel 98*, pp. 111–23.

Mahanama Thera, Ven. (1912) *Mahavamsa – the Great Chronicle of Sri Lanka*, trans. W. Geiger.

Maher, D. T., I. R. Santos, D. R. Tait (2014) 'Mapping methane and carbon dioxide concentrations and δ13C values in the atmosphere of two Australian coal seam gas fields', *Journal of Water, Air and Soil Pollution*, 225, 18 November.

Malin, S. (2013) 'There's no real choice but to sign: neoliberalization and normalization of hydraulic fracturing on Pennsylvania farmland', *Journal of Environmental Studies and Sciences*, 2014(4): 17–27.

Markle, G. E. (1999) 'The Holocaust and sociology', in P. Hayes (ed.), *Lessons and Legacies 111: Memory, Memorialization, and Denial*, Illinois: Northwestern University Press, pp. 33–40.

Marx, K. and F. Engels (1967) *Capital*, vol. III, New York: International Publishers.

Masalha, N. (1992) *Expulsion of the Palestinians: The Concept of 'Transfer' in Zionist Political Thought, 1882–1948*, Washington, DC: Institute for Palestine Studies.

— (1997) *A Land without a People: Israel, Transfer and the Palestinians 1949–96*, London: Faber and Faber.

— (2000) *Imperial Israel and the Palestinians: The Politics of Expansion*, London: Pluto Press.

— (2005) *Catastrophe Remembered: Palestine, Israel, and the internal refugees: essays in memory of Edward W. Said (1935–2003)*, London: Zed Books.

— (2011) 'New history, post-Zionism and neo-colonialism: a critique of the Israeli "new historians"', *Holy Land Studies: A Multidisciplinary Journal*, 10(1): 1–53.

— (2012) *The Palestine Nakba: Decolonising History, Narrating* the Subaltern, Reclaiming Memory, London and New York: Zed Books.

Massad, J. A. (2006) *The Persistence of the Palestinian Question: Essays on Zionism and the Palestinians*, London and New York: Routledge.

Matar, D. (2011) *What It Means to Be a Palestinian*, London and New York: I. B. Tauris.

Mayer, J. (2010) 'Covert operations: the billionaire brothers who are waging a war against Obama', *New Yorker*, 30 August, www.newyorker.com/magazine/2010/08/30/covert-operations.

McDermott-Levy, R., N. Kaktins and B. Sattler (2013) 'Fracking, the environment, and health: new energy practices may threaten public health', *American Journal of Nursing*, 113(6): 45–51.

McDonnell, M. A. and A. D. Moses (2005) 'Raphael Lemkin as historian of genocide in the Americas', *Journal of Genocide Research*, 7(4): 504–5.

Meadows, D. H. et al. (1972) *The Limits to Growth: A Report for the Club of Rome's Project on the Predicament of Mankind*, New York: Universe Books.

Mobbs, P. (2013a) 'Sheet E1. Peak energy: the limits to oil and gas production', Free Range 'Energy Beyond Oil' Project, www.fraw.org.uk/publications/e-series/e01/e01-peak_energy.html.

— (2013b) 'Economically and politically fracked: "behind every picture lies a story" – statistical reality versus PR-hype within the political project of unconventional gas in Britain', *Mobbsey's Musings*, 25 July, www.fraw.org.uk/mei/musings/2013/20130725-behind_every_picture_lies_a_story.html.

— (2014) 'With sub-$60 oil, fracking and tar sands losses threaten the whole financial system', *The Ecologist*, 17 December, www.theecologist.org/News/news_analysis/2679765/with_sub60_oil_fracking_and_tar_sands_losses_threaten_the_whole_financial_system.html.

— (2015) '"Environmentalists" oil price panic reflects their own existential crisis', *The Ecologist*, 8 January.

Moore, C. W., B. Zielinska, G. Petron and R. B. Jackson (2014) 'Air impacts of increased natural gas acquisition, processing, and use: a critical review', *Environmental Science and Technology*, dx.doi.org/10.1021/es4053472.

Moran, A. (1999) 'Aboriginal reconciliation: transformations in settler nationalism', *Melbourne Journal of Politics*, Special Reconciliation Issue, University of Melbourne Press.

Morgan, R. (2004) 'Advancing indigenous rights at the United Nations: strategic framing and its impact on the normative development of international law', *Social and Legal Studies*, 13(4): 481–501.

Morris, B. (2004) *The Birth of the Palestinian Refugee Problem Revisited*, Cambridge: Cambridge University Press.

Morsink, J. (1999) 'Cultural genocide, the Universal Declaration, and minority rights', *Human Rights Quarterly*, 21(4), November.

Moses, D. (2000) 'An Antipodean genocide? The origins of the genocidal moment in the colonization of Australia', *Journal of Genocide Research*, 2(1): 89–106.

— (2002) 'Conceptual blockages and definitional dilemmas in the "racial century": genocides of indigenous peoples and the Holocaust', *Patterns of Prejudice*, 36(4): 7–36.

— (2004) 'Genocide and settler society in Australian history', in D. Moses, *Genocide and Settler Society: Frontier Violence and Stolen Indigenous*

*Children in Australian History*, New York and Oxford: Berghahn Books, pp. 3–48.

— (2008) 'Empire, colony, genocide: keywords and the philosophy of history', in D. Moses (ed.), *Empire, Colony, Genocide: Conquest, Occupation, and Subaltern Resistance in World History*, Oxford: Berghahn Books, pp. 3–54.

— (2010) 'Raphael Lemkin, culture, and the concept of genocide', in D. Bloxham and A. D. Moses (eds), *The Oxford Handbook of Genocide Studies*, Oxford: Oxford University Press.

— (2011) 'Genocide and the terror of history', *Parallax*, 61(4).

Moses, A. D. and D. Stone (eds) (2006) *Colonialism and Genocide*, Abingdon: Routledge.

Moshman, D. (2001) 'Conceptual constraints on thinking about genocide', *Journal of Genocide Research*, 3(3): 431–50.

Muggah, R. (2008) *Relocation Failures in Sri Lanka: A Short History of Internal Displacement and Resettlement*, London: Zed Books.

Murray, J. and J. Hansen (2013) 'Peak oil and energy independence: myths and reality', *Eos*, 94(28): 245–52.

Nikiforuk, A. (2010) *Tar Sands: Dirty Oil and the Future of a Continent*, Greystone Books.

Nirmal, D. R. (2013) '"History" after the war: historical consciousness in the collective Sinhala-Buddhist psyche in post-war Sri Lanka', ICES Research Paper no. 09, International Center for Ethnic Studies.

Obeyesekere, G. (1984) *The Cult of the Goddess Pattini*, Chicago, IL, and London: University of Chicago Press.

Office of the Chief Economist (2011) *World Energy Outlook: 2011*, Paris: International Energy Agency.

Osborn, S., A. Vengosh, N. R. Warner and R. B. Jackson (2011) 'Methane contamination of drinking water accompanying gas-well drilling and hydraulic fracturing', *PNAS*, 108(20), 17 May, www.pnas.org/cgi/doi/10.1073/pnas.1100682108.

Palast, G. (2002) *The Best Democracy Money Can Buy: An Investigative Reporter Exposes the Truth about Globalization, Corporate Cons and High Finance Fraudsters*, London: Pluto Press.

Palmer, A. (2000) *Colonial Genocide*, London: Crawford House Publishing.

Pappé, I. (2006) *The Ethnic Cleansing of Palestine*, Oxford: Oneorld.

— (2011) *The Forgotten Palestinians: A history of the Palestinians in Israel*, London and New Haven, CT: Yale University Press.

Paradies, Y. C. (2006) 'Beyond black and white: essentialism, hybridity and indigeneity', *Journal of Sociology*, 42: 355.

Parsons, T. (1937) *The Structure of Social Action*, New York: Free Press.

— (1960) *Structure and Process in Modern Societies*, New York: Free Press.

Patz, J. et al. (2005) 'Impact of regional climate change on human health', *Nature*, 438: 310–17.

Peebles, P. (1990) 'Colonisation and ethnic conflict in the Dry Zone of Sri Lanka', *Journal of Asian Studies*, 49(1).

Peiris, G. H. (1981) 'Agrarian transformations in British Sri Lanka', *Sri Lanka Journal of Agrarian Studies*, 2.

Perry, S. (2012) 'Development, land use, and collective trauma: the Marcellus Shale gas boom in rural Pennsylvania', *Culture, Agriculture, Food and Environment*, 34(1): 81–92.

Perugini, N. and N. Gordon (2015) *The Human Right to Dominate*, New York: Oxford University Press.

Petersen, K. (2007) 'Oil versus water: toxic water poses threat to Alberta's indigenous communities', *The Dominion*, 48, October.

Pilgrim, S., C. Samson and J. N. Pretty (2009) 'Rebuilding lost connections: how revitalisation projects contribute to cultural continuity and improve the environment', University of Essex iCES Occasional Paper 2009–01, Interdisciplinary Centre for Environment and Society, www.essex. ac.uk/ces/esu/occ-papers.shtm.

Piterberg, G. (2008) *The Returns of Zionism: Myths, politics and scholarship in Israel*, London: Verso.

Porter, J. N. (1993) 'The Holocaust as a sociological construct', *Contemporary Jewry*, 14: 184–7.

Powell, C. (2007) 'What do genocides kill? A relational conception of genocide', *Journal of Genocide Research*, 9(4): 527–47.

Power, S. (2003) *A Problem from Hell: America and the Age of Genocide*, London: Flamingo.

Pretty, J., B. Adams, F. Berkes, S. de Athayde, N. Dudley, E. Hunn, L. Maffi, K. Milton, D. Rapport, P. Robbins, C. Samson, E. Sterling, S. Stolton, K. Takeuchi, A. Tsing, E. Vintinner and S. Pilgrim (2008) 'How do nature and culture intersect?', Plenary contribution for the conference Sustaining Cultural and Biological Diversity in a Rapidly Changing World: Lessons for Global Policy, organized by AMNH, IUCN-The World Conservation Union/ Theme on Culture and Conservation, and Terralingua, New York, 2–5 April. Copy on file with author.

Pritchard, S. (1992) 'The rights of indigenous peoples to self-determination under international law', *Aboriginal Law Bulletin*, www.austlii.edu.au/au/journals/ AboriginalLB/1992/16.html.

Purdey, S. J. (2010) *Economic Growth, the Environment and International Relations: The growth paradigm*, Oxford: Routledge.

Qumsiyeh, M. B., S. S. Zavala and Z. S. Amr (2014) 'Decline in vertebrate biodiversity in Bethlehem, Palestine', *Jordan Journal of Biological Sciences*, 7(2): 101–7.

Rahula, W. (1956) *History of Buddhism in Ceylon: The Anuradhapura period, 3rd Century BC – 10th Century AC*, Colombo: M. D. Gunasena.

Ram, U. (2007) 'The colonization perspective', in Ilan Pappé (ed.), *The Israel/Palestine Question: A Reader*, 2nd edn, London and New York: Routledge, pp. 53–77.

Rashed, H. and D. Short (2012) 'Genocide and settler colonialism: can a Lemkin-inspired genocide perspective aid our understanding of the Palestinian situation?', *International Journal of Human Rights*, 16(8): 1142–69.

Rashed, H., D. Short and J. Docker (2014) 'Nakba memoricide: genocide studies and the Zionist/Israeli genocide', *Holy Land Studies*, 13(1): 1–23.

Reynolds, H. (1996) *Aboriginal Sovereignty: Three Nations, One Australia*, NSW: Allen and Unwin.

Rodinson, M. (1973) *Israel, a Settler-Colonial State?*, New York: Monad.

Rogan, E. (2009) *The Arabs*, London: Allen Lane.

Rogers, J. D. (1990) 'Historical images in the British period', in J. Spencer (ed.), *Sri Lanka: History and the Roots of Conflict*, London and New York: Routledge.

Romm, J. J. (2008) *Hell and High Water: The Global Warming Solution*, New York: Harper Perennial.

Rose Johnston, B. (2000) 'Human environmental rights', in A. Pollis and P. Schwab, *Human Rights New*

*Perspectives, New Realities*, London: Lynne Rienner.

Rosenbaum, A. S. (1995) *Is the Holocaust Unique?: Perspectives on Comparative Genocide*, Boulder, CO: Westview Press.

Roy, S. (1987) 'The Gaza Strip: a case of economic de-development', *Journal of Palestine Studies*, 17(1): 56–88.

Sa'di, A. H. and L. Abu-Lughod (eds) (2007) *Nakba: Palestine, 1948, and the Claims of Memory*, New York: Columbia University Press.

Sakhnini, N. (2005) 'The 1948 war: a cover up for ethnic cleansing', *Al Awda*, 16 November, www.al-awda.org/zionists4.html.

Samson, C. (2003) *A Way of Life that Does Not Exist*, London: Verso.

— (2009) 'Indigenous peoples' rights: anthropology and the right to culture', in R. Morgan and B. Turner (eds), *Interpreting Human Rights: Social Science Perspectives*, Cambridge: Cambridge University Press.

Samson, C. and D. Short (2006) 'Sociology of indigenous peoples' rights', in L. Morris (ed.), *Rights: Sociological Perspectives*, London: Routledge.

Sartre, J.-P. (1967) *On Genocide*, www.brusselstribunal.org/GenocideSartre.htm.

— (1990) 'Introduction', in A. Memmi, *The Colonizer and the Colonized*, London: Earthscan.

Satchi, P. (1983) *Sri Lanka: The National Question and the Tamil Liberation Struggle*, London: Zed Books.

Schabas, W. (2000) *Genocide in International Law*, Cambridge: Cambridge University Press.

Schafft, K. A., Y. Borlu and L. Glenna (2013) 'The relationship between Marcellus Shale gas development in Pennsylvania and local perceptions of risk and opportunity', *Rural Sociology*, 78(2): 143–66.

Schafft, K. A., L. Glenna, B. Green and Y. Borlu (2014) 'Local impacts of unconventional gas development within Pennsylvania's Marcellus Shale region: gauging boomtown development through the perspectives of educational administrators', *Society & Natural Resources: An International Journal*, 27(4): 389–404.

Schaller, D. (2008) 'Colonialism and genocide – Raphael Lemkin's concept of genocide and its application to European rule in Africa', *Development Dialogue*, 50, December.

Schaller, D. J. and J. Zimmerer (eds) (2005) 'Raphael Lemkin: the "founder of the United Nations's Genocide Convention" as a historian of mass violence', *Journal of Genocide Research*, 7(4): 441–578.

— (eds) (2009) The Origins of genocide?: Raphael Lemkin as a historian of mass violence?, Abingdon: Routledge.

Shaw, M. (2007) *What Is Genocide?*, Cambridge: Polity.

— (2010a) 'Sociology and genocide', in D. Bloxham and A. D. Moses (eds), *The Oxford Handbook of Genocide Studies*, Oxford: Oxford University Press.

— (2010b) 'Palestine in an international historical perspective on genocide', *Holy Land Studies*, 9: 1–25.

— (2013) 'Palestine and genocide: an international historical perspective revisited', *Holy Land Studies*, 12(1): 1–7.

Shelley, T. and T. Opsal (2014) 'Energy crime, harm, and problematic state response in Colorado: a case of the fox guarding the hen house?', *Critical Criminology*, 22(4): 561–77.

Sherbok-Cohn, D. and D. El-Alami (2001) *The Palestine–Israeli Conflict*, Oxford: Oneworld.

Shlaim, A. (2000) *The Iron Wall: Israel and the Arab World*, London: Allen Lane.

Short, D. (2003) 'Australian "Aboriginal" reconciliation: the latest phase in the colonial project', *Citizenship Studies*, 7(3): 291–312.

— (2007) 'The social construction of "native title" land rights in Australia', *Current Sociology*, 55: 857.

— (2008) *Reconciliation and Colonial Power: Indigenous rights in Australia*, Aldershot: Ashgate.

— (2009) 'Sociological and anthropological perspectives on human rights', in M. Goodhart (ed.), *Human Rights, Politics and Practice*, Oxford: Oxford University Press, p. 102.

— (2010a) 'Cultural genocide and indigenous peoples: a sociological approach', *International Journal of Human Rights*, 14(6/7), pp. 831–46.

— (2010b) 'Australia: a continuing genocide?', *Journal of Genocide Research*, 12(1/2): 45–68.

Short, D., K. Hulme and S. Bohm (2014) 'Don't let human rights fall to wayside in fracking debate', *The Conversation*, 24 March, theconversation.com/dont-let-human-rights-fall-to-wayside-in-fracking-debate-24652.

Short, D., J. Elliot, K. Norder, E. Lloyd-Davies and J. Morley (2015) 'Extreme energy, "fracking" and human rights: a new field for human rights impact assessments?', *International Journal of Human Rights*, dx.doi.org/10.1080/13642987.2015.1019219.

Smith, A. (2005) *Conquest: Sexual Violence and American Indian Genocide*, Cambridge, MA: South End Press.

Smith, A. D. (1986) *The Ethnic Origins of Nations*, Oxford: Blackwell.

South, N. (1998) 'A green field for criminology?: a proposal for a perspective', *Theoretical Criminology*, 2(2): 211–33.

— (2010) 'The ecocidal tendencies of late modernity: trans-national crime, social exclusion, victims and rights', in R. White (ed.), *Global Environmental Harm: Criminological perspectives*, Cullompton: Willan.

South, N. and A. Brisman (eds) (2013) *The Routledge International Handbook of Green Criminology*, London: Routledge.

Stainsby, M. (2007) 'The richest First Nation in Canada: ecological and political life in Fort McKay', *The Dominion*, 48.

Stott, P., D. Stone and M. Allen (2004) 'Human contribution to the European heatwave of 2003', *Nature*, 432: 610–14.

Stretesky, P. B., M. A. Long and M. J. Lynch (2013) 'Does environmental enforcement slow the treadmill of production? The relationship between large monetary penalties, ecological disorganization and toxic releases within offending corporations', *Journal of Crime and Justice*, 36(2): 233–47.

Tambiah, S. J. (1986) *Sri Lanka: Ethnic Fratricide and the Dismantling of Democracy*, Chicago, IL: University of Chicago Press.

Tennent, J. E. (1860) *Ceylon: An Account of the Island; Physical, Historical, and Topographical*, 2 vols, London.

Thomas-Muller, C. (2007) 'We speak for ourselves: indigenous peoples challenge the fossil fuel regime in Alberta', *The Dominion*, Tar Sands Issue, 48, Autumn.

Timoney, K. P. (2007) 'A study of water and sediment quality as related to public health issues', *Treeline Ecological Research*, Sherwood Park, AB.

Tomuschat, C. (1996) 'Crimes against the environment', *Environmental Policy and Law*, 26(6): 243.

Trivett, V. (2011) '25 US mega corporations: where they rank if they were countries', *Business Insider*, 27 June, www.businessinsider.com/25-corporations-bigger-tan-countries-2011-6?op=1.

Tully, J. (2000) 'The struggles of indigenous peoples for and of freedom', in D. Ivison, P. Patton and W. Sanders (eds), *Political Theory and the Rights of Indigenous Peoples*, Cambridge: Cambridge University Press.

Turner, G. (2007) 'A comparison of the limits to growth with 30 years of reality', *Socio-Economics and the Environment in Discussion*, CSIRO Working Paper Series 2008–09, Canberra: CSIRO Sustainable Ecosystems.

Van Kreiken, R. (1999) 'The barbarism of civilization: cultural genocide and the "stolen generations"', *British Journal of Sociology*, 50(2): 297–315.

— (2004) 'Rethinking cultural genocide: Aboriginal child removal and settler-colonial state formation', *Oceania*, 75(2): 125–51.

— (2008) 'Cultural genocide', in D. Stone (ed.), *The Historiography of Genocide*, London: Palgrave Macmillan, pp. 128–55.

Vengosh, A., R. B. Jackson, N. Warner, T. H. Darrah and A. Kondash (2014) 'A critical review of the risks to water resources from unconventional shale gas development and hydraulic fracturing in the United States', *Environmental Science and Technology*, dx.doi.org/10.1021/es405118y.

Veracini, L. (2006) *Israel and Settler Society*, London: Pluto Press.

— (2013) 'Constructing "settler colonialism": career of a concept', *Journal of Imperial and Commonwealth History*, 41(2): 313–33.

Vivian, A. and B. Schokman (2009) 'The Northern Territory Intervention and the fabrication of "special measures"', *Australian Indigenous Law Review*, 13(1): 7.

Waller, L. (2008) '"We can no longer be sacrificed": First Nations resistance to tar sands development is growing', *Briarpatch Magazine*, 9 June, http://briarpatchmagazine.com/articles/view/we-can-no-longer-be-sacrificed

Weisberg, B. (1970) *Ecocide in Indochina*, San Francisco, CA: Canfield Press.

Weiss, G. (2011) *The Cage: The Fight for Sri Lanka and the Last Days of the Tamil Tigers*, London: Bodley Head.

Westing, A. H. (1974) 'Proscription of ecocide', *Science and Public Affairs*, January.

Whitaker, M. (1990) 'A compound of many histories: the many pasts of an East Coast Tamil community', in J. Spencer (ed.), *Sri Lanka: History and the Roots of Conflict*, London and New York: Routledge.

White, B. (2009) *Israeli Apartheid: A Beginner's Guide*, London: Pluto Press.

— (ed.) (2010) *Global Environmental Harm: Criminological perspectives*, Cullompton: Willan.

— (2013a) 'Resource extraction leaves something behind: environmental justice and mining', *International Journal for Crime and Justice*, 2(1): 50–64.

— (2013b) *Crimes against Nature: Environmental criminology and ecological justice*, London: Routledge.

Wilson, J. (1988) *The Break-up of Sri Lanka: The Sinhalese Tamil Conflict*, London: Hurst.

Wolfe, P. (1999) *Settler Colonialism and the Transformation of Anthropology*, London: Cassell.

— (2006) 'Settler colonialism and the elimination of the native', *Journal of Genocide Research*, 8(4): 387–409.

— (2012) 'Purchase by other means: the Palestine Nakba and Zionism's conquest of economics', *Settler Colonial Studies*, 2(1): 133–71.

Woodward, E. (1974) 'Aboriginal Land Rights Commission: Second Report', Parliamentary Paper no. 69, April.

Zalasiewicz, J. et al. (2008) 'Are we now living in the Anthropocene', *GSA Today*, 18(2): 96.

Zierler, D. (2011) *The Invention of Ecocide: Agent Orange, Vietnam, and the Scientists Who Changed the Way We Think about the Environment*, Athens: University of Georgia Press.

Zimmerer, J. (2008) 'Colonialism and the holocaust – towards an archaeology of genocide', *Development Dialogue*, 50, December.

— (2014) 'Climate change, environmental violence and genocide', *International Journal of Human Rights*, 18(3): 265–80.

Zinn, H. (1995) 'Introduction', in D. A. Grinde and B. E. Johansen, *Ecocide of Native America: Environmental Destruction of Indian Lands and Peoples*, Santa Fe, NM: Clear Light Publishers.

Zureik, E. T. (1979) *The Palestinians in Israel: A Study in Internal Colonialism*, London: Routledge.

# INDEX